THIS IS YOUR TOMORROW ... AND TODAY

GETHSEMANI'S *SALVE* WINDOW

"Our Life . . .

Our Sweetness . . .

Our Hope"

REV. M. RAYMOND, O.C.S.O.

THIS IS
Your
TOMORROW
...and TODAY

THE BRUCE PUBLISHING COMPANY
MILWAUKEE

NIHIL OBSTAT:

Fr. M. Thomas Aquinas Porter, O.C.S.O.
Fr. M. Gabriel O'Connell, O.C.S.O.
Censores

IMPRIMI POTEST:

Most Rev. Dom. M. Gabriel Sortais, O.C.S.O.
Abbas Generalis

NIHIL OBSTAT:

Rev. Joannes F. Murphy, S.T.D.
Censor Librorum

IMPRIMATUR:

✠ Romanus R. Atkielski
Administrator Milwauchiensis

January 8, 1959

Unless otherwise noted, the quotations in this book from the New Testament are from the Kleist-Lilly translation.

*The Library of Congress catalog entry for this book appears
at the end of the text.*

To
THE IMMACULATE CONCEPTION
as tribute
to mark the centenary of her apparitions
at Lourdes
and
testimonial of
her tender mothering of
Charlie and Kay

Foreword

GOD did it. He, the Three-Personed God shattered a resolution of twenty years' standing. This book is the result of His shattering. But for these bits I bless Him, and pray that you will, too.

If the living God took hold of your heart, and not only held it, but for twenty months tightened His grip on it day by day, would you not drop a practice of twenty years — especially when you saw that that practice had basis only in your personal preference? If the all-holy Face of the invisible God looked out at you from happening after happening, until you came to know His every feature as well as you know your own, would you not relinquish your hold on a determination that had been the result really of your own particular temperament? If our ever incomprehensible God brought you into ways which Holy Writ has rightly called inscrutable, but, because He was the Light of your path, you found these ways understandable and saw clearly just where they led, would you not abandon your own fixed way of doing things and cheerfully follow His lead? I would, and did. For our ever incomprehensible God showed me so many of His inscrutable ways with such compelling clarity that the practice of twenty years was thrown aside wholeheartedly and this book cast in a mold I had once resolved never to use. Faith demanded that I do it.

That explanation of how it happened is not an apology; it is an *apologia*. For the living God and His demands on a creature never call for an apology.

But if Faith explains the manner of this book, it is Fidelity that explains the matter. For just as no sculptor rests easy as long as his statue is only in clay, and no painter is content if his picture is only in outline, so no teller of a romance can be without disquiet so long as he has not portrayed the happy ending. Fidelity to the Mother of

God, then, demanded that the romance begun by the unfolding of the fact that *Love Does Such Things,* then carried on by the presentation of *A New Way of the Cross,* which led to *God, a Woman, and the Way,* should be completed by proving to all that THIS IS YOUR TOMORROW . . . AND TODAY!

When it was shown that the *Joyful Mysteries* in the life of Christ and His Mother were the one source of all the real and lasting joy in the lives of Christians, a trilogy was begun. Then, when those *Sorrowful Mysteries* which led the Son of God to a Calvary where He became a Criminal dead upon a cross, and brought the Mother of that Son of God to a borrowed tomb outside of which she sat as the world's brokenhearted *Pietà,* were presented as Mysteries which alone give real meaning to life, the second part of that trilogy was finished. To stop there would be to present a drama minus its denouement. Indeed, it would be to tell only half the truth about the living God and about the life He would have us lead. The full truth of the matter is that neither Christ nor His Mother was made for only joy and sorrow. They, and every Christian under Them, were made for life in the glory of God and life with the God of glory.

Yet what Faith and Fidelity demanded called for a Fortitude that was anything but meager. For the task was not only difficult, it was delicate — and my hands are heavy. No prudent man talks about himself in private, let alone in public, without real reason. No wise family member introduces outsiders into the loving intimacy of his own family unless he has assurance that the sacredness of this secret center will be reverenced, and that this reverence will be tinctured with love. For a silent monk to talk about himself and take the public into the intimacy of his family there must be something akin to a divine command. But though that command was heard it has not rendered this task any less delicate or any less difficult.

Since it was God, through His representatives — my superiors — who had given me the assignment to write, I resolved twenty years ago to keep myself out of the picture and to do with truths for His sake what He had done with His only Word, who is Truth, for our sake. I would "incarnate" them. They would be clothed in flesh and blood. They would be human yet ever resplendent with the Divine. They would be living truths and truths that we could live.

To date, the carrying out of my resolve has been fairly easy. My subjects have all been not only truly human and really divine, but big enough to fill any canvass and thus keep the painter out of the picture. But now the entire scene seems to have been shifted; for the author must appear on almost every page.

Why this sudden and seemingly complete reversal of form? — God is the answer. But while He has utterly shattered the determination to remain unseen, He has enabled me to keep my other and much more important resolve; namely, to "incarnate" truth. It was He who gave me the "incarnation" — and one may not sin against the Light! Nor may one ever "grieve the Spirit." Gratitude to God the Father, loyalty to God the Son, loving appreciation of God the Holy Spirit demanded that the truth about the Glorious Mysteries of the Rosary — those Mysteries which so wondrously crown the lives of Jesus and Mary — be shown "incarnate" in the life of one who was dying, and shown in such a way that each of us may learn to live gloriously, and die the same way: "in Christ Jesus," mothered ever by her who is "our life, our sweetness, and our hope."

If this "incarnation" — which is so personal to me — proves nothing else, it will show with a marvelous clarity that God is nearer than we know, and that His Christ, and that Christ's Mother enter every happening in our lives — sin alone excepted — with an intimacy we seldom recognize, to give them a meaning of which we are too frequently unconscious. We were made for *glory*. That is incontestable. For we were made by God, and God, omnipotent though He be, and possessed of infinite freedom though He is, can make nothing save for glory — His very own glory. Since His Son shattered the tomb as Conqueror of death, there is not a person living who need ever die! Nor is there a dying person who need ever live but in *glory*. That is the message Mary gives us in these final Mysteries of her Rosary. But this is the way God "incarnated" that truth. . . .

Contents

THIS IS YOUR TOMORROW...AND TODAY

CHAPTER ONE

A Bolt From the Blue

"It's a gift!" I said to myself. A great gift. But how can I ever get them to see it that way?

I glanced again at the excited scrawl my sister-in-law had air-mailed to me the day before:

> I can't write. The worst has happened. It is cancer and it has gone too far. It is outside the lung. I don't know what to do or where to turn. You were my first thought.
>
> Love,
> Kay.
>
> P.S. I'll write when I compose myself a little more.

How different that was from the long, chatty letters of the previous three weeks! True, I had felt her nervousness in each of them, and even read the anxiety she had left unexpressed. But along with that nervousness and anxiety had come bubbling cheerfulness, brave hope, decided composure. But who could blame her now for being anxious and upset? To have what had actually begun as something of a lark turn into this seeming catastrophe was enough to shake strong men, men who had emotional control and possessed real financial security. But what did Kay, the ever lighthearted one, have now? A husband who was doomed; for inoperable cancer of the lung allows for no argument. A family of seven young children — the oldest just entering her teens, the youngest still teething. To cap the climax she was without a trace of financial security; for it was only a few years back that

Charlie, her husband, had sunk his all — and much more than his all — in their little Cape Cod home. He had never carried hospital insurance on himself, and had allowed even his life insurance to lapse. No, Kay could not be blamed for not knowing at the moment "what to do or where to turn." But I knew both. And I would have to tell both Charlie and herself just where to turn and precisely what to do.

This would be no new role for me. I had begun to fill it in some small way the very year they were married, just a few months before I left to join the Trappists. Off and on, for slightly over twenty years now I had kidded them, cajoled them, occasionally chided them; but always managed to console and encourage them. For to me they had never ceased to be the two happy youngsters who had moved into their tiny apartment just after their honeymoon — blissful in their possession of one another, and seemingly oblivious of the fact that that was all they did possess.

Strange how vivid one's memory can be at certain times. As I again glanced at the excited scrawl before me, I saw in the clearest detail the parlor of that first apartment. I could trace the pattern on the upholstery and even feel the oily fringe on the leather of the ash tray that hung on the arm of the chair into which I had occasionally sunk. And there before me stood the two happy youngsters, as confident as any world conquerors — and much less fearful of their futures.

But now. There was Kay down on the Cape not knowing "what to do or where to turn," while Charlie lay on a hospital bed up in Boston with a cancer in his lung which one of the best thoracic surgeons in the state had pronounced inoperable. Humanly speaking, this was a stunner! But, while always fully understanding and completely sympathetic with the human side of things, I had persistently striven to make this pair see beyond the human. I knew now that my task was to get them to see only the divine. Could I do it? I most certainly would try; and my tactics, if they can be called such, would be open honesty and the fullness of truth. I would write a letter telling Charlie not only what he had, but what he could expect. In it I would speak to Kay, urging her to focus with her whole mind and heart on the fact that we have as Providing Father no one less than God.

For me cancer was not only a very old, but it had become a very intimate acquaintance. My father had died from one in 1935. Mother had come down with another in 1948. And before she had the recurrence which took her to God in 1949, I had been found to have a sizable one inside of me. They called it "adenoma carcinoma," and said it was "just above the sigmoid flexure." How I smiled to myself now as I recalled the question I had put to the medical man who was taking my history just before surgery and seemed so interested in the family record of cancer. "Are you boys now working on the theory that cancer is hereditary?" I asked. That it ran in the blood of my family seemed fairly obvious. Why, even lovely Sheila-Mae, Kay and Charlie's first-born, had died of cancer of the blood — leukemia — before she was five. So cancer was nothing new in my life — nor in that of Charlie and Kay. But could I get them to see now that it was both a gift from God and a bit of His Glory?

Played by Ear, the autobiography of Daniel A. Lord, S.J., was on my desk. He had but recently died from lung cancer after giving the world a blood-stirring example of faith and fortitude by working up to the very last minute, conscious all the time that the minutes were waning as cancerous cells multiplied. I would send that to Charlie; for he had known of Father Dan from high school days and his years in Our Lady's Sodality. I would tell him not only to read Dan's life but to lead it in his own. I would remind him of the quiet, heroic, thoroughly supernatural way both Mother and Dad had taken their cancers. I would also tell him about Joan Gasser, a student nurse at St. Joseph Infirmary, Louisville, who was discovered to have Hodgkin's disease just three months before graduation. The discovery had been made only a few days after my own operation. Between that time and the day of my discharge I came to know Joan Gasser quite well. Here indeed was a girl God had endowed not only with looks, personality, and keen intelligence, but had given her a greater gift in a vibrant faith. They told me she was heard crying the night the diagnosis was made. But I never saw her any way but brightly smiling. "I'm lucky," she said. "I know what I've got and what I can expect. I'll make the best of it." She not only went on to graduation, but took the Kentucky State Board examinations, passed them, then went home to Owensboro, joined the staff of Our Lady of Mercy

Hospital, and for three years showed the world around her how one should meet life and death. It was a joyful Joan who ministered to the sick in that hospital, and who finally became a patient in that same hospital. And it was a holily joyful Joan who died with a smile on her lips after three years of living with such a holy joy in her heart that it radiated from her person.

I would mince no words in this letter to Charlie. He would read the truth of what had been found in him, and what it meant. But he would read some other and much more vital truths in this same letter. He would read of what God had made of him by Baptism, and what this same God had a right to expect from him after this latest gift. I would insist upon the reality of the Mystical Body of Jesus Christ, and tell how special members are graced with the privilege of "filling up what is wanting to the Passion of Christ," as St. Paul has phrased it, and thus help God save mankind. Then I would urge my brother to look *ahead*. That would be my greatest objective. For experience had taught me how the clammy fogs of earth and human considerations are quickly dissipated by the white light of eternity which streams from the very throne of God — for those who have eyes to see it.

That letter was a long one. I humbly felt it was a good one. I prayed God to let Charlie see anything I had left unsaid, and to understand fully all that I had actually written.

Charlie never saw the letter. I was without the address of the new Carney Hospital in Boston, so I sent the letter to Kay on the Cape. I wanted her to read it anyhow; for I well knew she would have to get these stabilizing truths about God and life in Christ Jesus beating in her own blood if she was to face the future with any calm. She read them all right, but came pounding back at me with a plea that I write another and an entirely different letter; for Charlie was still in the dark; had no idea of what had been found in him; in fact, was quite convinced that he was a well man and would be back to work within a few days or a few weeks at most.

I sat back from that letter smiling at the fact that we can use words, at times, to do just what Talleyrand said we should make them do: conceal the truth. The surgeon who operated on Charlie had told him the truth — but because of the difference between the technical meaning of "positive" and the usually accepted meaning, Charlie had come to possess anything but the truth. The doctor had begun by saying: "Well, Charlie, we found a tumor in your lung. . . ." Before he could complete the sentence Charlie had broken in with: "Was it positive?" meaning, of course, was it "benign" or "favorable." The doctor very honestly replied that it was positive. "I excised it," he said, "and had it examined. . . ." Charlie again broke in. "Good," he said. "Did you tell my wife?" And the greatly relieved doctor replied: "I sure did. I called her from surgery and gave her all the facts." And Charlie sank back under the influence of the sedation they had given him.

I did not blame this doctor; for I had discussed the advisability of telling patients about inoperable cancer with more than one physician, and had found that most were opposed to the telling. They claimed the revelation would kill the morale necessary to carry on in life bravely. Some had even cited cases where real despair had set in almost as soon as the information had been given. I could understand all that. But, as a priest of God, I always felt that the patient had a right to know, and claimed that all that was needed for a morale booster was proper orientation to God and Heaven. I surmised now that the Boston surgeon was of the school that believed it inadvisable to acquaint their patients with the facts. But I was writing no different letter to Charlie. Instead I was writing a very spirited letter to Kay, telling her that the soul was infinitely more important than the body; that the priest has a right and a duty as well as the physician; that Charlie was a Catholic college graduate who knew not only how to put first things first, but very definitely how to face what Theology calls "The Last Things."

That second letter was sent air mail, special delivery; for Charlie was now back on the Cape and due home from the Barnstable County Hospital there in a day or two. But my spirited effort to keep that particular letter from Charlie was what actually put it in his hands. For the special delivery boy arrived at 33 Blanid Road just a few hours after Charlie had; and in all good faith the boy placed the letter in Charlie's hands. Without even looking at the "Mrs." on the address, Charlie tore it open and read what set him questioning Kay.

Her next letter told me that she had managed to dodge the real issue and left Charlie wondering just what it was that I knew which the others did not know. At the close of her letter Kay admitted that, after all, it was providential that Charlie had intercepted that letter; for, when the discovery would come, it would not be such a shock and disappointment to him.

It was more than a month later that the discovery did come; and it was made in my presence. In early January of 1957 I had been in St. Joseph Infirmary in Louisville for a check on my own cancer. While telling a friend about Charlie's case I was called to the phone. It was Charlie calling from Osterville, Massachusetts. When I told the friend who was on the other end of the line, he said: "Ask him if he can come down. Tell him I'll pay for the ticket." At this news, Charlie gasped. Then in suppressed emotion came the words: "Joe, this is almost unbelievable. Only last night I was saying to Kay that the one thing on earth I wanted was a visit with you."

That was how it came about that I saw my brother for the first time in twenty-one years. It is easy to see why I grew keenly conscious of the nearness of God. When I had left Gethsemani for Louisville, Charlie was on my mind, but never a thought that before I returned to the monastery I would have seen him and that he would be traveling back with me. It is also easy to see why I suspected that this lung cancer meant much to Heaven. So many utterly unexpected things were coming to pass, while the carefully planned affairs were all going awry.

When Charlie walked in on me one Friday afternoon looking the picture of health and aglow with love and excitement, the first thing I did was welcome him warmly to our "Cancer Club." In some ways this is only a name. In other ways it is a tremendous reality. It has no officers, no meetings as such, no dues. Yet its members, if you can call them that, meet every morning "in Christ Jesus" and pay their dues daily by earnest prayer that each and every other member will be granted the grace to fulfill the purpose God had in mind when He favored them with the privilege of suffering for Him with cancer. This very loosely organized group came into being when so many priests, nuns, and layfolk — all rather close acquaintances — found themselves visited by the same disease. Sister Margaret, supervisor of surgery at St. Joseph Infirmary and a charter member of this "Club," dropped in on me shortly after Charlie's arrival. She sized up the situation immediately and joined me in initiating Charlie into his duties and privileges as member of this organization. It was all done in a light, offhand manner, but there was no missing the point of all the banter. Charlie stood up to all of it without blinking an eye. He even added his bit to the very enjoyable badinage.

We then went on to tell of different members of the "Club," naming their specific type of cancer and outlining the treatment they had received. We even mentioned some of the former members who had completed their task for God. We used no "double talk" whatsoever; we did not even employ what many would term a "diplomatic approach" to the difficult subject. So it was not too long before I felt I had accomplished all I had intended by that first long letter which Charlie had never seen. I was more than relieved by the manly way my younger brother seemed to accept the entire matter.

But that night, as I lay reflecting on the session, I found a question rising in my mind because of the perfect calm with which Charlie had taken the almost bald presentation of a very personal fact. I wondered whether God had blinded him momentarily to the full import of inoperable cancer, or whether Charlie himself had been rendered numb by the impact of the truth, and had covered his numbness with a smile and those almost too ready words. I could not question him immediately; for he had been taken into the hospitable home of my surgeon, the late Doctor Michael Joseph Henry.

A few days later, however, when Charlie complained of chest pains, an X ray was taken of his lung. We were both present when the technician brought the film in and handed it to Doctor Maxwell, one of the Infirmary's radiologists. He read it for us then and there. The shadow in the upper lobe of the right lung was easily discernible. The doctor, however, was psychologist enough to run the end of his pencil over the rest of the lung and enthusiastically remark: "You have plenty of breathing space there, Charlie." So I abetted him by saying to my brother: "By the looks of that, instead of going to Heaven, you'll have to go back to work." But I had seen enough X rays to recognize why it was that the surgeon in Boston had closed Charlie's chest without excising that tumor, convinced that the case was beyond surgical skill. Doctor Maxwell made no mention of cancer or reference to the tumor. So it was a light-hearted younger brother who set out with me for Gethsemani late that same afternoon. During the fifty-mile drive he talked often about going back to work soon. Again that question of the first night arose in my mind: Did the boy really understand his condition?

The Right Reverend Dom James, Abbot of the Monastery, gave us a royal welcome. When we finally left the Abbot's room I stopped to pick up a handful of mail that had accumulated in my absence, then led Charlie down through the passages of the subcellar to the quiet and hidden room allowed me for my writing. As I entered I said: *"Ecce catacumba mea!"* While Charlie was looking around, I selected from among the mail a large envelope bearing the stamp of "Barnstable County Hospital" and extracted the letter.

It was from Doctor Julius G. Kelley, superintendent of the hospital in Pocasset, on Cape Cod. I had asked this good man, some weeks earlier, to favor me with a full report on Charlie's case, giving even his prognosis. The letter began by telling how Charlie had been found "to have a round infiltrate in the right upper lung field during an X-ray survey on September 18, 1956." That was the date Charlie was not likely to forget; for it happened to be the day for voters to register, and he and Kay had gone to do their duty. As they came out of the building after registering, Kay saw a mobile X-ray outfit across the street and cried: "Let's have our chests X-rayed, Charlie."

"What for?" was the rather dampening reply, but he crossed the street with her to the van.

Less than a week later, when a card arrived at 33 Blanid Road, advising Charlie to report to the nearest hospital for further study of his chest, he had only disdain for the suggestion. When Kay urged him to take the card seriously he cried: "Why, good heavens, girl, I never felt better in my life."

Doctor Kelley's letter went on to tell me that Charlie finally did report "for further diagnostic studies on October 18." He then confessed that they had been unable to make a definite diagnosis at Pocasset, but that "since this type of lesion is often serious, it was decided that he should have his chest opened as a therapeutic measure." I knew all this. So did Charlie whom I had beckoned to read the letter over my shoulder. But, the letter went on: "This procedure was carried out by Dr. Francis E. Woods of the Overholt Thoracic Clinic, who is on the staff of the Carney Hospital in Boston, on November 14. An epidermoid carcinoma was found which was inoperable because of the extensive involvement of the glands of the mediastinum. It was decided that the tumor could not be removed and the chest was closed. . . ."

The only real news for me in that passage was the name of the cancer. But it was all news to Charlie, and I could all but feel his growing excitement. I hurried down through the paragraphs describing the nitrogen-mustard treatment, its nature, and its purpose, to the last paragraph. It read: "I am sorry to have to inform you that this situation is getting progressively worse, and the outcome is his eventual death. We hope to prolong his life so that he may be with his family as long as possible. At the present time he is free from pain except for some disability in the region of the chest wound, but we can assure you that his difficulties will be kept at a minimum with the proper use of pain relievers."

When I got that far, I turned to find a somewhat white-faced and wide-eyed Charlie staring down at the letter. All I could do was smile a brotherly, love-filled smile and say: "There it is for you, boy."

He did his best to smile back, but his best was not quite good enough. He finally whistled: "Whew! No pulling of punches there, is there?"

The bell was ringing for Vespers, so I hurried him to his room, showed him how to get to the refectory in the Guest House and promised to be back in his room before he had finished his supper.

I was up to his room long before anyone would normally be out from the Guest-House supper. But Charlie was there before me — and it was evident that he had been crying. "Don't you like our food, Chic?" I asked as airily as possible.

He did not rise to such bait. He took a long inhale from his cigarette, let the smoke out slowly, then said: "Guess I can't take it, Joe. Your food looked wonderful. But I got thinking. . . . It's Kay and the kids. . . ." He took a few more puffs from his cigarette, then while snubbing it out said: "You know, I never believed I had cancer until I saw that letter. I had read your special delivery to Kay. It made me suspicious. I asked some questions up at the hospital in Pocasset.

Their cozy replies made me more suspicious. But I have been feeling so good. . . . Then there was Doctor Woods' answer the day of the operation. . . . So, even when you and Sister Margaret welcomed me to the 'Cancer Club,' I still did not believe it. The X ray at St. Joe's and the way that young doctor read it confirmed me in my belief that whatever I had, I did not have cancer. But now. . . ." He looked away, and I saw he was filling up again. He drew out his handkerchief, and blew hard.

I laid some reading matter I had brought on the table and quietly said: "Well, Chic, I'm glad you learned the truth in a place named after the place Christ learned the truth, and that you are crying out somewhat as He did. Don't let your tears bother you, boy. Jesus Christ, the strongest Man who ever lived, did something more than weep in His Gethsemani. When He saw death before Him He sweated blood. There's nothing to be ashamed of in your tears. . . ."

"Oh, Joe, I'm not afraid to die. But Kay and those kids. . . . Does she know all you know?"

"Every bit, Chic; and has known it all along."

"That poor kid! What a life I've given her. And she carried it off so well! When I read your letter I questioned her sharply; for your lines had shaken me. I was just home from the hospital and thought everything was rosy. . . . Yet she satisfied me with her answers and actually quieted my rising fears. What a girl! . . ."

Again he began to pace back and forth, and again I could see tears forming in his eyes. I find it difficult to look on any man in tears. But when that man was my own brother, and when I knew the reason for those tears, I found myself choking up badly. I knew something should be said. But I could not trust my voice. Charlie had the advantage of a cigarette over me. He could draw in big inhales and let out much of his tensions with the smoke. All I could do was clear my throat noisily and vigorously blow my nose. But finally I found my voice and said: "Listen, boy. We have Compline in five minutes. I've got to go. After that there is *Salve.* I want you to be present at that, and I want you to place yourself, your case, your wife, and your kids in the Immaculate Heart of Mary. She is our Mother, you know. We must never forget that fact! After *Salve* I have some Office to make up. So you go directly to bed. I'll call you for Mass in the morning. God love you, boy, and grant you deep sleep!"

With that I hurried away. My heart was aching for the one I had just left and for his family up on Cape Cod. My head filled with memories, even as flashes of the possibilities for the future stabbed their way between those memories. Yet, I honestly believe that it was these distractions that made me so recollected that night and had me praying so intently and intimately to God.

The Office I had to make up took me longer than I had anticipated. I was genuinely surprised to find that it was after eight o'clock when I closed my breviary. I stole up to the corridor in the Guest House and was startled to find light streaming from under the door of Charlie's room. I knocked quietly and immediately entered. There was my brother at the side of the table snuffing out a cigarette in a tray that was piled high with other butts that had been snuffed out with a hard, nervous hand. He had not even taken off his coat. And his face was wet with tears.

I crossed the room quietly and sat on the side of an extra bed that was there. It was time of Sacred Silence and I should have been asleep for over an hour by this time. But I felt sure that Christ would never leave any soul in such distress.

Charlie flung himself into a chair and blurted out: "Who's going to take care of those kids? How can Kay ever bring them up alone?"

I waited a moment before saying as softly and as kindly as I could: "Chic, I can answer both of those questions, but you wouldn't even hear me unless you do now what I'm going to beg you to do so long as you're down here — and so long as you live." He waited now, so I had to go on. "If we think of Kay and those kids along merely natural lines, Charlie, we're beaten. But we don't have to think along those lines! God is God. He's asking us to believe as we never believed before. And the first thing we've got to believe with all our being is that He knows what He is doing. You don't want this cancer. Neither do I. But obviously God wants us both to have it. So why not rejoice? We're always saying: 'Thy Will be done.' Let's do it. As for Kay and the kids. Let's realize something we may never have fully realized before. They are His kids much more than they are yours. He is their Father much more completely than you could ever be. You and Kay brought them to birth. But who gave them their being? God, of course. We don't believe enough in Divine Providence, Chic. That's why we get panicky. Don't you see that since God is the Father of your kids He is obligated to care for them? Yes, I said obligated! We pray the Our Father often enough, but we live the Our Father all too seldom. You're going to learn your Faith as you never learned it before — and you're going to live it as you never lived it before. God will take care of those kids. He has plans for their futures more complete than anything you could dream. What's more, He can make His plans come true. We don't trust God enough, Chic — and I believe it hurts Him. Show yourself to Him as you love your kids to show themselves to you. Your immediate concern is not the kids — or even Kay. Your immediate concern is to ready yourself for the most glorious moment of your existence: the moment of your meeting God face to face!"

I looked at my brother closely and saw that my softly spoken but intensive words had but slightly distracted him from his preoccupation. For a moment I was baffled. When I saw him nervously light up another cigarette, I took off my cowl, turned down the covers on the extra bed, and said: "I'm staying with you tonight."

He gasped, "Can you?"

"Looks as if," said I nonchalantly, and emptied the overfilled ash tray into a wastebasket. Inwardly I was kicking myself for not having realized how frightened the boy was. My mere physical presence was enough to transform him from a grown man afraid to take off his clothes and lie down with his fears, to an eager, trust-filled, and happy young brother.

When his gratitude came out in a boyish: "Oh, gee!" I chuckled, sat on the side of the bed and said: "Since you're so wide awake, young fellow, let's get down to brass tacks. Some people would say you read your death warrant as you looked over my shoulder this afternoon. But I say you read your passport to Heaven; you looked on the visa that will allow you into the Presence of God. People will say: 'Hard luck, Charlie. Truly a tough break.' But I say you're one of the luckiest stiffs alive. We've all got to die. But not many ever get anything like the clear indication of their specific way Home that is now yours. Death is nothing to fear, Chic. In fact, it's something to love and to look forward to. For it's our only way to God — and glory!"

He seemed to be listening closely, so I went on with: "Actually, it is not death that men fear; it's the Judgment. But now I'm going to let you in on a little lesson I received in what I call 'Applied Theology.' When I was first in St. Joe's for my cancer, Father Gerard, a fellow monk, came in from Gethsemani with pneumonia. Of course I was allowed to visit him and speak with him — something I hadn't done in the thirteen years we had lived together. Somehow or other we got off on the subject of Purgatory. Now frankly, we know very little about this place of purification save that it is a mystery of God's love, mercy, and justice. But after we had chatted for some time, this good young priest just about took my breath away with the statement that he did not expect to go through Purgatory. Just then, Sister James Marion, the nun in charge of that floor, happened to look in. I called to her: 'Come in, Sister, and meet a man who expects to go directly from earth to Heaven.' She looked at me quizzically so I told her the discussion we were having and the statement Father Gerard had made. She looked at me very levelly and said: 'I don't expect to go to Purgatory, either, Father.' I whistled much as you did earlier today, sidled toward the door and said: 'You two will excuse me, won't you? I've often thought I'd be lucky to land in Purgatory.' With that I went over to my room and began to think the matter through. I must confess that since I gave all my merits to Mother Mary as a Jesuit novice I practically never think of this matter of Purgatory and the possibility of avoiding it entirely. But as I sat in my room there in Louisville reflecting on the Dogma of Indulgences, thinking of all the merit and mercy that must be heaped up by assistance at Mass, then dwelling on the doctrine of the Communion of Saints, trying to measure at least in some vague way all the satisfaction being given to God by the many martyrs of our own days, I saw the possibility — and even the high probability — of many earnest Religious and generous layfolk going directly to Heaven. I crossed the corridor and looked in at Father Gerard and Sister James Marion and laughed as I said: 'I'm the heretic, not you people.' Just think, Chic, of all the merit a hospital nun must amass in a single day when she does everything for the glory of God. Her every step can serve to pay off that temporal punishment due to sin."

He nodded slowly, then surprised me with the comment: "I hope it is not only hospital nuns and Religious who can do what you say. I hope we lay people do much the same. I can understand your Father Gerard and your Sister James Marion; for I myself hope to go direct from earth to Heaven."

The temptation to whistle my astonishment was strong. I managed to suppress it and say: "Good for you! That's the very point I was going to make about this cancer of yours. It can easily be turned into real cash; made the kind of currency God will accept as payment for anything you may owe Him in the line of temporal punishment. While you are here at Gethsemani, Chic, talk very honestly, intimately, and seriously with God and His Mother. Tell Them how glad you are to take this thing for the glory of our Father, who is God, and for the sake of our fellow men who are sinners. Thank God sincerely for this privilege He is according you. Ask Mother Mary, and all Heaven, for the grace to live joyously from now on out — until you join Them. Actually, Chic, when we think deeply and rightly, we see that we have no reason whatsoever for not living gloriously all the time."

He studied the slow spiral of smoke that rose from the cigarette he had just snuffed out, then began quietly and slowly: "You want me to fly high, don't you?" Then with gradually mounting intensity he said: "I can take it, Joe. Yes, as far as I am concerned personally I think I can do all you ask. But Kay . . . and those kids. . . . They've got to live, you know; and living takes money. . . ."

He swallowed hard. I could guess what was coming. I, too, had thought of the financial angle and the long future before those seven youngsters. But this was no time to go into that. So I hurriedly interjected: "Now look, Charlie. While you're here I'm going to pound some truths into you. Truths by which we live. The first is one you do not seem to have comprehended as yet. It is this: Those kids are God's far more than they are yours. Hence, you can leave them in His very capable hands. Get that?"

There was the faintest trace of a smile on his face as he pushed my playfully threatening fist away. "The same goes for Kay," I went on. "If you ask me, I'll say she's lucky to have God for a provider. I know you haven't asked me. But I'm telling you anyhow. I'm also telling you that we have to get up early in the morning, so we're going to say the Glorious Mysteries of the Rosary; then you're going to bed."

"Glorious?" he questioned. "Wouldn't the Sorrowful ones be more appropriate?"

"That's why I chose the Glorious. Just to be appropriate. You don't realize it yet, but this day's discovery was one of the most glorious things in your life. And if you'll be wise you'll say nothing but the Glorious Mysteries from now until you join Him who ascended and her who was assumed. For the most prudent thing you can do from this moment on is to focus your gaze on your future — your ultimate, glorious future."

As he fumbled for his beads and arranged his chair to serve as prie-dieu, I went on: "You know, Chic, it often appears to me that we Catholics do not have the foggiest idea of who we are or what we are doing. For instance, have you ever realized that you are actually living the Mysteries of the Rosary every day of your life, and especially the Glorious Mysteries?"

He turned toward me and a frown gathered on his forehead as he said: "I am living the Resurrection this very day when I just read my death warrant?"

I fingered my crucifix preparatory to blessing myself, left his question resting in the air for a moment, then said: "The first Glorious Mystery is Christ's Resurrection from the dead, Charlie, not ours. Yet it is thanks to that very Mystery — to that Resurrection — that you and I are alive this moment with the life that need never die — the life of glory! But more about that tomorrow. Our first intention tonight will not be Kay and the kids, much as your heart desires it. It will be gratitude to God — an expression of our warm thanks to Him for cancer. Believe me, boy, it is going to work wonders! It already has! Thanks to it, you and I are now together for the first time in twenty-one years. Let's be very grateful. In the name of the Father, and of the Son, and of the Holy Ghost. Amen. . . ."

CHAPTER TWO

A Promise About Mysteries

ON WEDNESDAY Charlie got his first taste of monastic life. He was up early; served my Mass in the Crypt under Gethsemani's Basilica; then went to breakfast. In the short period of time between breakfast and Tierce I briefed him as well as I could on the Divine Office and the Conventual Mass. He assisted at both. Having reported to my first Superior concerning the happenings in my "Catacomb" and Charlie's room the day before, I obtained full permission to spend all time possible outside of choral duties with Charlie, and was even granted the rarest of all permissions — that of staying the night with him in his room. Armed with this freedom I made Charlie put on his hat and coat after Mass and took him outside the walls.

We headed for the milking parlor on a knoll to the west of the Monastery from which the full panorama of Gethsemani can be taken in. The weather was sunny but the temperature was fourteen above zero, which is cold for Kentucky. We were both glad to gain the shelter of the milking parlor. Pointing out the various details of this modern establishment took so much time that Charlie was well warmed up when I invited him outside for a view of Kentucky's knobs.

Far to the east of us Rohan's Knob stood out in cold clarity. I pointed to it and told my brother how the first band of Trappists who had come to America in 1803 had settled at its base after living a short time close to Bardstown. I summarized their various moves: from Bardstown to the base of Rohan's Knob; from there to East St. Louis; from there to what is now the site of St. Patrick's Cathedral on Fifth Avenue, New York City. Charlie jerked his head toward me at mention of that detail. I laughed and said: "That's the historic fact, Chic. They were certainly nomadic Trappists. They went back to France after the defeat of Napoleon at Waterloo. But even at that, one of them got stranded in Nova Scotia and actually founded the monastery which gave New England its present monks. Eight of the monks of that group of traveling Trappists lie buried at the base of that Knob. I was sent to see if I could get the bones one day. The good pastor told me I was welcome to them if I could find them, but it was his opinion that God alone knew where they were buried. A monument erected in the churchyard gives the names of the monks, but the monument is over no grave. The name of that church Charlie, is the same as that of your Alma Mater — Holy Cross."

That led me to tell my brother of the first procession of the Blessed Sacrament ever to be held in Kentucky. It was one that made its way from the Trappist Monastery to the Church of the Holy Cross — a distance of about a mile. Then I pointed out that we were now standing in the middle of what Michael Williams had called "America's Holy Land." To the left of us was Nazareth, motherhouse of the Sisters of Charity, who had a Bethlehem Academy in nearby Bardstown. A bit to our left was Loretto, motherhouse of the Sisters of Loretto, the second All-American community of Sisters, founded very shortly after the first, that of Nazareth. We were standing on ground called Gethsemani and looking to a veritable Mount of Calvary slightly to the north of us. Around about us lay St. Vincent's, St. Francis', St. Mary's. On a clear day the bells of the various motherhouses, Monastery, and parish churches could be heard calling to one another, announcing, as it were, the grand news that "the Angel of the Lord declared unto Mary" — and that the "Word was made flesh."

When my brother asked how the locale happened to be so thoroughly Catholic I told him some early colonial history that is not recounted often enough. I told him of the all-Catholic county of St. Mary's in Maryland whence some sixty families came in 1785 to settle on Pottinger's Creek, part of which ran through our property of Gethsemani, and how they eventually brought into being the first Catholic diocese west of the Alleghenies with its Cathedral at Bardstown. I could not resist the temptation to tease my brother by saying: "By the way, Charlie, that settlement in Maryland outrivals what you have on the Cape. You have Plymouth Rock with all its memories of the Puritan Fathers and the *Mayflower*. But Maryland has memories of an *Ark* and a *Dove*, Lord Baltimore, and what Cape Cod never had — religious toleration. That is why I dare to say you are standing on ground right now that is more American than anything you have up around Boston, despite Paul Revere, Lexington, Concord, and the Minute Men. For, you see, the *Ark* and the *Dove* dropped anchor in Chesapeake Bay just a little over a decade of years after the *Mayflower* had stood off the shore of Plymouth; but they brought to America something the Puritans never brought — real religious freedom."

Charlie's comment was: "I'm not going to argue for Cape Cod or the Massachusetts Bay Colony. All I'm going to say is that I live with Kay and the kids on the Cape — and it's a beautiful place to live. I'll even add I find them beautiful people to live with. I suppose there are a few Puritans around but I have no dealings with them. But, tell me, what is that huge cross on that hill opposite us?"

"Not many know it, but that is almost Gethsemani's tombstone. We call that little rise 'Calvary Hill' but few of the present community realize how aptly it is named. That cross marks the original site of the Gethsemani School for Girls — a thing the first monks thought they were committed to by a promise a speaker made the day the first community opened its drive for funds to build our Monastery. He wasn't even a monk at the time, yet he told the people that if they would contribute to the building of a home for the monks, the monks would see to it that two schools were built for their children and that their boys and girls were really educated. The monks kept that promise, Chic; but keeping it almost killed them and the Monastery. It's too long a story to tell now. It brings in abbots, bishops, nuns, parish priests, and what not. But I'll say now that when looking on those two hills: the one with the cross and the other over there with the statue of St. Joseph on it, you are looking at two hills that hold and hide history and heartbreak. Where St. Joseph now stands there once stood a full-fledged college. It burned down in 1912, and most of the monks were happier than the schoolboys. Some of them even said the fire was sent from Heaven; for conducting a college is no job for contemplatives."

"Speaking of fire, Joe, let's find one. I'm frozen!"

"Oh, Charlie, excuse me! I forgot all about your light coat. When I get wound up I guess I get warmed up. . . ."

"You're still the same, Joe. Twenty years of silence has not slowed up your flow of talk. In fact, I think it has speeded it up a bit. But we can see some of this country from the window in my room. You can tell me more of its story from there."

I hurried him down through Aden Nally's yard, telling how Aden's father had worked for the monks until he was over eighty-three, and how Aden had followed in his father's footsteps, and would celebrate his golden jubilee of service this coming May. When I added that I considered Aden more saintly than many a silent monk, Charlie, who was puffing slightly, asked: "Who said the good die young?"

Once back in his room and the chill not yet out of his system, Charlie showed that, despite his keen interest in all the history that had been poured out, the really absorbing consideration of his being was the discovery he had made yesterday and all that it connoted for him and his own. For we were hardly seated when he asked: "What's the straight dope on a general confession, Joe?"

I looked at the clock and saw that I had but a few minutes before Sext, so I hedged with: "Take it easy, fellow. You're not ready for the last rites yet."

"I know. But I also want the straight dope on confession. When should a man make a general confession?"

"That's easily answered, Chic. Maybe never." When he frowned I went on. "I know a nun who was hurried to Boston from the Midwest for a very serious operation at the Massachusetts General. When her Reverend Mother tried to break the news to her just how serious it all was, and quietly urged her to prepare for possible immediate Judgment, the nun laughed and said: 'Get me a confessor, Reverend Mother. But know well I'm not going back any further than my last weekly confession. I've always tried to make a fully honest confession. So I'm going to show God I trust Him.' To me, Chic, that is the sanest attitude possible. It's also, in a way, a tribute to God. He said to His Apostles — and to all His priests: 'Whose sins you shall forgive, they *are forgiven.*' To go back over old sins and reconfess old confessions is something like questioning God's sincerity. Take Him at His word. He said those sins are forgiven. So forget them." Charlie made no comment, so I went on. "Just before my own operation for cancer, I had visions, and even hopes, of dying. So, like just about everyone else in a similar position, I thought of a general confession. I sent for my Abbot. But by the time he arrived I had reconsidered the matter. I laughed and said I was sorry for the trouble I had put him to but was glad he was present. I then told him my thought processes on the matter of general confession and concluded by confessing from my last weekly confession. I'd do the same tomorrow if I were in the same position. I trust God."

"So do I, Joe. But as you know, not all of us have put in years behind protecting monastery walls. When should a fellow make a general confession?"

"I've got to hurry to Sext, Charlie, but I can give you the fullest answer in fewest words. General confessions are either necessary or simply useful. They are necessary when one is absolutely sure he has made a bad confession — deliberately concealed some sin that was serious, for instance — then went on living as if he had made a good confession. That man or woman can only get right with God and self by going back to the last good confession he or she made before that bad one, and making a general confession of all since. General confessions are useful before the big events of our lives; before marriage, ordination, final vows, or the like. You're not before any of those just now, so I'll see you after dinner."

That afternoon was spent within the enclosure. There are many things that interest an outsider within a Trappist monastery: the church, the choir, the stalls, the choir books; the sacristy with its vestments and sacred vessels; then the various "regular places" such as chapter room, scriptorium, refectory, dormitory, and workroom. While showing these places to a visitor one can very easily give him the history of the house and enlighten him on the spirit of the Order. Then there are the gardens, garth, tiled cloister, and Stations of the Cross to be seen. I showed my brother all such places and gave a running commentary on their specific uses. I found him exception- ally silent through it all. In the cemetery, where I showed him the graves of the various abbots and monks, I noted he knelt long at

Brother Joachim's grave, but it was only months later that I learned how he had asked and obtained from "The Man Who Got Even With God" what he called a "moral miracle."

After I had shown him the various shops, garages, barns, the smoke-house, the meat-processing plant, along with the cheese factory, laundry, bakery, and water purifying system, he exclaimed: "Boy, this is a little world all its own."

"That's how St. Benedict wanted it, Chic. He wanted his monks to have everything they needed right behind their cloistering walls so that they could live not only for God alone, but with God alone."

"St. Benedict would be satisfied with Gethsemani, I'm sure. Above all, Joe, you have something here I've felt since the moment we arrived. You have peace. I have felt it everywhere I've been — even up in the milking parlor this morning. I used to pity you being locked in down here. Not any more! Now I only envy you."

When we got back to his room late that afternoon, we found that Father Prior had set out some very welcome refreshments. As we partook of them Charlie again brought up the matter of a general confession. "It's not necessary, thank God. But I think it would be useful," was his comment.

"You're the boss, there, Charlie. But be sure you know what you're doing and why. If you really want to make a general confession I'll get you a good confessor. We have plenty. After all, it might be a very smart thing to do. And surely, you couldn't get a better place to prepare yourself for it than Gethsemani."

"That's what I thought, too, Joe. But you don't have to look up any confessor. You'll do."

"I . . . ? You want to make a general confession to me?"

Charlie could not miss the surprise, the warning, and even the anxiety in the question. Yet he only nodded his head affirmatively.

I think I made a quick recovery. I am not sure. But I know I said: "O.K. You're the boss in that matter, too. Come to think of it, I made a similar choice once. Just before coming down here I made something of a general confession to Jack." Jack is our eldest brother, Director of the Jesuit Mission Band of New England.

"So I'm following good example, am I not?" said Charlie with a smile.

"Improve on it, Chic. There's no immediate rush in the matter. Take tonight and tomorrow morning for a real preparation. Pray God to give you all the light you need. Pray Mother Mary to grace you with real contrition. Divide your life into periods: grammar school days, high school, college, premarital period, married life. Recall the specific duties of each state in your life and see how you fulfilled them. Go over the Commandments in order — and the Precepts of the Church. It's not so difficult an affair. I'll help you all I can. But, Chic, before you even begin your remote preparation I must tell you that I will not even hear your confession unless you promise me right now never to go back over your past life again — even on your deathbed."

He shook his head and gave a slow but firm "O.K."

That night I was allowed to stand beside him in the gallery of our Basilica while the Community below us sang the *Salve*. It was an experience for me to hear the manly prayer of praise and petition rise in the dark from the depths below. I entered into that prayer and praise with exceptional fervor; for I was very mindful of a lung cancer case I had seen in the hospital this past year. Gus Hayden had been just Charlie's age. He had been even more sturdily built. Like Charlie he had come to the hospital with no inkling of what was wrong with him. Yet eight months after his operation Gus was dead. I knew this most likely was the last night we would be together on earth. I knew we could not spend it in any better way than we were at that moment: calling on the Queen of the Universe and naming her "Mother of Mercy, our life, our sweetness and our hope"; begging her to turn her motherly, merciful eyes toward us, and to show us at the end of our exile — Jesus.

I made Charlie file out with the Community to receive the Abbot's blessing at the door of the Basilica. We monks are used to this. We do it every night of our lives. But, apart from the Conventual Mass, nothing at Gethsemani so deeply impressed my younger brother.

It had been a long day. Charlie should have been tired out and ready for bed. But when he got to his room he was full of talk, especially about his children. He gave me the special feature that marked each as an individual, illustrated their characteristics with stories of their accomplishments, and let me see more of his heart than he realized as he tried to make me see his youngsters. The elder girls were exceptionally fine swimmers, according to this proud father; Charlie, Jr., was at times a tease, sometimes even a torment, but never anything but completely lovable. Keven, it appeared, was something of a thinker. "I call Charlie 'the Mayor,' for he knows everyone in town, and everyone knows him. When I walk down the street with him, he greets everybody, and practically everybody greets him. He knows ever so many more people down there than I do. But Kev I call 'the philosopher.' I don't think anyone in our family was ever so quiet or self-contained."

That led us into a discussion of the members of our large family. There had been ten of us: six boys and four girls; but one of the boys had died before Charlie was born, so he always thought of us as numbering nine. The elder five had gone into religion: three priests and two nuns; Jim, the second eldest of the family, had died as a result of the flu in 1918. So that left the family domain to Charlie and the two girls, Peg and Betty. Peg married. Betty became a schoolteacher. It was very enjoyable to go over the old days, and quite enlightening to go over some that were not so old. Charlie had some truly keen observations to make not only on the younger, but also on the older members of the family.

He told me of his recent travels in North Africa, Turkey, and Saudi Arabia, where he had gone as representative for a construction company engaged in the building of our overseas' air bases. He had some fascinating stories to tell of his various experiences, but I noted that he always came back soon to his family and our own Mother and Dad. Undoubtedly Doctor Kelley's letter had done things to Charlie's mind and memory. Unquestionably, too, God was doing some very rare things to his soul.

We ended the evening with the Rosary, and again I insisted on the Glorious Mysteries. I told him that he was to say nothing for the rest of his days but the same Glorious Mysteries.

Next morning he served my Mass and assisted at the Conventual Mass. Then, before I could make a single suggestion, he said: "Let's make that general confession now."

When he rose from his knees after absolution had been given, he smiled, lit a cigarette, and after a first long inhale said: "So all

I have to do is 'live joyfully,' huh? That's the queerest and the easiest penance I ever received."

"Are you sure? You're liable to be greatly surprised. You may yet find that I've given you the hardest penance of your existence. But, Chic, I'm convinced that God wants us to live joyously. Chesterton was right when he said, 'Joy is the secret of the Christian.' I believe it's the secret of the Christian saint. But did I actually say: Live *joyfully?*"

"You did."

"Well, let it go. I meant to say live *gloriously.* There's a shade of difference in the meaning. I don't think too many people are aware of the fact that we are members of the glorious Christ, the Man-God who came back from the grave. Nor are there so very many who fully realize they live their supernatural life only by actually sharing in those Mysteries of Christ we call Glorious. You asked me something about the Resurrection the other night. Do you realize that you have already risen in Christ?"

"Now, as Father Eddie would say, you're talking like a mystic."

Father Eddie is our brother who joined the Oblates of Mary Immaculate four years after I had joined the Jesuits, but who was ordained priest of God two full years before me. Eddie was the readiest wit of the family and possessed of a seemingly inexhaustible stock of stories, but he was impatient with anything that sounded obscure or appeared intangible. "The guy's a mystic" was his summation of any and all who did not deal in a spirituality as palapable as bread — and just as wholesome.

I jumped at Charlie's remark, and made ready to defend myself from what I considered a real slur, but just then word came that Mrs. Henry, widow of the doctor who had so expertly excised my cancer, was at the Gate House, ready to take Charlie back to Louisville and his plane. "We won't keep her waiting, Chic, but before you or I die, I'm going to make you eat those words — and like their taste. I'll tell you what I'll do: I'll write to you as often as my Abbot will allow — and I believe that will be about every two weeks — and I'll prove to you that you, Kay, and all your children — that every right living Catholic — is actually living the Mysteries of the Rosary; not only the Joyful and Sorrowful, but very especially the Glorious ones."

"Boy, will I look forward to those letters! And have you your work cut out for yourself. I can see that we live some of the Joyful Mysteries. At least joy is the characteristic of Gethsemani and her monks. I've seen it and felt it everywhere and in everyone. I know we share in the Sorrowful Mysteries. This cancer business. But the Glorious? . . . Well, as I say, I'll be looking for those letters."

As I bundled Charlie into his seat after having blessed him, I laid my hand on the door and said: "See you in Heaven, old boy, if I don't see you again on this earth." As if cued by the line, Mrs. Henry came right in with: "Don't talk nonsense, Father Raymond. Charlie is going to bring his wife and family down this summer, and they are going to spend some time with me." I believe my brother took that all-but-impossible picture to his heart rather than the much more highly probable reality I had presented with my words.

I walked back to the main building of the Monastery a rather lonely monk, shaking my head over all the omissions that marked the visit. I had not told him how to pray; how to make prayer a conversation and not a monologue; how to listen while at prayer and not always to be talking. What had I told him anyhow?

By the time I reached my workroom I realized two things: first, the visit had been so highly charged emotionally that I was really tired; second, without any premeditation on my part, I had been inspired to mark out a road not only for Charlie to walk, but for me to follow.

As I sat at my desk I wondered how much time I had to show Charlie just how intimate a life we should live with Jesus and Mary. No one of his medical men had so much as hazarded a guess as to his length of days. I myself was inclined to think his time was short. So I resolved to get to work right away on a task I humbly hoped and earnestly prayed would open his eyes to reality as they had never been opened before. My focus would be on the Glorious Mysteries not only as they had been and are being lived by Jesus and Mary, but as they should be lived by himself, Kay, his children, and all Catholics.

CHAPTER THREE

"The Living Man ... Is ... the Glory of God"

HAVE you ever tried to talk to one you thought was standing on the brink of the grave? It is one of the most rewarding experiences of life. For it makes you look at earth, and all things on earth, and see them in proper light. It forces you to view time in the only proper perspective: that of its relation to Eternity. It compels you to examine your own beliefs minutely. In brief: it brings you face to face with God.

The day after Charlie left Gethsemani we Trappists entered our annual retreat. Many people are amazed to hear that we walled-in monks make a yearly retreat, and are even more amazed when told that not only we, but Carthusians, Carmelites, Poor Clares, and every other cloistered contemplative in the Catholic Church are bound by law to make a retreat every year of their cloistered lives. "What in the world do they want with a retreat?" "Aren't such people always on retreat?" are the usual questions. Yes, we are "always on retreat." Yet Holy Mother Church, wise with the wisdom of almost two thousand years of experience, knows that no matter how divine a human being may strive to be, he or she will always retain much that is distinctly human, and ever remain in a nature that has fallen and can yet be deceived. She also knows that no matter how high we may have climbed in our ascent to God, there is always a peak just beyond that is yet to be conquered. Actually, for most contemplatives, retreat time is the happiest and holiest time of the year; for we go, as it were, into deeper cloister where we hold more intimate rendezvous with God and His Mother. There we strive to learn just what it is They wish from us in the coming year.

This particular year of 1957, after eight days of very real intimacy with Them, I felt it was Their desire and, therefore, my duty that I cultivate with ever greater care the virtue called *Pietas*. That was my one resolution; for with the passage of the years I have learned not only to follow the advice of all skilled directors of souls and make few resolutions, but I have managed to reduce my resolution to a single word. This year it was the word *Pietas*. For that word not only sums up the whole story of the God-Man's life on earth, but is a perfect word picture of Jesus. Further, it holds within itself practically all the directives of the Gospel; for it is that special virtue which marks a man as a loving son of God.

Is it not astounding that we can say a thing to ourselves in all sincerity hundreds and hundreds of times, yet never grasp the full meaning of what we are saying? During a retreat a monk often wakes up to the truth of things he has held as true since his early childhood, but which have never truly lived for him. I believe I had some such experience in this retreat; for I became acutely conscious of a need for a more intimate living with God both *as* His son and *in* His only Son. With greater clarity than ever I realized that my sainthood depended upon my becoming by grace what Jesus Christ is by nature — a *son of God*. For I saw that sanctity is nothing other than being "alive to God in Christ Jesus," and that being "alive to God in Christ Jesus" is nothing less than a participation in the glorious life of the Only-Begotten of the Father. But what could that participation be but *Pietas?*

Of course I knew I had been made a son of God by Baptism. But during this retreat it came home to me with special force that the whole problem of living is really a question of "becoming what we are." We are human, free, intelligent, and rational beings. But what a lifetime of struggle it takes to become any of those! So, too, with Christianity. We are all Christ — made so by Baptism. But to become Christ — what endless battles have to be fought, and won!

Reading the first Epistle of St. John the Apostle one day during retreat, I wondered if he did not have this very idea in mind when he wrote: "See what kind of love the Father has bestowed on us, that we should be children not merely in name but in reality. . . . now we are children of God, and what we shall be has not yet been manifested" (1 Jn. 3:1, 2).

Mulling over this idea of being "children of God" made me go to St. Peter's second Epistle and read that passage which tells how we "become partakers of the divine nature" (2 Pet. 1:4). That certainly reveals that we are not children of God by any mere legal fiction but in very fact. It is not only a thrilling truth, it is even somewhat frightening, for we well know that "actions follow nature"; that if we actually partake of the nature of God our actions should be Godlike. Hence there is fright until we remember that our life's work is to "become what we are" — and that a life's work is done only in a life's time. Possibly Peter had something like this in mind, and that is why he exhorted the earliest Christians "to supplement faith with moral courage, moral courage with knowledge, knowledge with self-control, self-control with patience, patience with piety, piety with brotherly affection, brotherly affection with love" (2 Pet. 1:5-7).

In time I realized I had Peter, Paul, and John in the one word *Pietas*. For retreat time is the most apt time for mulling over all matters of eternal importance. "Mulling" is the exact word; for you have time to pulverize and even atomize truths, then slowly heat them with your constant attention to them, then, by your will action upon them, spice them as you would a rare wine. In this way you come to "savor" these truths, as St. Ignatius of Loyola always exhorted retreatants to do, and come at last, at least in some remote way, actually to "taste God."

I was "mulling" this idea of "son of God" because of the impact the word *Pietas* was having on me. Soon, with real force and clarity it came home to me how essential it is for every monk — and every other man — to realize in the strictest sense of that word "realize," just who he is and what he is doing; how necessary it is for all Christians to be vividly and vitally aware that they are the "continuation of the Incarnation."

To get that truth in sharp focus you have to "mull" over the facts that authentic Christian life and actual Christian living are nothing else but a flowing of the divine life from the Father to the Son, from the Son, through His humanity and under His Spirit, into the Church, and from the Church into each member of the Mystical Body. That sets one's mind and heart right in the center of the Holy Trinity. Then to be realistic one has to conclude that Catholic

Christians, in all truth, *are* Christ; hence, the one work He came on earth to perform, they are on earth to complete. Men live to be loving sons who will give their Father the glory that is His due. Obviously, that can be done in only one way: by being Jesus Christ. For only the God-Man can offer God the glory that is His due; for only the God-Man is holy, as we sing in the *Gloria* of the Mass, and it is only through that unique holiness that He is glorified who is worthy of infinite glory. Hence, since the first and final vocation of the monk, as well as the first and final vocation of every man, is to give glory to God, it follows, inescapably, that the one work for every man and for every monk is none other than to be "alive to God in Christ Jesus" (Rom. 6:2) as St. Paul wrote to his Romans, or *Vivere in Verbo,* that is, live in Jesus Christ, as SS. Augustine and Bernard were so fond of phrasing it. So once again I saw that the word *Pietas* told the whole story for God as well as man. It could serve admirably as the simplification of life and living; for it would be the unification of all efforts and strivings.

How Christ loomed as the one answer to every vexing question! By His birth and His being He is the *Verbum Divinum,* the adequate expression of God's glory. St. Paul had told the Hebrews that truth when he wrote: "This Son is the radiant reflection of God's glory, and the express image of his nature" (Hebr. 1:3). We monks sing that truth almost daily; for in one of our hymns for Matins we hail Christ as *Splendor Paternae Gloriae.* What happiness to recall that this Splendor was seen shining from human eyes — for *Verbum caro factum est* — the Word was made flesh. What joy to go on and realize that He has incorporated us into that *Caro* — by becoming Head of a Body of which we are members. What a relief it is to see that we can fulfill the purpose for which we were made since "in Him, and with Him, and through Him," we can give God the Father a glory that is adequate, substantial, and, thanks to Jesus, infinite!

After such reflection, *Pietas* took on fuller meaning; for identification with Christ is not only the one answer to life's fundamental question, it is the solution to every problem that springs from any sense of frustration. For once you so identify yourself with Christ as to bring the virtue of piety to whitest heat, you are able constantly to lift to the Father, in fullest adoration, the very face of Christ. More than that: you are able to express your glowing gratitude to God adequately; for you can lift to Him the mind and will of Christ Jesus. Finally, to repair the outrages of mankind, your own among them the first, you are enabled to lift to God the nail-imprinted hands of Christ. To me it appeared that the one virtue that would seal into my soul the very face of Christ and thus enable me to be what I should be to the one, true, and only God, whom I am privileged to call "Father," was the virtue of piety.

That, then, was my retreat for 1957. But that was not all of it. Each day, as I said my Rosary, I thought of Charlie, Kay, and those children on the Cape. All that God was granting to me during these days I resolved to share with them as soon as my retreat ended. For this virtue of *Pietas* fitted in with all I was thinking as necessary for their lives now that God had touched them so intimately. For years I had visualized the family escutcheon as carrying but two words: *Fides* and *Fortitudo*. I had never told Charlie about this. Yet, as I pondered over what he would need most, and what Kay would require in real abundance, I could think only of Faith and Fortitude. I had planned to acquaint them with my concept of what our coat of arms should carry. But now that God and His Mother had made Their demand, as I felt, for piety, I would add a third word to the two very essential ones.

I wrote a long letter that can be summed up in three words: *Fides, Fortitudo,* and *Pietas.* Then I sat back waiting for replies. The first letter that arrived from Massachusetts was not a reply. It had crossed my long one in the mails. But it actually was a reply to many questions that were in my mind and heart. First it told how Charlie had flown home to Boston where he was met by Kay, whom he then kept up half the night talking about Gethsemani — and his cancer. Then it related how they had gone back to Osterville where Charlie immediately plunged into a remodeling of his little home. I rejoiced at that bit of news; for work is of supreme medicinal value to mind and nerves. But when Charlie concluded that part of his letter with: "I want to do all this while I am physically able. My only discouragement is that I tire so quickly," I realized that my brother was not only conscious of the possibilities latent in cancer of the lung for a speedy death, but also that the disease was at its dread work. For Charlie was so robustly built that the painting and light carpentering he had described should have stimulated rather than fatigued him.

A third question that was in my mind and heart had to do with the effect of his visit to Gethsemani on his mind and heart. I got my answer in a passage which ran: "How good God has been to me: granting so many pleasant hours with you; helping me to learn to trust Him implicitly; giving me a glimpse of monastic living and an insight into what real living is."

That would have been more than ample recompense for all effort exerted, but then came something which not only touched the heart but actually brought tears to my eyes: "I'm living joyfully, but how about that promise of yours?"

Lent was approaching, so I used that fact as my point of departure as I plunged into the task of keeping my promise. I told my brother how St. Benedict bids all his monks to enter the holy season with joy and spend the entire forty days in the same joyousness as "with spiritual joy and desire" they "await the holy Feast of Easter" (Rule, Chap. 49). Of course he asked each of them to "lead lives of greatest purity and atone for all the negligences of other times"; he also asked them to pray more, and do more penance — but always with joy — because all Lent, and all Lenten practices, are but a preparation for the Feast of all feasts and the Solemnity of all solemnities: Easter. I then reminded him that Bishop Fulton Sheen never tired of pointing out that while pagan orgies ended in fasts of some sort, every Christian fast ended in a feast.

I remarked that while the early Christians used to take pagan celebrations and, as it were, "baptize" them, turning them into Christian feasts, we modern Christians seem to have reversed all that. We seem to have allowed the present-day pagans to take our Christian feasts and so materialize them that they are too nearly now pagan celebrations. "And I'm not talking about the commercialization of Christmas," I wrote. "I'm talking about the Feast of all feasts, the one you are to focus your whole attention on as Christ gives you the privilege of helping Him save mankind by 'filling up what is wanting to His Passion.'"

To prove that point I took three events with which we were well acquainted in the years that had passed, but which I hoped were still current and popular: Surnise Service in the Hollywood Bowl, the egg-rolling contest on the White House lawn, and New York's Fifth Avenue Easter Parade. I began by saying I supposed there would be thousands of people crowding into Hollywood's Bowl this coming Easter dawn just as there used to be when I was without the walls. I hoped many would be participating actually in a religious service. "But," I asked, "how many present at that Service, as they called it, would be conscious of the fact that they were but repeating a ceremony that was Catholic in origin and completely Christian in intent?"

I then told how the people of Medieval Europe gathered in great crowds on Easter morning to watch the sun issue in the day. As it came up over the rim of their world, they broke forth into joyous religious hymns; for they saw that sun as a symbol of the Risen Christ. "Even today," I added, "in the Alpine regions of Austria, the same custom lives. But with these people it is always Christ that is seen in the rising sun. What is it with us? How many in the Hollywood Bowl would actually see in the Easter sunrise what should be seen: the symbolization of His Resurrection who is 'the Light of the World,' and who, in all truth, 'illumines every man'? (Jn. 1:9.) How many would see in the break of that day a symbol of His breaking of the bonds of death? How many would find in that dawn's mounting radiance a reminder of the life which He diffuses, and in which every man can share if he but will.

"That is the life you live, Chic and Kay. That is the life that pulses in your children, and has pulsed ever since they were baptized. That is the life we Catholics actually breathe. For what Paul said of himself, we can say of ourselves: 'In Him we live, and move, and have our being' (Acts 17:28). Kay, get all your youngsters to realize who they are. Tell each: You are a breath of God — and one He is still breathing."

The egg-rolling contest on the White House lawn was my next example. I asked how many of those who witnessed that affair would see in it a symbol of Christ's conquest over death, and recognize in the eggs a sign of that new life which could be theirs, thanks to that same Christ and that same conquest. I closed that illustration of my point by saying: "That kind of thing is as Catholic, and almost as old, as the Catacombs; but how many are aware of it?"

The third example, while it seemed the most secular of all, was the one freighted with the deepest religious significance. I did not stop with New York's Fifth Avenue, I crossed the continent from New York to Los Angeles, missing none of the big cities on the way, nor any of their places of promenade. I even reminded Charlie of the miniature "Easter Parade" we used to watch — and even take part in — on Dorchester's Columbia Road; then told Kay I supposed she would outfit her youngsters with new clothes for the day and have them "parading" somewhere on the Cape. Then I made my point by asking how many of those who put on new clothes at Easter ever thought while putting them on that they were symbolizing that reality of all realities: "the putting on of the new man — Christ?"

These "Easter Parades" I wrote were a paganization of what were once religious processions. In the old, and much more leisurely, days, the faithful were accustomed to take a walk through the fields after Mass. Soon wise parish priests were leading these walks with a lighted Paschal candle; turning what was once a stroll into a procession, and thus keeping alive in the minds and hearts of the people the truths and sentiments of the Easter Mass at which they had just assisted — especially that thrilling truth that the Dead Man of Calvary was alive with a glorified life in which all the baptized shared.

At the end of my letter I asked Charlie and Kay if they or any of their children could tell me why it is that, on Sundays, we say the *Angelus* standing and not kneeling. It was a question whose answer I learned from the side reading I was doing to shape these letters about the Glorious Mysteries. Back in the year 325, the Council of Nicea decreed that on Sundays all Christians should pray standing, to show that they had *risen* with Christ. I also learned that the Eastern Churches are much more practical than we of the West; for over there they keep their peoples alert to the fact that our Christ is a living, and even a gloriously living, Christ, by calling every Sunday "Resurrection."

The reply I received was not a reply but a review of what he had gone through at Pocasset as the medical men gave him his course of treatment with nitrogen-mustard, the specific for lung cancer. But there were references enough to actualities in his soul-life to justify me in becoming more serious in my next letter and stressing the fact that in his Epistle to the Colossians St. Paul had boldly called Christ "your life" (Col. 3:4). I insisted that our Catholic Christian religion is a religion of *life*, not of death. I called my brother's attention to those strange-sounding, but wonderfully truth-telling words that St. Paul had coined in order to show our oneness with Christ, and very especially our oneness with the risen and glorified Christ. In Greek, all the words Paul had coined began with a *"sun"* or a *"sum";* while in Latin they had as prefixes *con* or *cum*. In English the best we can do is use the word "with." Yet this suffices to convey Paul's stirring truths. He teaches that we suffered *with* Christ (cf. Rom. 8:17; 1 Cor. 12:26); were crucified *with* Christ (cf. Rom. 6:6); died *with* Christ (cf. 2 Tim. 2:11); were buried together *with* Him (cf. Rom. 6:4 and Col. 2:12); but then even more emphatically he goes on to teach that we rose from the dead *with* the same Christ (cf. Eph. 2:6; Col. 2:12 and 3:1). In more than one place Paul expressly states that we are "alive *with* Christ" (Rom. 6:8; 2 Tim. 2:11).

Once I had got that deeply into St. Paul I decided to go further and insist that Kay, Charlie, and each of their children had been called by God to be witnesses *to* the Resurrection of Jesus Christ.

I meant that to startle them. So I reminded them first of the fact that there were no witnesses *of* the Resurrection. The soldiers who guarded the tomb had been conscious of an earthquake and saw an angel roll back the stone; but they had not witnessed the rising of Christ. I hazarded the surmise that just as God alone witnessed Creation, it was fitting that God alone should witness this climax to His re-Creation. At any rate the fact remains: there were no human witnesses *of* the Resurrection, but every human being should be a witness *to* the triumph of Christ over death and the grave. It is a duty for Christians; for, as St. Paul taught his converts at Ephesus, Galatia, and Corinth; "in Christ Jesus" every baptized individual had been made a "new man," had become a "new creature." Since that is so, they should prove it by walking in a "newness of life" (Rom. 6:4); show forth a "newness of spirit" (Rom. 7:6); and manifest a "newness of mind" (Rom. 12:2). "If we do that," I told Charlie and

Kay, "we will be witnesses *to* the Resurrection of Christ; for we will be showing the world that we are 'alive to God in Christ Jesus' (Rom. 6:12) and to be thus alive is to live gloriously; for that is the way He lives. We, and every Christian, should be able to say with equal vigor and utter truth what Paul so vigorously and truthfully said: 'for me, Christ *is* life!'" (Phil. 1:21.)

I was keenly aware of the fact that I was talking of nothing but life to a man who, according to all medical expectations, was very near death. Therefore I stressed a truth too many Catholics are unconscious of: the fact that for those who are in the state of grace, Heaven has already begun; for they actually possess God. To enable my brother to grasp this truth I almost belabored the fact that grace and glory are not two distinct entities, but one single entity possessed in two different environments.

"Grace is glory in time. Glory is grace in eternity," I wrote my brother and his wife. "Since that is true, you, thanks to grace, possess God in time, just as really as they who are now in eternity possess Him, thanks to the light of glory. There is a difference in the vision, but there is identity in the possession. You live with God now just as truly as you will live with Him in eternity. A veil, only a veil, stands between you and the face of Father, Son, and Holy Spirit. And thanks be to the Triune God, that veil becomes thinner with every heartbeat. It is translucent now, thanks to grace; please God it will one day be transparent, thanks to glory."

I insisted once again that we Christians are "alive to God in Christ Jesus" — and only "in Christ Jesus"; that He is the Risen One, the Glorified One; hence, we live a glorious life and share in the first Mystery of the Glorious Rosary. Thus I paid the first installment on that promise I had made.

Before I paid the second installment I had to change my tack and write a brief letter in which my main endeavor was to boost their morale. Charlie was impatient with his doctors since they would not allow him to go back to work, and Kay was depressed by the seeming hopelessness of the situation. I wrote them that God was now giving them an opportunity to do more for Him than they had ever done in all their married life. They could now preach to their neighbors, relatives, and all their friends as no eloquent priest could ever preach; for God had entrusted them with a work that only they could do. They could show their little world Christ Jesus as He had not been seen through them at any time before. I was out to thrill them with the realization that the most important hour of their lives was just now striking. In it they could prove to all who knew them that we "earth-born and earth-bent" creatures have been made for the very glory of God. All they had to do was smile not bravely, but cheerfully, and thus show all around them that they were children of God who trusted their Father absolutely.

"Do that," I wrote, "and you will be showing the world that glory which is to be found in the face of the Risen Christ. That is what Paul told his Corinthians. That is what I am telling you: 'God, who commanded light to shine out of darkness, has shone in our hearts, to give enlightenment concerning the knowledge of the glory of God, shining in the face of Christ Jesus' (2 Cor. 4:6). Since we are alive with Christ, how could it be other than that His glory should shine out from our faces?"

Lest that strike them as something too new, I quoted from St. Irenaeus, one of the earliest of the ecclesiastical writers. But for the sake of effect, and for the sake of insuring some continuity in our letters, I left the quote incomplete. I said: "The living man is the glory of God."

I asked Charlie and Kay to look up St. Paul's second Epistle to the Corinthians and read the fourth chapter; for that chapter reads as if it had been written for Charlie. Paul tells how "We carry about with us in our bodies at all times Jesus' condemnation to death, so that in these same bodies of ours the living power of Jesus may become evident" (2 Cor. 4:10). That would have been enough, I knew. But I also knew Charlie and Kay would read further and learn that: "for the sake of Jesus every moment of our lives we are condemned to death, so that the living power of Jesus may become evident in our weak selves so liable to death." That should help boost their morale. Paul's next lines would keep Charlie looking not only ahead, but even looking up, as I especially wanted him to do. "We are convinced," says Paul, "that he who raised Jesus will also raise us with Jesus, and will place us near him . . . although the physical part of our being is wasting away, yet its spiritual element within is being renewed day after day. For our present light affliction is producing for us an eternal weight of glory that is beyond all measure, while we direct our gaze not at what is seen, but at what is unseen. What we see is temporary, but what we do not see endures forever. In fact, we are certain that when our earthly dwelling, which is but a tent, is destroyed, we have an edifice made by God, a dwelling not made with hands, everlasting in the heavens" (2 Cor. 4:11–5:1).

That resounding passage would prove in very truth that "the living man is the glory of God" and enable me to go on to show the aptness of the remainder of the quote from St. Irenaeus: "The life of man is the vision of God."

CHAPTER FOUR

"The Life of Man ... Is ... the Vision of God"

THOSE two letters brought no immediate response. I began to wonder, as a preacher often wonders in the pulpit, and a teacher occasionally in class: Was I using the wrong words to convey a truth that set me tingling and should have had the same effect on Charlie and Kay? A week passed. Another was more than half gone and I was growing more conscious every day of the distance between Gethsemani and Cape Cod. But then I received a three-page letter:

> I feel as though I had been rung through a clothes ringer. I had a lot of nausea through the night. I suppose I should expect it; for I always get it when I have my first dose of nitrogen mustard.
> Dr. Kelley was in for a brief chat last night. He put me in a private room — it's the same one I had when I came home from Carney. It is a very pleasant room and I am able to get all the rest I want. It also affords me the time and opportunity to do a little reading. I have been reading what you sent — I am delighted to come to the realization that I am an "associate in the Redemption" when I "make up for what is wanting to His Passion." I *joyously* accept my small pains; for I am inspired to aspire to the heights of life — I want to go Home! I want to be ready so that I may be accepted into my Home. . . .

That was the first page. The two lines about being "delighted to be an associate in the Redemption" and that other reference to "joyously accepting" his small pains told me that my brother was thinking and remembering. I was quite happy with that indirect reply. But his statement that he "wanted to go Home" was the one I found most revealing. I wondered if God and His Mother had already effected that *metanoia* by which a man is made so completely God-conscious that everything and everyone is seen in reference to

38

eternity and to God. It seemed too sudden to me. Yet "all things are possible to God."

The next page read:

Humanly speaking, I have wondered why I have been so afflicted. I have gone over my past life and though realizing I have done many wrongs — of which one alone could bring down a denouncement from my Creator — yet, comparing my faults with the faults of others, I humanly argued that there was no comparative justification. Sin is to be punished and is to be punished according to the law of God — Well, that passage you have about the boy struck blind in one of your books —that helps me realize what you have been telling me so often and in so many ways: "Chic, how God loves *you!*"

That paragraph showed me my brother as I expected to find him — and yet showed him progressing faster and farther than I yet expected. His reference was to the story in the Gospel of the man born blind of whom the Apostles asked Jesus: " . . . who has sinned, this man or his parents, to account for his being born blind?" and received that answer so pregnant with meaning for all who suffer in the New Dispensation: "Neither this man has sinned, nor his parents. No. God simply wants to make use of him to reveal his ways" (Jn. 9:2-3).

If Charlie had caught all that Christ was saying in that line; if he believed this cancer, which could be used as payment of the temporal punishment due to his sins, was also an opportunity for him to "reveal the ways of God," then I had no need for questioning the impact of my last few letters. God and His Mother were working on a soul that was still very much the soul of a husband and father, but was growing ever more conscious of the fact that it was also the soul of a son of God.

The next few paragraphs held what seemed a very healthy attitude toward reality. "I hope to get home Saturday," he had written. "And I hope I get the drive necessary to continue my house painting. I have two bedrooms to complete; then I intend to start on the outside of the house. I have a lot of raking and cutting to do, too, to help landscape the place. I must get to it."

That kind of thing would keep him from slipping into self-pity. And when he said that he was teaching Kay how to drive, he made it clear that he was not hugging any illusion to his heart.

His last page made me smile broadly:

Tell Father Abbot that he is remembered daily in all our prayers. The children were very anxious to know how old he was, was he fat, did he wear a beard, did he speak English, etc? Now there is a picture they get from the various TV programs. When I told them how much you two look alike, Charlie, Jr., pops out with: "Well, they are brothers, aren't they?" Now there's recognition for you — Brothers in Christ. — Thank him again and again for his generosity to me.

Well I am surprising everyone with the way I look. I weigh 174, have good color — but am just too lazy. I am looking forward to Passion Week.

I received a phone call from Betty the other night. She is back teaching school and feeling much better. If this good weather keeps up maybe we'll visit one another. . . .

The reference to Passion Week puzzled me. The solution came in the very next letter dated March 14. "Am looking forward to Passion Week and Jack's Mission down here in our parish."

That sentence showed me God at work again. In February some unexpected business in Boston connected with her social service work had brought Sister Mary Clare down from Halifax, and allowed her an opportunity to go to Cape Cod and visit with Charlie for the first time in fifteen years. What that had meant to Charlie came out in a letter that was radiant with happiness of heart. Now early April held an even greater boon — for Father Jack would not only visit Charlie, but give him a Jesuit Mission. What gratitude to God and His Mother this evident solicitude for the afflicted one demanded!

When word came from Doctor Kelley saying: "Financially the situation is well in hand — the Barnstable Department of Public Welfare is caring for the patient in part, and also helping with the children," my sigh of relief was profound, and my heart filled with gratitude to God and Mary Immaculate.

I well knew how hospital bills can mount. Charlie had made mention of some fund on the Cape to care for residents who suffered from tuberculosis, telling how he benefited by it when first he went to Pocasset; for the primary diagnosis of the lung shadow was TB. But I had heard nothing about that since, nor about any other source of funds. Then I could never forget one of Kay's earliest letters before the Boston operation. Nothing had been arranged by that time with county or state officials, but some agency had given her a food certificate worth thirty dollars. "My grocery bill, Joe, runs me thirty-five every week. Then I have to pay ten dollars for milk. . . ." Such statements sent one to God and His Mother with pleas that were next to importunate.

That Charlie was not unresponsive to so much kindness from God and His Mother was proved by this same Doctor Kelley who on April 1 wrote: "Your brother, Charles, is a very happy, contented man; and this is unusual in a patient who suffers from cancer. I can assure you that it has been a lesson to all of us here. We thank you from the bottom of our hearts."

I had more reason than the doctor to express thanks from the bottom of the heart; for in our correspondence he had confessed that Irish though his name was, and Catholic though all Irish seem to be, he was without faith, and his parents had been Baptists. I could now tell my brother that one of the reasons God had blessed him with cancer was the superintendent and staff at Barnstable County Hospital, and insist that quite definitely he was "God's ambassador" who was to manifest Christ.

Before I had an opportunity to congratulate my brother on the work he was doing for God I received a short letter in which he said: "You ask me how I feel. I tell you I want to go Home to God — but His will be done. If He can use me on earth, then I must await my call Home."

I remembered hearing, almost forty years before, this same brother of mine crying, "I want to go to God! I want to go to God!" That was 1918. The Spanish influenza had struck the family. Everyone in the family was down with it but myself. Charlie's case was the worst of all; for he developed empyema and such a high fever that he became delirious. As I stared at his letter now I relived those two endless days and nights that were filled with the cry: "I want to go to God! I want to go to God!" I saw a wearied and somewhat hurried doctor perform the necessary operation on Charlie right there in my mother's room. I watched and knew relief as the youthful sufferer grew quiet. Then with joy I saw him gain strength day after day, until finally he was up and out on the streets playing again with his favorite Scotch collie, Tango.

I used that memory as introduction to the next long letter that went north, pointing out that, quite obviously, his desires and God's plans were not too closely alike. But then I reminded him that forty was a mystical number in Holy Scripture and may yet have some bearing on his longing and the good Lord's seeming denial of fulfillment. Thirty-nine years lay between his first cry and this latest. "Take heart and have high hope!"

Then I became serious; for it was evident to me that while the cancer had not yet begun to pain Charlie physically, it could begin to gnaw away at him psychologically. That must be prevented, if possible. Since there is an "occupational therapy" that keeps hands busy and helps toward mental health, why could we not devise an "occupational therapy" for the mind that would keep the intellect and will busy and thus help toward healthiness of soul? If I could present mysteries to Charlie that were almost tangible, yet always just out of reach, would I not absorb his attention?

St. Irenaeus' quote, which had been left incomplete, was taken up again. "The living man is the glory of God" is truth enough to spellbind any thinker. But, as yet, I had received no reaction to it from Charlie. So I completed the quote and told my brother that "the life of man is the vision of God," hence, I would help him to live by showing that the first Glorious Mystery is ours as well as our Lord's and prove beyond doubt that our Religion is a Religion of joy.

Mr. Frank Sheed supplied me with a telling illustration. I told my brother how this man had visited many a church and celebrated cathedral both in Europe and America but had come out of most shaking his head, saying: "They are neither liturgically correct nor theologically true." That statement he explained by showing that while on every wall there was a crucifix, it was only occasionally, and then usually high up in stained glass, that one got any glimpse of the Resurrection. "That should never be," was Mr. Sheed's concluding comment. I asked Charlie if he could tell Kay what Frank Sheed was thinking about when he said such a thing.

Gilbert K. Chesterton was used to support Frank Sheed's contention; for shortly after his conversion this jolly genius remarked that practically everywhere he found statues of the *Pietà* and the *Mater Dolorosa*. Being Chesterton he had to ask: "Where is the *Causa*

Nostrae Laetitiae?" Again I asked my brother if he could tell Kay what this great man was hinting at.

Charlie was then reminded that ten of the fifteen Mysteries of the Rosary are crowded with joy, while the other five are but steps to greatest glory. Lamentations are heard in our churches but three days of the year, but the joyous *Alleluia* resounds on more than three hundred days in the same year. It was conceded that we have a Lent, and that it is a severe fast of forty days. But that concession was merely to heighten the fact that the remainder of the year is filled with seasons overflowing with joy.

That our Religion is a Religion of joy and not a cult of suffering was driven home by the fact that Holy Mother Church interrupts her penitential season of Advent with a Sunday that is a shout of *Gaudete,* and her stricter season of Lent with a Sunday that sings of *Laetare.*

The argument is not unassailable. For one can always ask: Why the Cross? To forestall any such comeback from my brother I reminded him of the difference between means and ends, then referred him to the second verse in the twelfth chapter of St. Paul's Epistle to the Hebrews, where Paul says: "in view of the joy offered him" Jesus "underwent crucifixion with contempt of its disgrace." That surely is proof enough that Calvary is the turning point in the Christ Drama, not the last act. The Cross and the cruel Crucifixion were means, not ends; and means to highest joy. God the Holy Spirit says precisely that in this passage from St. Paul.

It had to be immediately admitted that there is no such thing as "Christianity without tears." But with mounting insistence I told my brother that there can be no true Christianity that does not see sunshine through its tears and thus find a rainbow in every sorrow. "There is no pleasure in suffering, Chic, but there should be joy; for we, His members, when we suffer, are one with Him who is not only the Man of Sorrows but the King of Glory and the Source of all joy. Live in Him and you will give meaning to what seems meaningless, and divine purpose to what appears to humans so pointless and unprofitable — pain. By knowing who you are and what you are doing you can transmute suffering into that gold which alone can purchase accidental glory for God — and eternal glory for man."

That was asking my brother to do something that not only challenges the best in human nature, but actually demands special help from almighty God. I was asking him to find real, substantial joy in the very thing that was seemingly blotting out all joy from his little world and his life. I was saying that he was not to be a Christian in the too commonly accepted sense of that word, but in its realest signification. I was telling him he must be Christ. Put as bluntly as that, it seems to be asking the utterly impossible. Yet what other demand lies implicit in Baptism? What other reality can one see in the doctrine of the Mystical Body of Christ? What other truth is so fundamental to our dogma of sanctifying grace?

There was a purpose even more personal to Charlie in my citing St. Paul's Epistle to the Hebrews in anticipation of a possible objection to the theme I was propounding. I felt sure my brother would not only look up that text but read it in its context. If he did, it would arouse echoes of what I had been telling him about himself and Kay being special instruments of God to show those near them on the Cape that God lived and was nearer than life itself. It would also give him and his wife the courage they needed to fulfill their task. For St. Paul opens that twelfth chapter with the words: "That is why we, too, surrounded as we are by such a throng of witnesses, should cast off every encumbrance that weighs us down, especially sin, which so easily entangles us. Let us eagerly throw ourselves into the struggle before us, and persevere, with our gaze fixed on Jesus, the pioneer and perfect embodiment of confidence."

Those lines should throb with meaning for Charlie at this particular time in his life. For he was learning the depths of Christianity from this encounter with cancer; and those depths are the divinity and the humanity of Christ. Not the Jesus of Bethlehem, Nazareth, or faraway Galilee. Not the Christ of twenty centuries ago. But the Jesus Christ who is nearer than blood to our veins — the Man-God in whom "we live and move and have our being." The concluding verse in this particular passage is the exhortation to "meditate on him who in his own person endured such great opposition at the hands of sinners; then your souls will not be overwhelmed with discouragement" (Hebr. 12:3).

Before that letter had reached the Cape I was studying one that had come from there. Kay had written a letter that showed she was stunned by the successions of submissions that God had asked of her. The Christmas before Charlie was found with cancer had been clouded for her because a vacation one of her brothers took in Florida ended by his body being flown back to Boston after he had drowned while surf bathing. The following January her next oldest brother was found dead in his boardinghouse, evidently from a heart attack. Last August her brother-in-law took his only child off to the White Mountains on a Sunday, thinking that Kay's sister would join him in the middle of the week. That brother-in-law came home Thursday to find Kay's sister dead of a cerebral hemorrhage. "I am not complaining, Joe," Kay had written, as she told me of Charlie's growing weakness, "but I am wondering why God asks so much faith of me."

The answer to that very understandable question came the very day I had read Kay's letter. I was saying the first Glorious Mystery with Kay's case somewhat forward in my mind as I thought on all that the Resurrection must have meant to Mary Immaculate. Suddenly, with a clarity that stopped me in my slow stride, I saw that in the Resurrection we are at the heart of all Mystery, and that in it is to be found the answer to every problem.

As has happened more than once, the five Glorious Mysteries were not completed that day. I did not so much as finish the first. But I did find an answer for Kay. I wrote that God asks so much faith of her "because you are a true daughter to your glorious Mother"; then went on to show what faith the Triune God had asked of Mary Immaculate — not only at the Annunciation, but all through her earthly life.

Does anyone think enough on what God asked of that little Jewish maiden whom all generations have called and yet will call blessed? An angel appeared to her and told her that she, a virgin, would conceive, yet remain a virgin; that she would become a mother without losing her precious virginity; that she need not know man but would be overshadowed by "the power of the Most High." That angel went on to tell this humble girl of very lowly circumstances that the Son she was to bear would be given "the throne of his father David"; that He would be "acclaimed 'Holy' and 'Son of God.'" Was there

ever such a succession of high improbabilities and seeming impos-
sibilities? Then, as if reading the exclamation that leaps into the
human mind: "Impossible!" this same angel goes on to say: "Nothing
indeed is impossible with God." He even added what can, perhaps,
be called a *motivum credibilitatis* — a confirmatory sign that leads
the human mind on to assent more readily to what seems difficult to
accept. He told her about her aged cousin, Elizabeth.

God always rewards faith. Mary "set out in haste to go into the
mountainous region" — not to seek for proof of the veracity of God
but to prove her own belief in what the angel said and to help
her cousin who was "now in her sixth month." The joy of that
meeting still rings in our world whenever the *Magnificat* is sung
or said; the tender beauty is recalled in every *Hail Mary* — for it
was Elizabeth who first said: "Blessed are you beyond all women!
And blessed is the fruit of your womb!"

But all life, even the spiritual life, and the very life of the
Mother of God, is undulant. She came back from the radiance, and
even the effulgence of grace and God that had marked the Visitation,
to the worried gleam in Joseph's eye and the pain-filled frown on his
forehead. We know Mary was silent, but who can doubt that she
had to quiet her loving heart again and again by telling it what
Gabriel had first told her: "Nothing is impossible with God."

And God rewarded that faith. For soon the man who had frowned
and known fear was filled with reverence not untinged with awe,
and more glowing with love than ever before. His attention to his
betrothed breathed with an admiration that was not too different from
adoration. Joseph, undoubtedly, was an ecstatic lover after he had
heard the angel say: "Her conception was wrought by the Holy
Spirit. She will bear a Son and you are to name him Jesus; for he
will save his people from their sins" (Mt. 1:21).

But Caesar Augustus interrupted that bit of bliss and sent a woman
heavy with Child and an anxious husband on the road to Bethlehem.
Then the closing of the doors! But Mary went on believing, and
more than likely encouraging Joseph with the words: "Nothing is
impossible with God."

How every trough is followed by a crest in Mary's life! How
wondrously was her every act of faith rewarded. Her own ancestral

town had no room for her or her Child, but angels sang to shepherds, and soon Magi came from the East. To such a crest there had to be a correspondingly deep trough, so Joseph is awakened and told to "Take with you the child and his mother and flee into Egypt!" (Mt. 2:13.)

If Mary were tempted to reason as human beings so often are, what questions could she not have asked. Did the Son of God have to fly before the threats of a weak kinglet such as Herod? Was Egypt with its teeming idols the fit place for the Only-Begotten of the one true God? And as she looked at that Helplessness cuddling close to her breast could she not have asked: "Can this be the Omnipotent?" But we know that with Mary there were no questions after that first one to Gabriel. We can safely surmise she stilled them all by the statement that "Nothing is impossible with God." But what faith was asked of her!

My sister-in-law, being woman, wife, and mother, would have insights into the mind and heart of Mary that are denied men. I banked on that as I told her to think how Mary had to *believe*, and deny all the evidence of her senses, as she fed, bathed, clothed the Child that had come from her own physical being, yet tell herself all the time that He was God.

"She did for Him what you have done and are still doing for your own little Christy," I wrote to Kay; "yet she had to believe all the while that He was Omnipotence. Has God ever asked such faith from any other?"

I went on and showed that Nazareth was not all joy and sunshine as some are led to think. It was while at Nazareth, as far as we know, that Mary Immaculate was made a widow. I hesitated long before using that word and that illustration. For "widow" is a lonely word — and Kay knew only too well that soon she would be made a widow. But if she could be convinced that all such bereavements made her more and more like the Mother of God; if she could be led on to realize that it is those who are nearest and dearest to God, those whom He feels He can trust, who are visited by such afflictions, it would be worth the momentary stab of pain she was bound to feel as soon as she read the lines.

If the sisters of Lazarus would one day cry out: "Lord, if you had been here, my brother would not have died" (Jn. 11:32), what could not Mary Immaculate have asked as her husband lay dying? Yet she looked at Jesus and believed with all her being that He was the Author of life and death. If thoughts of the future entered her mind; thoughts about her means of support, of how she was going to care for the carpenter shop and the trade, she silenced them all, no doubt, with: "Nothing is impossible with God."

Elizabeth had said: "Happy is she who believed . . ." (Lk. 1:45) and no one can hesitate to accept the testimony, but neither should any question the fact that, humanly speaking, it cost Mary to believe when so many and such unexpected things came into her life — and all because of Jesus.

I asked Kay to weigh some of the facts in Christ's Public Life in order to appreciate what was demanded from Mary the Mother of God in the way of absolute trust and unwavering faith. Cana's water did, as one has happily put it, "see its God and blush" — and all because Mary had asked for the miracle. But from then until she held Him a corpse on her lap, what joy was there in those two or three years?

"You are about to enter Passiontide, Kay," I said. "Enter it with Mother Mary. Spend it thinking what the first Passiontide was like for her. Then you will see how dear you are to God; for you will realize what He asked of His Son's Mother in the way of faith and all that goes along with faith: trust, hope, love."

No one knows — no one will ever know — just what Christ's last days on earth meant to His Mother. But it does help to appreciate how she loved God, and how much she was willing to suffer for men, if one but takes the time to think prayerfully on the facts of her widowhood and her motherhood, if one dwells long and lovingly on the truth that Mary was not only human, but the perfect human. Kay was busier than usual with her household, now that Charlie was ill. But with the Mission coming on in Passion Week and the question about God's demands churning in her soul, this was the opportune time to turn her attention as fully as possible to the human side of Mary Immaculate and thus win complete dedication to her Immaculate Heart for life.

Kay was alerted to Mary's widowhood by insisting on her warm womanly love for Joseph. Then she was led on to think of all it meant to this lonely widow to be robbed by God of her only Child — and that, not by any ordinary death, but by a condemnation as a criminal. To have that condemnation pronounced by the "very best people" in the land: the High Priests, Pharisees, Scribes, Doctors of the law, and by ruling Roman officials; to have even the ordinary people cry out for His crucifixion — what must it have cost Mary Immaculate?

I quoted from the poet Rilke, who, in his *Before the Passion*, clarifies our concepts and shows us how poignantly human Mary was when he has her say:

> Oh, if you wished this, you ought not to have dared
> to issue forth from any woman's loins;
> saviors should be hewn from mountain-mines
> in which the hard is broken from the hard.

Mary is all mother as she goes on talking to her Son. Finally she asks:

> So richly it was promised I should bear you —
> why didn't you fiercely burst from me and leave?
> If you need only tigers to break and tear you,
> why was I reared in the woman's house, to weave
> and make for you a soft clean swaddling-gown
> in which was not the smallest seam to chafe
> your body? Even so was my whole life —
> now suddenly you twist nature upside down.*

Nature was "turned upside down" for Mary when Christ was nailed to the Cross, but we should never so turn the supernature upside down as to forget that it builds on nature, or to imagine that the world's most valiant woman stood beneath that Cross without the world's greatest heartache and heartbreak. That Man on the Cross, nailed there hand and foot, was her Son. That was her own flesh up there, torn from scourging, writhing in agony. That was her own blood that trickled from underneath that crown of thorns to mat in His hair and blur the vision of His eyes. This lonely widow had to stand there hour after hour after hour, watching the life she had given Him ebb away. She, His Mother, had to wait and wait and wait — until He died.

* Raisaer Marie Rilke, *Life of the Virgin Mary*, translated by C. F. MacIntyre (Berkeley and Los Angeles: University of California Press, 1947), p. 29. By permission.

Rilke's lines vibrate with verisimilitude. It cost heavily to be the Mother of God. The price she paid is simply inestimable. Yet, on Easter morn that exorbitant outlay seemed paltry indeed when He, as Rilke says, "went toward her . . . wholly resurrected." How like St. Ignatius of Loyola this modern German sounds in the poem "Consolation of Mary With the Resurrected Christ" as he insists:

> Oh, first to her. How they were then
> being healed unspeakably.
> Yes, they were healing. That was it.
> They did not need to touch each other firmly.
> Barely an instant
> he laid his soon-to-be-eternal hand
> upon the womanly shoulder.
> And they began,
> silently as trees in spring,
> infinitely together,
> this season of their uttermost communion.*

If Kay could be brought to realize how human Mary Immaculate is; if she and Charlie could be led to live as intimately with her up there on Cape Cod as did John the Beloved and Peter, the blusterer, back in Judea; if they could be made as conscious of her motherliness as their own children were of the love of their parents, then the future was safe: faith would bring the fortitude to externalize *Pietas*. They would be children of God — children without fear.

As Easter came on that year of 1957 the thought of Mary and her faith was very much a part of me. The suspicion that our recognition of her superlative privileges has blinded us no little to the realities of her life grew to a conviction. We know how close she was to Jesus; we know He is God; but, too often, we forget that this Mother of God looked on her Boy and saw only a Man. Thus we fail to remember that her whole life — even to Easter and after Pentecost — was a life of faith.

Thomas of Aquin said she "borders on the infinite." But that very truth can lead us into error about the reality of Mary's life and living. She became the very Mother of God, yet always remained *ancilla Domini* — just a creature who served her God. A little Jewish maiden became a wife, then a mother, then a widow, then a Childless

* *Ibid.*, p. 33.

widow — and all the time she was but an individual human being who had to believe. Her life was what every human life should be — a life of faith.

But while pondering this fact there came back to me memories of the days spent as a student in Theology trying to analyze an Act of Faith. It is a fascinating, albeit an almost frustrating, process; for one has to deal with more than human mind and human will; one has to deal, in no slight degree, with Divine Mind and the Divine Will — for one has to take into consideration the grace of God. But, because it was Passiontide, and because it was faith I was pondering, I was seized by a concept that was to serve me well when it came time to write about Easter.

In the analysis of an Act of Faith there is what we call a "preamble" to the Act. In that preamble there is a step called "the judgment of credibility" — that point in the process when after looking at some revealed fact we say: "This truth can be believed." It is a human judgment. There is some dispute, but not very much, among theologians whether or not grace is required in making such a judgment. I do not see any necessity for supernatural help in this matter and I have always been fond of using "Ockham's razor" — which says *entia non sunt multiplicanda sine necessitate* — "we are not to demand more than is actually demanded." So this step in the preamble, where motives are found for believing, always looked to me like one we could call "the enticements of God" — for they are usually palpable facts that can give us reasons for accepting facts that are anything but palpable. The Vatican Council spoke of them as external signs which God willed us to have as arguments and proofs of His omniscience and omnipotence. It went on to say such signs could be easily understood by any and every intellect and recognized as certain signs of Divine Revelation.

That looks very much like an abstract way of presenting what Jesus Himself made manifest in a very dramatic manner, and at one of the tensest moments of His public life. The Jews were ready to stone Him because, as they said, He, "a man," made Himself God. Jesus said: "If I do not act as my Father does, then do not believe me; but if I do, then believe on the strength of my actions even if you do not believe my words" (Jn. 10:37, 38). At the Last Supper

Christ used the same argument: "Had I not done in their midst what no one else has ever done, they would have no sin" (Jn. 15:24). And St. John tells us, at the close of his Gospel: "Jesus gave many other proofs of his claims in the presence of his disciples, which are not on record in this book" (Jn. 19:35). Each was an "enticement" to believe His word. Yes, each miracle was a motive to take Christ for what He claimed to be. The Vatican Council speaks of "miracles and prophecies" as among what I call "enticements." But it was St. Paul who confirmed me in my determination to make all this clear to the family on Cape Cod. When writing to his Corinthians he became trenchant: "If Christ was not raised [from the dead], then there is nothing to our preaching, there is nothing to your faith" (1 Cor. 15:14). The fact of the Resurrection, then, is the foundation for our faith; for it was both miracle and fulfillment of prophecy. That fact was concretized for me in the empty tomb. That emptiness was a real "enticement" to believe that whatever Christ said was true. I had my tangible for all that was intangible about Easter and its Mystery.

Chesterton's advice to "stare at a familiar thing until it begins to look strange" seemed very sound. His promise that "then you will be seeing it for the first time" spurred me on to ask Charlie and Kay to concentrate their thoughts upon the empty tomb that once had held the corpse of God, and to keep on staring until it began to look strange. They would do this if they would first look at some other tombs that were full. Both had heard of Mary Baker Eddy. Both knew where the church of the Christian Scientists stood in Boston. But had either of them ever heard what might be idle gossip and false report, namely, that within the gray granite mausoleum which is Mary Baker Eddy's tomb there is a telephone and there used to be an attendant waiting for it to ring? That was the story a Cambridge man had told me years ago. He said that the foundress of Christian Science had promised to communicate with her disciples after she was dead. I do not know how much truth there is in the story; but of this I felt quite sure: that phone had never rung; that tomb was still full.

Their gaze was then turned from Massachusetts to Moscow, where a mightier tomb than Mary Baker Eddy's holds the corrupted or cor-

rupting corpse of Communism's "Messiah" — Vladimir Ilich Ulyanov
Lenin. If that tomb had ever been found empty and its former occu-
pant reported as risen from the dead, what would happen to our
world? But there is no reason for alarm. That tomb is still full, and
that very real and realist "Religion" called Communism utterly
foundationless.

It seemed profitable to have my brother and his wife gaze thoughtfully toward Berchtesgaden in Germany and to recall that Adolf
Hitler, the upstart Austrian house painter who had risen to complete
domination of Germany, had once chosen this spot for his home. He
had done so because Richard Wagner had written that Siegfried the
Invulnerable, who had had one reincarnation in Frederic Barbarossa,
was to have another in a "hero wondrously divine," a man who would
be "the savior of his race"; and that this man would make his home
where the bones of Siegfried and Barbarossa are supposed to lie
buried: Berchtesgaden. Neither Charlie nor Kay had to be told that
those bones still lie buried or that Hitler was not even a demigod,
let alone "wondrously divine." They well knew that his "Religion"
of Nazism had been delusion not untouched with dementia.

Then their gaze was brought back to the one and only tomb that
does lie empty — the tomb of Him who *had* to rise from the dead. For
to friend and foe, at various times and in varied places, under different and often critical circumstances Jesus had spoken of the "Third
Day." Christ, Himself, had made the emptiness of that tomb an
"enticement" to believe. In fact He had made it the test of His
veracity. In all truth, it is the one sign He gave to His own generation — and to all succeeding generations. That empty tomb is the
foundation stone, the immovable rock on which rests our life-giving
Faith; it is the unshakable sign that Christ's Religion is the only true
Religion, and that He is the Only-Begotten of the one, true God.

Once they had concentrated long enough on the very familiar
Tomb, it did, I hope, begin to seem strange. When they had seen it
for what it actually is, then they could understand Paul's stinging
phrases about "If Christ be not risen . . ." That passage to the Corinthians was made more personal by the lines: "If Christ be not risen
— then this Monastery of mine is a mausoleum housing the living
dead, and the sanctuary lamp, flickering before the altar in your

church at Osterville, is dancing its life away before a tomb and not a Tabernacle. If Christ be not risen — the Host on our altars is hollow, and the Mass a mere memorial; and while your Baptism may have been something in the nature of a bath it most certainly could not be anything in the nature of a rebirth. Furthermore, if Christ be not risen, our Catholic Church, although a magnificent organization, is not a mystic organism; consequently, the Mystical Body is a corpse and not a *corpus* — for it is only a risen Christ who could be *Vivifier*. Feel the power in those words of St. Paul: 'If Christ be not risen, vain is your faith; for you are still in your sins' (1 Cor. 15:17). See now what Easter really means to you! He has risen! The tomb is empty. The first Glorious Mystery of Mary's Rosary is truly glorious — and, thanks be to God and His Christ, you and I and every other baptized Christian are living it."

That Easter letter brought us back not only to our promise about the Glorious Mysteries, but led us on to an appreciation of Mary's faith and our own. She was calm even on Calvary. She knew true peace of soul even as she heard God, in what sounded like despair, crying to God: *"Eloi, Eloi, lama sabachthani"* (Mk. 15:34). Mary was filled with faith even as she saw God die. And we . . . I harked back to that idea about the "motives for credibility" being "entice-ments" given by God to have us assent to His revelations. Once they had the concept clearly, they would see how much more fortunate they were than those who lived when Christ walked the earth, or those who came into the Faith shortly after He had left it. How many more "enticements" to believe has God given us since then! Every Hail Mary we say or hear said is such; for it is a fulfillment of that prophecy Mary uttered about herself when she sang her *Magnificat*. Every new day is such; for every new day we see a ful-fillment of Christ's final prophecy when we look upon the Catholic Church and see that the "gates of Hell have not prevailed." Those "gates" have striven to prevail every single day from Calvary to Com-munism. But Christ is faithful to His promises.

Then I hazarded a startling statement: "How much more ready to believe should we be than Mary was!" Then I explained how we had the empty tomb before us from the very beginning of our Cath-olic existence, whereas Mary had this tangible "enticement" to believe only at the end of hers. I went on to show the numerous motives for credibility that lie all about us, which Mary never had. Hence, if her Act of Faith had a "preamble" parallel to ours, then ours should be readier and much more easily made — all other things being equal.

I felt that this constant concentration on the first Glorious Mystery was giving them what they, and every other human in our very troubled human race, needed in these days of tension: it was giving them *reassurance*. Since there is so much wisdom in the adage: "I was full of pity for myself because I had no shoes, until I met a man who had no feet," I thought it wise to capitalize on this reassurance that comes to all right-thinking Christians at Easter time. So I told Charlie and Kay that they ought to pour their very hearts out in gratitude to God for giving them in such high degree what so many in the world about them lacked entirely — rock-deep reassurance. How the millions imprisoned behind the Iron and Bamboo Curtains must long to be assured that life on earth is not sheer madness; that human existence is more than fear, constant and inescapable suspicion, oppression, brutal domination, and a despotism that allows for not one truly free breath.

"Not only those poor peoples," I went on, "but every thinking person needs the reassurance that life on earth is not what Macbeth once called it: a 'tale told by an idiot, full of sound and fury, signifying nothing.'" Yes, every one of us who wakes to a new day needs the reassurance that our years here on earth, few as they are at most, filled too often with frustration, never completely satisfying, and often enough inducing real despair, are as meaningful as Divinity and as purposeful as God. We need to know! We need to know that despite our groping intellects, our unstable wills, despite our open wounds of anger, envy, gluttony, and sloth, our bleeding stigmata of lust and pride, our stumbling leads somewhere. We need to know that life is not a rat race; that we humans are not on a treadmill. Our minds must have some one truth to cling to with complete assurance, even though everything else in our universe falls away. That one truth is the Resurrection of Jesus Christ from the dead!

Thanks to the empty tomb we can raise our heads and say that we earth-bound mortals are creatures who are "walled around by God"; that we live by a belief that is more firmly fixed than the very foundations of the world. That is why our hearts are ever ringing with "Alleluia!"

"The life of man is the vision of God, Charlie and Kay, as you can learn from looking at your Mother," I wrote. "Mary Immaculate had God ever in her vision — not the 'face-to-face vision' that is going to be Heaven, but the vision granted you and me and all believing Catholics thanks to the light of Faith. May yours be a *glorious* Eastertide!"

Charlie and Kay must be convinced that under Mary and in Jesus they actually were living the Glorious Mysteries of the Rosary. As that particular letter was posted I wondered if I was through with the first Mystery. I did not scruple the time nor the length of the letters; for Paul's words "If Christ be not risen . . ." force us to look at living truth and shape our lives truthfully. Too much time cannot be spent on such a task.

CHAPTER FIVE

"... Be Turned Into the Holiness of God"

THE monks of Gethsemani give all their attention on Easter Sunday to the newly risen Christ. It is only on the following day that the mail accumulated during Lent is distributed. In the little stack awaiting at my place were envelopes bearing cancellation stamps of Boston, Halifax, Detroit, Stoughton, and Louisville. All the family had been mindful of me. But the two I extracted first bore the stamp of Osterville, Massachusetts. The first was brief. It had been written just before Easter but held references only to Passion Week and what it had meant to the adults and children of 33 Blanid Road.

In it Charlie spoke of how hard it was to get around to writing a letter. "I have an excuse for last week," he wrote, "for I was kept quite busy making the Mission and enjoying daily visits with Fr. Jack. Yes, he came down to spend a few hours with us every day."

That gave me a little start; for I well knew Father Jack's rule while on a Mission. He claimed his work was to give a Mission and, hence, there was no time for visiting. The parish at Osterville was not large, it is true, but for Father Jack to depart from his rule told me that he was making the most of the opportunity presented by God. The letter said that the children were all well, and that they had a grand time with Father Jack during the week.

About the Mission Charlie had little to say other than "Jack gives wonderful, straight-forward talks. I was so happy to be able to make the entire Mission. Jack was thorough in his explanation of who we are and what we are doing. He told us about our gifts from God and our obligations to Him. It was a wonderful week in every way and Fr. Jack is truly a man of God."

57

I knew Jack himself, disdainful of all compliments, let alone of flattery, would be pleased with that last sentence; for no real priest longs for any other name or fame.

Charlie made one reference to his sickness. "I was at Pocasset a week ago. I have had a lot of pain lately, and they decided that if the pain continues I shall have another series of treatments. I shall go back to Pocasset some time in May, if not before then."

That seemed scant reference to what would ordinarily absorb a person. I began to wonder if my youngest brother had inherited some of his dad's reticence when it came to his own sufferings. How well I remembered Mary Clare's report on Dad in his last days when the cancer was really painful. She came into his room as quietly as nuns do such things and found Dad with face contorted and teeth clenched. "Are you in awful pain, Daddy?" she asked. He opened his blue eyes, actually managed a bit of smile, and said: "I must have been dreaming, Mary. I must have been dreaming that I was back in the Old Country and a white donkey was stepping on my toes." Could Charlie be like that?

When I opened the second envelope a half-dozen snapshots cascaded to the floor. They were a set taken last Christmas. There was one of the entire family grouped in their sitting room. I studied it closely. The children were lovely — each of them.

As I studied those children's faces I found myself choking up, for it came home to me that Charlie had to look on this heart-winning beauty and innocence day after day and realize that soon, maybe sooner than even he suspected, he would see them no more. He had to look at Kay as she cared for the youngest and think ahead into the years when they would be grown up. . . . The pictures blurred before my vision, but I had newer reason to turn to Mother Mary and beg her to fill my brother to the brim with fortitude.

It took me some time to quiet my own heart as I wondered if I could ever do what Charlie was doing and, from all reports and evidences, doing with such spirit that no one could so much as guess what was going on within him. Mary Clare had described him as "so alive, so brave, so pleased to have been with you and to see his big sister." She went on to say that he "seemed on top of the world" and that it was "difficult to believe that he was doomed to die from cancer." She closed her account with "he is on his way to Heaven with a joyous courage." I had thanked both God and His Mother the moment I first read that letter. I thanked Them again now as I recalled it — and then went on to plead for ever more joy and ever more courage, admitting that were I in Charlie's position, with so much beauty, innocence, and love before me in those seven children I would need Heaven's full store of courage to go on.

After that prayer I opened the letter in which the snaps had been sent and read:

> Do you remember that perennial favorite of the old radio days — Jimmie Gallagher? Well, as he always used to say: "I'm still hanging on." My old legs have been giving me quite a time, so finally I got in touch with Doctor Niles. He told me I've had so much poison injected into my blood stream this is the usual effect.
>
> I'm glad to have that explanation for the pains in my legs would wake me up from a sound sleep, and I could not understand why they were causing me such discomfort. Doctor told me to take more codein, and I've felt better the past few days. I feel quite dopey — that is, more so than usual! — and I sleep a lot during the day. I find it quite an effort to get around; for my legs won't do what I want them to do. Boy, you should see me: the old man of the mountain!
>
> We were pleasantly surprised Tuesday. Kay had to go to her dentist. She has her new "store teeth" and he wanted to see how they fitted. They make her look lots younger and even more beautiful. Well, when we got back from Hyannis we found Fr. Jack had come down for a visit.
>
> He looks very tired for he has been on the road. He was able to take supper with us, and I can assure you we all enjoyed his visit so much!
>
> Charlie Junior plays for the Sealtest Little League baseball team. On Wednesday night Kay and I went over to watch him play. He led off the second inning with the first hit of the game. He's lightning fast. He stole second, then got to third on an infield hit. With one out he danced down the third base line. The catcher chased him back a little toward third, then made the mistake of tossing to the third baseman. The ball was just out of his hand when Junior Jet Flanagan set sail for home. He stole home by running right over the catcher. I got quite a kick out of it. In the last inning the catcher got hurt, so in from center field comes the mighty mite to take his place behind the plate. The shin guards came up to his hips, but he caught a good game.
>
> Maureen takes her exam for swimming instructor next week. If she passes she can get a job teaching children how to swim. I hope she makes it, for then she can earn money for her future education.

Kathy got herself a steady job baby-sitting for the summer. She will work nights. I want her to get as much sun as possible so, since she will have the day time to herself, she will be able to get to the beach all right.

Kevin is beginning to play baseball now. So I have hopes that he'll come out of his shell.

Patty graduates from kindergarten Sunday. She looks grand in her purple satin costume. They put on a show, then dress in cap and gown to receive their diploma.

Christy still keeps us on our toes. Even Mary finds it hard to keep up with her. . . .

That certainly read like "joyous courage" to me. The details about each member of the family sent me back to the snaps to identify them and conjure up what I could of their personalities and characters. I marveled at the way Charlie was maintaining his sense of humor. Not a syllable of self-pity had yet appeared in his lines. Knowing something of human nature, especially as it is found in men, I thanked God and His Mother for the graces They were giving my brother. Then when I wrote I urged him to even fuller co-operation with God's grace as I told him he could mint that suffering of his into the only coin God will accept — the currency which bears the image of the Only Son. I spoke of the Mass, but spoke of it in relation to Easter and the first Glorious Mystery of Mary's Rosary.

I asked my brother if he had ever stopped at the *Fifteenth* Station as he made the Way of the Cross. Of course no Catholic church in all Christendom has a fifteenth station on its walls; yet for the fullness of truth about our Redemption and the wondrous work wrought by Christ a fifteenth station is needed. For, though every Creed and Council, every catechism and text book of theology teaches and has taught that we were redeemed by Christ's "Passion and Death," each expected and yet expects us to understand more than they have expressly stated and state.

It is a fact well worth pondering; for it makes Easter what it should be: the Feast of all feasts and the Solemnity of all solemnities. It also sets the first Glorious Mystery in proper perspective. For it is only Easter Sunday morning that makes the Friday afternoon in Holy Week "Good." The Cross is the sign and symbol of our Faith only because there lies beyond Golgotha's grim mound an empty tomb.

Had there been no radiant Christ standing alive in the rose of Easter's dawning, then, as far as we would know, an execution took place on Calvary on Friday afternoon, and not our expiation. In short, had there been no Resurrection, there would have been no Redemption. That is how important Easter and the first Glorious Mystery are to the Catholic Christian Religion.

Once I had got my brother to reflect on these facts I felt I had him in position to look at the Holy Sacrifice of the Mass and see it, perhaps, in an entirely new light. We have been so steeped in the truth that Calvary was the one and only Mass of the New Law's one and only High Priest, and that the Mass is Calvary re-presented, that we seldom, if ever, think of Christ's Resurrection in connection with the New Law's Only Sacrifice. In the Mass the Priest and Victim are the same as the Priest and Victim of Calvary — and this makes it the identical acceptable Sacrifice; nevertheless the state of that Priest and Victim in the Mass is not the same as was the state of the Priest and Victim on Calvary — and it is this that makes the Mass so acceptable. But while that can be stated in a sentence, it can be comprehended only by slow and thorough thinking — especially by those who have not received a formal training in Theology.

Neither Charlie nor Kay had received such a training, so I proceeded slowly. I told how Martin d'Arcy, S.J., had marveled at finding so many manuals of Dogmatic Theology neglecting the Resurrection. He had reason to marvel; for the Cross and the empty tomb are correlated. The sagging Corpse of Golgotha and the resplendant beauty of the Easter Christ are complementary. No one should ever speak of Christ's Passion and Death except as Jesus did; that is, by always and immediately adding something about the "Third Day."

The couple on the Cape were then asked to look at the prayer every priest must say just after he has offered the bread and wine in the Mass. Every celebrant bends over and asks the all-holy triune God to accept what he has offered as a "memorial of Christ's Passion, Resurrection, and Ascension." If the Mass is a re-presentation only of Calvary, why does every priest have to speak of the Resurrection and Ascension?

"It is vital, Kay and Chic, that you grasp this point firmly. Not only for a proper understanding of Christ and His Sacrifice, but for your offering of your Christhood and your sufferings. For, let me put it plainly: a gift is a gift not when it is offered, but only when it is received. So, too, with suffering: it is sacrifice not when there is a human oblation or offering, but only when there is a divine acceptation of the offering. Now let us review a little Sacred History and learn some Theology. . . ."

I referred then back to the first book of the Bible so that they might see Cain and Abel making *oblation*. Each made an offering to God. But only Abel's became sacrifice; for only his was acceptable and accepted. Then I asked them to read in the First Book of Kings how Saul smote Amalec "from Hevila to Sur," and how the King of the Chosen People had been commanded to spare nothing, to slay ox and sheep, camel and ass. But then to read how the people "spared the best of the sheep and of the herds that they might be sacrificed to the Lord." They were saved to be offered as holocaust. Those animals were slain and offered. But there was no sacrifice made that day; for those slain offerings were not acceptable to nor accepted by God. Obviously, then, there is more to sacrifice than what is technically called *oblation* and *mactation* — though both of these are essential. From the examples before them, Charlie and Kay could see that while there must be a slaying and an offering of the victim, there is no sacrifice unless there is an acceptation of what has been slain and offered. Three elements, then, were seen as necessary for sacrifice; and of these, the third, or *acceptation*, loomed as the most important as far as we are concerned.

The point is so essential that it cannot be overstressed. So Charlie and Kay were taken to Mt. Carmel and allowed to witness a most significant drama, which taught a lesson that would mean so much to their own lives, their understanding of the Holy Sacrifice of the Mass, and their transformation of all their living into a "Mass."

They were shown Elias, the lone Prophet of God, entering into contest with four hundred and fifty priests of Baal. Were odds ever so uneven? The conditions governing the contest were clear: two altars for sacrifice were to be erected; on each the separate parties were to place the bullock they had slain, dressed, and divided as was the custom for holocaust. But no fire was to be kindled under either altar. That was to decide the contest; for it had been agreed that "the God that shall answer by fire" was evidently the true God. Obviously, then, both parties knew that it is the third element in sacrifice, namely *acceptation*, that differentiates sacrifice from mere slaughter.

The priests of Baal made sacrificial *mactation* when they slew and dressed their bullock. They made sacrificial *oblation* when they cried: "O Baal, hear us!" But there was no sacrifice; for there was no sacrificial *acceptation*. From Scripture it is evident that they must have cried all morning; for the Third Book of Kings tells us that "when it was high noon, Elias jested at them saying: 'Cry with a louder voice: for he is a God, and perhaps he is talking, or he is in an inn, or on a journey, or perhaps he is asleep, and must be waked.'" The priests of Baal followed this advice and "cried with a louder voice"; and "they cut themselves after their manner with knives and lancets, till they were all covered with blood." But "there was no voice heard, nor did anyone answer."

It is a gripping story. Elias then goes to work. He builds his altar, prepares his wood, lays his bullock thereon, then pauses dramatically. The lone Prophet of God then has the people fill four buckets of water and pour that water over the bullock and the wood. He has them do this a second, and even a third time, so that not only were the bullock, wood, and altar thoroughly soaked, but the deep trench Elias had dug around the altar was filled to the brim with water.

Then the Prophet of God prays: "O Lord God of Abraham, Isaac, and Israel, show this people that thou art the God of Israel. . . . Hear me, O Lord, that this people may learn that thou art the Lord God. . . ." He was crying to Heaven for that third, and, as far as we are concerned, the most telling element in sacrifice — *acceptation*. He got it. For Scripture says: "Then the fire of the Lord fell and consumed the holocaust, and the wood, and the stones, and the dust, and licked up the water that was in the trench." It looks as if the Lord God is something of a showman, too. For that last touch of licking up the water in the trench is precious. No wonder the story concludes: "When all the people saw this, they fell on their faces and they said: 'The Lord, he is God. The Lord, he is God!'" (3 Kings 18:36–39.)

Fire from Heaven has always been the surest sign that the offerings of earth have been made true sacrifice by acceptation. It had fallen on the offerings of Abraham, Gideon, David, and Solomon. They were sure that they had offered sacrifice.

After that lengthy exposition Kay and Charlie would probably be wondering where was the fire in the New Testament, and very especially where was the fire in the Mass. So they were made to see where the three essential elements for Sacrifice lay in that Sacrifice of all sacrifices — that of Jesus Christ.

That there was *oblation* made, the Upper Room amply testifies. For there, Jesus, as Priest, took bread and said: "This is my body which is about to be given for your sake"; then over the cup of wine: "This — my blood, which is about to be shed for your sake" (Lk. 22:19, 20).

That there was *mactation* is only too cruelly evident from Calvary's Cross.

But if we stop there, we have not sacrifice; we have only brutal slaughter. For what is there about Golgotha that would tell any human being anything more than that a barbarous execution of a man had taken place? To human eyes everything about that Hill of Skulls is hideous. The arms of the Cross are as silent as the horns of any altar. The lips of the New Law's High-Priest are muted by death. How would we ever know that God had died and man had been redeemed if we were left with only that torn Corpse on the Cross as evidence? We need some sign that the offering was acceptable and has been *accepted*. We have it in the first Glorious Mystery.

"Fire from Heaven was the infallible sign in the Old Testament," I wrote my brother. "Fire from Heaven is the same infallible sign in the New. For the Uncreated Fire of Divinity came from Limbo with Christ's human soul, not to consume the Victim that lay in the Tomb, but to resurrect it from the dead. That Fire fell not to burn but to beautify; not to destroy but to glorify. The Resurrection of Jesus Christ is the one visible sign we have which enables us to fall on our faces, as did the peoples on Mt. Carmel, and cry: 'The Lord, he is God! The Lord, he is God!' For it is thanks to Christ's rising from the dead that we know the *Oblation* of the Upper Room and the *Mactation* of Golgotha have met with *Acceptation* by God. Now you can see the import of that prayer in the Mass which mentions the Resurrection and Ascension along with the Passion of Christ."

The tragedy of our day is not that our world is filled with so much suffering, but that so much suffering is not made into sacrifice by being placed into that Fire which is the risen Christ.

Charlie and Kay were not to live a tragedy, but to make their lives, with all their sufferings, exactly what God had planned them to be from the beginning: nothing less than a Divine Romance. They were told they could do that not by saying that prayer which has been attributed to St. Ignatius the founder of the Jesuits, but by living it. The *Anima Christi* was brought before them at this stage, for I felt that it would talk to them about Christ, His Mass, life, and real living. Further, it tied in neatly with the thesis they had been learning from the very beginning of this correspondence. Their gaze had been fixed and steadily held on the living, glorious Christ; for it appeared to be not only the soundest psychological approach but contained thrilling theological truth. Joy is of the essence of Christianity; and Jesus is the Source and Substance of that joy. Moreover, sanctity is the beginning and end of Christian living; and it is the risen Christ who is, in all truth, our Sanctification.

"Soul of Christ, be my sanctification" is the first petition of the *Anima Christi*. The prayer then goes on beautifully to beg: "Body of Christ, be my salvation. Blood of Christ, fill all my veins. Water from Christ's side, wash out my stains. Passion of Christ, my comfort be. O, Good Jesus, listen to me: Within Thy wounds I fain would hide; never to be parted from Thy side. Guard me should the foe assail me. Call me when my life shall fail me. Bid me come to Thee above, that with Thy saints I may sing Thy love for all Eternity."

My brother was told that he was to hide in the Wounds Christ carried in the Mass, but to note well that those Wounds were not bloody; they were glorious; they were afire with the Beauty which is God, and it was this Beauty which makes our sacrifices acceptable. "By all means make the Mass your life, Chic, and make your life a Mass; but be certain just what the Mass is: it is not only Holy Thursday and Good Friday; it is Easter Sunday and Ascension Thursday. It is even Pentecost and the Apocalypse!"

Such a presentation provokes questions. In answer to them I gave the doctrine Maurice de la Taille taught concerning the Mass. For

this acute Jesuit theologian, in magnificent fashion, has tied in the
Cenacle, Calvary, and what goes on endlessly in Heaven with what
we do when at our altars we celebrate Mass. Hence, the Gospels,
St. Paul's Epistles, and the Apocalypse are fused into such a unity
that we glory to find Christ so near. But the more specific purpose of
that kind of presentation was to alert my brother and his wife to the
fact that their sanctification lay in union, vital union with the Man-
God who, as St. Paul says, "rose for our sanctification" (Rom. 4:25).

The two on the Cape were not going to be allowed to lose sight
of the first Glorious Mystery nor of Mary who was the first to share
in it. They were told how our Mother is present at every Mass — and
how she longed, as only loving mothers can long, to help them make
their lives Christ's Mass.

They were reminded that the very best definition possible of us
humans, who are born one minute and seem to be moldering the next,
is that we are a "capacity for God." We are capacities that are to be
filled to the full with Almighty God — and it is Christ who has made
this filling possible. He did it by His Resurrection. For the breaking of
the Roman seals on that borrowed tomb was more than the stamping
of God's seal upon the action and Passion, the life and death of His
only Son. It was the opening of the sluice gates of life — the kind
of life that is sacred and sanctifying; the only kind of life worth living;
the only kind of life worth dying to achieve. Christ knew that. That
is why He was so anxious to die. But not enough of us Christians
realize that if Christ had not come out of the grave radiant with life
and glory, then all the God-filled assets won by His Agony in the
garden, that Scourging at the pillar, that staggering, stumbling Way
of the Cross, the Crucifixion, and Death itself — the full five Sorrowful Mysteries of Mary's Rosary — would have remained "frozen assets"
as far as mankind is concerned. Life comes only from the living.
Hence, it is not the dead Christ of Calvary, but the glorified Jesus
of Easter who can fill our capacities with God.

God the Holy Spirit teaches us this truth when He has St. Paul
tell us that it is only after His Resurrection that Jesus became a
"*quickening* — that is, a life-giving spirit" (1 Cor. 15:45). The same
Third Person of the Blessed Trinity clinches the lesson when He has
Paul write: ". . . being alive should no longer mean living with our

own life, but *with his life,* who died for us and is risen again" (2 Cor. 5:15).*

I had dwelt at length on this first Glorious Mystery. The season of the year allowed for it; for it was Eastertide, 1957. But had it been midwinter the same stress would have been appropriate; for in this Mystery lies the compendium and solution to all other Mysteries. It explains the five Sorrowful Mysteries in the life of Christ and His Mother. It explains every sorrowful mystery any man may have to endure on earth; for every man, no matter what his sorrows, was made for glory. St. Irenaeus was right: "the living man is the glory of God." He was even more right when he said: "the life of man is the vision of God." But that glory and that vision stem from and center in the risen Jesus.

That is why the fifth chapter in St. Paul's second Epistle to the Corinthians was so frequently brought to the attention of the two on the Cape. It is heartening to realize that "Christ died for us all, so that being alive should no longer mean living with your own life, but with His life who died and is risen again . . . henceforward we do not think of anybody in a merely human fashion . . ."; for ". . . when a man becomes a new creature in Christ, his old life has disappeared, everything has become new about him. . . ." All that would have very personal appeal to Charlie. I had reason to hope that both he and Kay would see the applicability of Paul's next few lines to both them and myself: "God appeals to you through us; we entreat you in Christ's name, make your peace with God. Christ never knew sin, and God made him into sin for us, *so that in him we might be turned into the holiness of God"* (2 Cor. 5:15 sqq.).*

"There's life in a line," I wrote in conclusion to one letter. "You two, along with your seven children, are to be turned into the *holiness of God* thanks to the risen Christ. That is what Baptism began. We are to live the Mysteries of Christ — especially the Glorious ones. You are not only living the Resurrection but soon you'll learn how you are living the Ascension."

* Knox translation. Emphasis added.

CHAPTER SIX

He Hears the Beat of Her Heart

MARY's month, those thirty-one days so filled with new life and promise, had almost passed in the year of 1957, and I was wondering just what it had done to the heart of my brother. As jonquils lifted their golden chalices to the sun here in Kentucky and as the robins built their nests while we monks planted and saw our seeds leap to life, I found a poignancy in all this beauty as I tried to imagine how it appeared to that couple on the Cape, who undoubtedly were conscious that this might be their last spring together.

My wondering ceased when a letter came which began: "Our Father who is up in Heaven watching so lovingly over me has given me much joy of late. In fact, He's spoiling me. . . . He sees me afflicted with something a little out of the ordinary, so He gives me much to offset this affliction. For instance, can you imagine me having a set of Gregorian Masses reserved for me."

That certainly sounded as if the very first lesson taught at Gethsemani, namely, that God *is* our Father, had been well learned. I thanked our Mother for that. Gratitude to Mary welled up in my heart; for I well knew how basic this truth is for all proper living. It is the granite bottom for *Pietas,* that virtue which shows God we know we are *His* children.

On the next page of that letter Charlie gave me more reasons for thanking Mary; for he wrote that he felt his life was "more useful than ever, more productive of grace" . . . that he was now "making up what is wanting to the Passion of my Brother, Jesus Christ."

If Charlie could hold those two truths about the Fatherhood of God and the need Jesus Christ has for our sufferings and sacrifices in the forefront of his consciousness, all would be well! I hoped I was not reading into his letter, but I saw so much of what he had left unsaid that I sang Mary's *Magnificat* to her and for myself. She it was who brought Christ to us. She it must be who brings us to Christ.

It was on the next page that I found the answer to my unphrased question of how spring with all its promise of life affected this man who was facing death. "The grounds around the house look beautiful at this time of the year," he had written. "The forsythia and bridal wreath have just about seen their day, but the colorful irises and beautiful begonia are just coming into full bloom. In another week's time we will have our roses. Our smaller flowers will fill up the gap during July and August. We have had a beautiful spring. . . ."

The things he had taken for granted year after year as God works His miracle in the birth of growing things were seen this year with keener eyes and a more clearly understanding mind and heart. And his own children. . . . What poignancy there is in the sentence, "I am looking forward to a grand summer with the children," when we know there is racing in his veins and eating at his body that which may take him from those children before that summer is over. But never once does Charlie set this possibility on paper. "With the new tires on the ranch wagon we will be able to enjoy ourselves," he writes. "But Kay must learn to drive, for I find it more and more difficult to do so. Coming up here to Pocasset I had to give up and let my neighbor take the wheel and finish the trip. Boy, when I give in you can be sure my legs really were hurting."

Yet once that admission is made he goes on: "Kathy is set for the summer with two baby-sitting jobs. Maureen will be at Spruce Tree Lodge from 8–10 a.m. and 6–8 p.m. . . . I hope to get Kevin and Charlie off to a boys' camp for a few weeks; it is sponsored by the St. Vincent de Paul Society of our parish. Patty, Mary, and Christy will, I hope, enjoy their summer with Mom and Dad at the beach. All this is contingent on God's Will, as I well know."

Charlie seemed to have just about everything in that paragraph. Husband, father, child of God are all in evidence — and that last sentence teems with thoughts and truths unexpressed. God-consciousness was assuming the ascendancy in my brother's life. I knew a great calm in my soul.

Two days later there came another letter, which began: "I'll spoil you by dropping you another line. . . . I write now while the talk I had with Doctor Gould is fresh in my memory. He had my chest X-rayed and my leg, too. Then in consultation with Doctors Wood, Sanbourne, Leadbetter, and Kelley — you see I have more doctors than the President — my case was thoroughly thrashed out." Who wouldn't smile at that remark about "more doctors than the President" — and admire the man who made it when the next page holds the lines: "I walk around in pain, I sit down in pain, I lie down in pain. If this were due to poor circulation, I would get relief by elevating my legs. I don't. I may not be a good diagnostician, but let me kid myself, anyway."

My brother was referring to the severe pain that had come into his legs which the doctors now attributed to the cancer in his lung. The X rays showed next to no growth of the tumor in his lung, so the medical men grew convinced that the nitrogen mustard had done some good. Another course of it was decided upon to see if it might not help the condition in the legs. Charlie wrote: "I had my second dose of rat poison last night and I was not sick after it. But boy, the other night, after the first dose . . . I usually say, after that first dose, that I'll never take another. I had even the nurses convinced that I meant it this time. But I took it in stride. They are all convinced that this stuff is doing a good job. I selfishly say I wish it weren't. But then, as you say, God's purpose must be served."

The letter cited first had closed with something new for Charlie. It read "Love, in the Loving Heart of Mary, your kid brother, Chic." I wondered if it was the month of May, or was it that Mother Mary was replying to the prayers of her monk with the generosity she has always shown. This present letter closed with "Tell your, or should I say 'our' Abbot, and all our brother monks that I join them in the loving Heart of Mary, asking her to obtain from her Divine Son the graces necessary for us, so that soon we shall all be a happy family with our Father in our Home." Then again the sign-off line: "Love always, In the Loving Heart of Mary, Chic."

That prompted a letter from me in which I spoke of Mother Mary. It must have prodded Charlie into some sort of a review. For in his next he told me how he struggled to get to Mass every morning, but did not always succeed. He then went on to show that he was making his life a Mass as he wrote: "since I found out what I had at Gethsemani I have been doing what you suggested in your letters. I remember you often as I suffer with my Brother, our Lord. I ask Him to take the pain as an offering to our Father and get you the grace you need to fulfill His purpose for you. Some nights and some days I offer it for Jack, Eddie, Mazie, Peg, or Betty — or for Kay and the Kiddoes.

"I'm no hero or martyr, but when I offer these pains for others, I get over many moments of despondency. I pray to hurry Home — but always add: Thy Will be done. I become afraid many times, but, thanks be to God, I do not fear for any length of time. I do not know what I'll do if and when it gets real rough, but I pray that I'm preparing for it by saying often: Thy Will be done.

"Many people say they admire my courage. If they only knew what a coward I am. If my Father in Heaven was not caring so much for me, I'd fail miserably; for by myself I'm so weak. He sees me through — without Him I am nothing. With Him I'm going to be a saint."

That paragraph told me how much Mother Mary had already accomplished! What *Pietas* Charlie was manifesting! What true humility, abandonment, and trust! "I'm going to be a saint" was just about the last thing I ever expected to hear my brother say. Yet there it was, and evidently written with determination.

He closed with ". . . summer is just about here with the Cape becoming crowded more and more each day. We are all quite tanned from the sea and the sun. The grounds around the house look lovely. I am with you daily in prayer."

Such a letter could not be acknowledged more sincerely than by quoting some lines from St. Paul's Epistle to the Philippians: "Rejoice! Rejoice in the Lord always; I repeat, rejoice." I told Charlie and Kay that the quotation marks were used out of honesty only. I had to admit the source of the line — but actually it expressed my heart. "And see," I wrote, "how perfectly the rest of that passage to the Philippians phrases my thoughts for me: 'Let your forbearance be known to all men. The Lord is near. Have no anxiety, but in every concern by prayer and supplication with thanksgiving let your petitions be made known in your communing with God. Then the peace of God which surpasses all understanding will guard your hearts and your thoughts in Christ Jesus!'" (Phil. 4:4-8).

Joy in the Lord, realization of the nearness of Christ, prayer that was not only humble petition and heart-deep thanksgiving, but also heart-to-Heart converse with God — all that was what I wished for Charlie and his wife. For these, and these alone, would give them that peace of soul which nothing in this world can disturb.

They were asked to read the entire Epistle aloud to one another and to hear in the tender voice of the Apostle my own loving accent. There is no doubt but that this is the most affectionate of all Paul's Epistles. Not even in his lines to Timothy is such tenderness and love made manifest. I wanted Kay and Charlie to realize that, like St. Paul, I was "praying joyfully" for them; that, like him, I was "convinced of this, that he who has begun this good work in you, will continue to perfect it until the day of Christ Jesus"; that I "had them in my heart"; and that "the object of my prayer is that your love may become richer and richer and be accompanied with a full knowledge and a keen practical insight, so that you may appreciate true values" (Phil. 1:3-10).

There was even deeper purpose in my request about this Epistle, for after telling how his own suffering had worked to God's gain and the spread of the Gospel and boldly stating that "Christ will be glorified by this body of mine, whether it lives or dies," Paul had turned to his beloved converts of Philippi and begged them to "let their lives be worthy of the Gospel of Christ" insisting that "you have been given the favor on Christ's behalf, not only of having faith in him, but also of suffering for him." That should mean much to anyone in the condition my brother was or in the position Kay found herself. But the statement in the third chapter to the effect that "I would know Christ and what his resurrection can do," along with the subsequent sentence: "I would also share his sufferings, in the hope that, if I resemble him in death, I may somehow attain to the resurrection from the dead" (3:8-11) was what I especially wanted the two on the Cape to hear and ponder.

When pain is persistent we must know what purpose it can serve, else we lose patience and may even become angry. That Charlie had grasped the fact that members of Christ can help complete the work of Christ had been evidenced in more than one letter. But now it seemed opportune time to show both Kay and him what a wondrous work they were doing for God's Mother and all mankind as they helped toward the speeding up of the triumph of her Immaculate Heart.

The signature which Charlie had come to employ so consistently served as introduction. "The Immaculate Heart of Mary has been ✗ pleading with you for over a century," I wrote. "All that is involved in this blessing from God called carcinoma is what she has wanted since 1830." Then they were told about Mary's many apparitions these past hundred and twenty-five years. The thesis proposed was that if they were willing to look upon Mary's Visitation to her cousin Elizabeth as something of an apparition, then they could say that our Immaculate Mother's every visitation or apparition from that at Ain Karin to that of Fatima has had but one ultimate purpose: Mary would bring Christ to mankind, so that she might bring mankind to Christ. This Mother of us all would be a channel of grace to every human being and set each of us dancing with the joy of sanctification, even as she had set the unborn Baptist jumping in his mother's womb. But since sanctification, for those of us who have attained to the use of reason, is a co-operative affair, she comes to tell us that the surest way to co-operate is by prayer and penance. She even specifies the prayer of special efficacy — her Rosary; and the penance of greatest worth — the specific duties of our state in life. It ✗ is all so simple that it may well confuse modern sophisticates. But it is all so much in accord with her own earthly life, that no true child of Mary can question the genuineness of the directive.

The first apparition was that which occurred on July 18, 1830, in the Motherhouse of the Daughters of Charity, which stands on the Rue de Bac, in the heart of Paris. On that day Zoé Catherine Labouré heard the Mother of God speak. But what was said that day was meant for Charlie, Kay, their seven children, and for all God's children who live today whether in or far from Paris. Mary had said then that the times were evil; that terrible things were about to happen; that the whole world would be convulsed by calamities. Hope for the people lay only in prayer. God's Mother insisted that special graces would be given to those who asked for them. It was from these apparitions that we got our Miraculous Medal; for Mary had asked the humble postulant to have one made. But our otherwise headlong and quite gullible people are hesitant and even skeptical when such matters are broached. So two full years passed before the first medal was made. If we look closely at the image on that medal we will note that there are some gems on Mary's fingers which emit no rays. The explanation was given by Mother Mary herself: they symbolize those graces that she has in her hands but which have never been asked for by needy men. Does it not seem that Mary Immaculate was but echoing the teaching of her Son who said: "Ask and you shall receive"?

Charlie and Kay were told that the message given to Catherine Labouré was for them. Mother Mary was saying: "Pray! Pray! Pray!" I urged them to ask for ever stronger faith, fortitude, and filial piety. For Christ's words, "Ask and you shall receive," contain both command and promise.

The next apparition, that of their Mother in tears, was at La Salette. But I pointed out that she was weeping not alone for those whose wheat would turn to dust that harvesttime of 1846, whose walnuts would be all worms, and whose potatoes nothing but rot. Melanie Mathieu and Maximin Giraud heard that the avenging hand of Mary Immaculate's Son was raised and ready to smite because of the desecration of the Sabbath and the abuse of His Holy Name. "If she wept for those who would know famine in 1846," Charlie and Kay were asked, "must she not be weeping more piteously for us whose lands produce surpluses, whose granaries are bursting, whose lives are lived in relative luxury, but whose world knows no genuine happiness because it lacks reverence for, and a keen awareness of, God?"

They were then told that they could dry Mary's tears by making every day something of a "Sabbath" by worshiping God and having their every heartbeat be something of an Act of Reverence for His Holy Name.

Lourdes and its apparitions were quite well known to them. But I pointed out that as our Lady stood above the rubbish in that cave at Massabielle and spoke to Bernadette, the message of La Salette was repeated in substance. Again it was: "Pray! Pray! Pray!" — and very pointedly to pray the Rosary. But this time there was an explicit call for penance.

The next apparition was one about which they knew little. They were told that our Lady-Mother did not wait for the invention of the airplane before she took to writing in the heavens. In 1871 two little French girls at Pontmain along with the Barbedette boys slowly spelled out the letters our Lady had formed in the skies, and finally read the words she had fashioned there: *Mais donc, priez mes enfants* — "Pray, my children, pray!"

"Don't you think that we who have seen our skies darken with wings faster than sound, who have watched rockets zoom up into the stratosphere, caught glimpses of man-made satellites, and listened to talk of space ships; don't you think that we who have seen pictures of those terrible mushroom clouds that rise from A-bombs and H-bombs need to read in our heavens those all-important words: 'Pray, my children, pray'?" was the question which brought that apparition into personal relation with our times.

Fatima needed less commentary than Lourdes; for the family on the Cape did not have to be told that our Lady did not shake the sun that rainy afternoon of October 13, 1917, just for those 70,000 who fell to their knees in fright. They knew she had done it for every man alive. The message she had for Lucy, Jacinta, and Francis was a message for Kay, Charlie, and each of their children, as well as for every other human being. The Mother of God once again placed in the hands of men the instrument that will bring about the conversion of Russia and give real peace to our world — the Rosary.

But they must remember, too, that Mary is always Mother. Whenever she seems to be asking something for herself, it is always of course a request that will bring blessings to her children. At Paris she had asked for a medal. She got it. But it was we who got the miracles. It is our Miraculous Medal. At Lourdes she asked for a chapel and processions. She finally got both. But with the cures worked near the chapel known to all mankind, and those taking place during the processions still startling the world, we well know for whose benefit she made her requests. It is the same with the prayer she most frequently asks for — the Rosary. From our recitation of it she undoubtedly gets some glory, but who can ever measure all

that we receive? "Right now," I told my brother, "we can convert
Russia with it and save civilization."

"That does sound like an exorbitant promise, Chic, until you consider who it was that made it. She is called the *Omnipotentia Supplex*
— which really means the Woman God cannot refuse. Doesn't she
show her power with God practically every day in those wonders that
are worked at her many shrines? We think of Lourdes almost exclusively, but she is showing herself *Omnipotentia Supplex* at many
other shrines. Fatima is becoming better known as a place for miracles
. . . and now there is Beauraing in Belgium." Then Charlie was told
how in 1932 five children saw our Lady thirty-three different times,
but very seldom did they hear her speak. When they did, they heard
what practically all her other seers have heard: a plea that they pray!
Here again our Lady-Mother revealed her Immaculate Heart, so these
apparitions should have special appeal for my brother if that signature
of his held all the significance it seemed to hold. Mary closed her long
series of appearances here by saying to one of the children: "Sacrifice
yourself." We were faced again, then, with her plea for prayer and
penance; that pressing need of our day which can so easily be
satisfied, thanks to Mary's directives.

Then there is Banneaux, a tiny town less than a hundred miles
from Beauraing, which already is rivaling Lourdes in the number, the
suddenness, and the unquestionably miraculous nature of its cures.

Charlie and Kay were told how, on the night of January 15, 1933,
eleven-year-old Mariette Beco was standing at the window of her
shabby little home in Banneaux. It was seven o'clock in the evening
as this little girl pressed her nose against the window pane and peered
out into the darkness. She was endeavoring to get an early glimpse
of her elder brother, Julien, whose supper she was trying to keep
warm. Mariette was the daughter of a lapsed Catholic, and so un-
learned was she in the things of God that thrice she had failed to
pass the simple test for First Holy Communion. Yet, it was to this
child that the Mother of God came. As Mariette peered out, looking
for Julien, she suddenly saw Mary Immaculate.

She told her family about it and, of course, was disbelieved. But
the next night the same thing happened. This time our Lady beck-

oned to Mariette to come outside. The child obeyed. The Immaculate Mother of God then led the girl to a spring by the side of the road and said: "This spring is for me."

On the third night when our Lady appeared Mariette found her voice and asked the Lady her name. "I am the Virgin of the Poor" was the reply. But then our Lady-Mother asked that a chapel be built by the spring; adding that these waters were for all nations, and that she had come to relieve the sick.

As usual there were all kinds of skeptical questionings, plus those customary cynical, searching tests. Here they went even further than they had gone at Beauraing; for not only whole panels of doctors but psychiatrists of world-wide repute examined this little girl who could not pass a test for First Communion. Yet she stood up so stanchly under the probings of these experts that they pronounced her perfectly sane, and credited her with having given a truly straightforward and utterly unwavering report.

At last, almost grudgingly, it would seem, ecclesiastical authorities accepted her story and allowed a chapel to be built. Then the wonders began. The sick came; many nations were represented. Mary showed her motherliness — and her power.

As one instance Charlie and Kay were given the colorful account of what happened to Benito Pelagri Garcia. The man was an anarchist who lived in Barcelona, Spain. One day he came home from work with his right arm so severely injured from a boiler explosion that the doctors said he would never be able to use it again. His wife, a Belgian girl, who held on to her Catholic Faith despite her husband's ridicule, had heard about Banneaux from her friends in the homeland. When she suggested a pilgrimage to the shrine in her native land, she received a bitter and taunting laugh in reply. The months passed. The injured arm did not improve. The unemployed Benito grew restless. One day he suddenly surprised his wife by saying they would go to Belgium. To her it was a pilgrimage. To him a change of scenery.

To humor his wife he agreed to her plan that they walk all the way. He even abstained from smoking and drink and lodged with her in the poorest of dwelling places. She was making it a true pilgrimage, a journey filled with prayer and penance. It is a long way from Barcelona to Banneaux, and this couple covered it on foot and in the heat of summer.

As soon as they reached the spring Benito savagely plunged both his hands into the water. He found that to his healthy left hand these waters were soothingly cool, but to his injured right hand they seemed to be boiling. Jerking both hands from the spring he stood for some time staring at the statue of our Lady-Mother above it. In his eyes there blazed anger, bewilderment, antagonism. Suddenly, thrusting both hands toward the statue, he blurted out: "If you are the Virgin of the Poor, prove it! Here is a poor man who has come all the way from Spain."

With that he showily plunged his injured hand into the waters again, then lifted it high for all who gathered near the shrine to see. Violently he pulled from that arm the tube that was in it for drainage. But as he looked at his arm the defiant laugh that was ready on his lips died; for the hole that held the drain tube was closing, the flesh about it was becoming solid, and the entire arm became perfectly sound.

Benito Pelagri Garcia dropped the pose of sophisticated skeptic, ceased to be an anarchist, and from that dramatic moment began to be a man.

"The real purpose behind all the wonders Mary works," I told my brother and his wife "is this: she cures bodies only to make souls sound. She is dramatic at times, but the drama is only to startle us into a consciousness of who we are, why we are living, and what we are actually doing.

"Aren't you two now, thanks to the realities you have had to face, in a position to admit that the world with all its rush actually anesthetizes us? We live and move in a state that is tantamount to unconsciousness as far as the real concerns of life and living go. Though immortal beings, we are absorbed by utterly temporal things. Though spiritual in the higher part of our composite nature, we allow the lower part to render us almost totally sensate. Though made for God, we are taken up almost exclusively with men. That is why the supernatural, which should be, and actually is, as normal as breathing, appears so strange to us.

"I can tell you two that cancer has already made you truly God-conscious. Since that is a fact who can question the statement that it is a blessing from God that has come to you through the hands of Mary? For let me insist once again that all her cures of human bodies are worked only that there will be real conversions of human souls.

"Perhaps you have wondered why I have not had you using Lourdes water, applying the Miraculous Medal, and storming her Immaculate Heart for a miraculous cure. I know how essential you are to Kay and the kids, Chic. I know a father's hand, a father's heart, a father's head will be wanted at 33 Blanid Road for years to come. I also know our Lady-Mother is 'omnipotent when she supplicates.' Yet I do not urge you, nor Kay, nor the children, nor any of our family or friends to pray for a miracle. I will even go so far as to say that miracles are parts of God's providence. Still I placed you, and got you to place yourself, and have asked Kay to place you, herself, and the entire family in the Immaculate Heart of our Lady-Mother, and rest satisfied with that, because I would have something better than a cure for each of you!

"The cancer victims she has cured at Lourdes will one day die. The sick she has made well at Banneaux will sicken again, and one day die. The cripples she has set upon sound limbs at Fatima and her other shrines will one day go to their graves. The eyes she has opened here, there, and almost everywhere in the world will one day close forever. But the souls she thoroughly sanctifies, the hearts she completely converts, the minds and wills she turns to Christ and keeps them thus turned, are far better off than any she simply cures of physical distress. Our Lady-Mother would never work such wonders simply for the sake of brittle clay. She would not disrupt the ordinary running of natural law just for the sake of time. Her aim is always something eternal. That is why I would have you rejoice in what she has already done to your heart, mind, will, and soul, and realize that every spasm of pain in your body is really a loving caress from the hand of your Mother of the Immaculate Heart. She is giving you opportunity not only to gain what is eternal for yourself, but even to speed on the temporal triumph of her Heart.

"I do not say, of course, that she may not yet cure you. All I

say is that you are in her loving hands to be cared for by her Immaculate Heart. She knows with certainty what is best for you and
all who are near and dear to you. I don't. I can only surmise. You
can be sure that she will get exactly what you and yours need —
even though, at first, that may not be precisely what you and yours
want or like."

Charlie began his next letter the way he usually signed off his
other letters.

> Soon we'll be in the Loving Heart of Mary for real.
> For the past several weeks time has been on my mind. I'd even say
> it has been uppermost in my mind. Its human facets — its human value
> — and the varied importance we humans give it individually.
> For instance — I did not think I'd be here now when I first read Dr.
> Kelley's report in your "catacomb." I didn't think I'd see Easter Sunday.
> It has come and gone.
> Now what has mostly been in my mind is how little I have used
> time to think of Eternity. Very specifically, I wonder how I dare class
> myself as a logical, a reasoning person when I see myself to have so
> often threatened my eternal happiness for moments of human pleasure.
> How good God, our Father, has been to *me!* I *grow* daily with this
> thought — and I can stand a lot of growing. . . .
> Pray that I go to my real Home soon, but only when I have finished
> the job Our Father gave me to do.
> Always in the Loving Heart of Mary. . . .

That closing reference to work to be done for God served as a lead
for my follow-up on Mary and her requests for prayer and penance.
Once again I reminded him that he was now in a position to do the
very best work of his life. He had his tools for this work in his pains
and her Rosary.

I reminded my brother that at Massabielle, Mary had let her
beads slip through her fingers as young Bernadette said the Rosary.
At La Salette, Melanie and Maximin were told by the Weeping
Woman to say the *Our Father* and the *Hail Mary* often — the prayers
that form the substance of her Rosary. At Fatima she was explicit. There she named herself "Lady of the Rosary" and asked
the three children — and through them, all mankind — to tell the
beads every day.

"Mary asks so simple a prayer of us," I told him, "because her

Rosary is at the same time the simplest and the sublimest of prayers. The unlettered can understand it. The most learned can never exhaust its meaning. It is a compendium of Christ's thrilling revelation; hence, every man's *Summa Theologica*. Finally, it serves not only to recall the Mysteries that filled the lives of Jesus and Mary, but as a mirror of the Mysteries that fill our nights and days and thus make up the lives of all who call themselves Christian."

It was then shown that we can call ourselves Catholics this day only because we have had an "Annunciation," a "Visitation," and have shared vitally in the "Incarnation." We are Christ's members! Having taken eight children to the Baptismal font, Charlie well knew that we have shared in the "Presentation in the Temple." As for the fifth of the Joyful Mysteries, who is there who has sinned, has been sorry for sinning, and has gone to confession who does not share in that heart-filling joy of the "Finding in the Temple"?

The proof that we live the Sorrowful Mysteries of the Rosary was hardly more than a reference to cancer. "That blessing," I wrote, "will allow you to share with Him that 'Agony in the Garden,' that 'Scourging at the Pillar,' and in your own way, to wear His 'Crown of Thorns.' We are all stumbling toward Calvary. We are all helping to 'fill up what is wanting to His Passion.' That is why we must meet Mary on the way of the cross. I say it again and again: we do not only say the Rosary, we live it. But let me insist that we shall never do that the way it should be done unless we realize with a dynamic realization that it is not only the Joyful and the Sorrowful Mysteries that are ours, but very particularly the Glorious ones. We are actually living them now, Chic. We are what we are only because we live in the *resurrected* Christ. That is the fact which makes life worth living; suffering something that can be courted; and death, far from something to be feared, seen as something to be loved — for it lets us in to that longed-for tryst with our Beloved. Believe me, boy, glory is ours today! We do not have to wait for tomorrow. So live your Rosary as well as say it."

But lest that seem too private and personal a work I again reminded my brother of the needs of the world and how he, whether home in Osterville, or up at the hospital in Pocasset, could satisfy those needs by his beads and his pains. Charlie had traveled far and mingled with many men. He knew, perhaps better than I, how many humans are lonely; how many call themselves orphans; how few count their lives other than meaningless. Yet God is Father to each; Christ, Brother; all Heaven, their kin; and there is no human breath or heartbeat without possibility of giving God glory and doing good to man. "You did a very good work for our nation, Chic, when you helped build those air bases in foreign fields. You can do even a greater work for our nation and for the men of all nations as you now suffer in, with, and for Jesus Christ and pray and live Mary's Rosary. The air bases protect us from physical harm, but your prayers and penance will protect millions more from spiritual hurt."

How we need to learn there is something better for pain than pain relievers! How we need to realize that we can take the pain and make it do something positive for God, His Mother, and our fellow man! When it grips us our only concern need not be how to get rid of it as quickly as possible, or how to minimize its effects on our human frame; we can take it and sublimate it into sacrifice and thus make it pay dividends to Jesus Christ as we turn it into that coin which can purchase light and liberty for many a fellow human. Above all we can offer it to God as something that will speed the triumph of the Immaculate Heart of Mary. Viewed in this light — and there is hardly any other proper light in which to view it — pain is seen as one of the most precious things in creation.

Charlie had been told something of the sorrow that afflicts the contemplative when he thinks on the poor return God the Father received from Creation, and what deeper sorrow he knows when he looks at the meager results Christ realizes from His all-out effort at re-Creation. Now he was asked to reflect on the fact that though the Mother of God has been speaking to men for over a hundred years, begging for prayers and penance, few have made anything like a generous response. The world has moved on since that day in 1830 when Mother Mary appeared to Zoé Catherine Labouré, yet, despite his breath-taking material progress, man's grasp on the things of the spirit seems just as feeble now as then — if not actually feebler.

To illustrate, I told Charlie how, during World War II outside the very Motherhouse of the Daughters of Charity on the Rue de Bac, wherein Mary had appeared to Zoé Catherine Labouré, a bullet fired by the occupying Germans struck a young member of the French Resistance. He fell mortally wounded. Two nuns rushed from the convent and drew the boy into the shelter of the convent's doorway. Seeing that he was about to die one of them bent over him and tried to prepare him for his meeting with God by saying: "You love the good God with all your heart, do you not?" Glazed eyes opened and the gasping reply came: "How can I say that I love this good God of whom you speak? I have not the slightest idea who He is."

Only a few gasps from eternity and he had to confess, there on the doorstep of the convent where the Mother of God had appeared, that he had not the slightest idea who God is.

But the deeper tragedy lies in the fact that this kind of thing seems typical rather than exceptional. Douglas Hyde in his book, *One Front Across the World*, tells about three hundred or so American G.I.'s who were on one of those Communists' death marches in North Korea. With them was a Catholic bishop and a handful of Catholic priests. To fall out of line was to invite a bullet or a bayonet into your vitals. A young G.I. did fall out. A Catholic missionary sidled over to him. Seeing that the boy was completely exhausted and could not possibly go on, the priest whispered: "Get ready to meet God, boy. Say you are sorry for your sins. Say you love God and I'll absolve you." The boy looked up. "I don't know what you're talking about, Padre. Haven't you got a cigarette on you?" One gasp from God — and he asks for a cigarette!

Just a few years back a book appeared in English with the title: *France, Pagan?* which was a devastatingly honest survey of Christians and Christianity in and around Paris made by two Catholic priests. They gave their manuscript to Emmanuel Cardinal Suhard, the then Archbishop of Paris. It is reported that for three days and three nights this Prince of the Church pored over that document, facing the facts and wrestling with the incontestable weight of the evidence. At the end of that wrestling the once careful and conservative Cardinal was so shaken by his study that he wrote a pastoral that will live as long as men live. He called it "The Meaning of God." He got his title from the fact that today men have lost the *real* meaning of God. As a consequence they have no true idea

of themselves, their purpose in life, or the meaning of the many
movements that have shaken their century and their civilization.

"Charlie," I concluded, "do you see what wondrous work you can
do not only in and for your own little world up there on the Cape
but for the wider world of men who need to know God? Live
joyously. Live gloriously; and you'll bring the true meaning of God
not only to those who see you, but, thanks to Mary's Immaculate
Heart, to countless others whom you'll never see until we all have
been resurrected from the dead and have ascended on high."

That last brought me back to my original theme. I was just on
time, too; for we were nearing Ascension Thursday when I addressed
myself to the task of showing Kay and Charlie that our entire Christian life is *ascensional*, hence, "it is Heaven all the way to Heaven,"
as some wise saint once said.

CHAPTER SEVEN

"...Our Exaltation"

In a world that many call "mad," it sounds a bit unrealistic, to say the least, to tell anyone that "it is Heaven all the way to Heaven." To a man who had to begin his very next letter with the words: "I have not been feeling too well lately: my legs have been giving me a lot of pain, and even my arms have been aching; that is the reason for my not writing sooner," such a statement would call forth a sneer were it not founded on faith and filled with fertile seeds of hope.

These two virtues seem so closely related that one is tempted to speak of them as one does of flower and fruit or of seed and stalk. Since that is fact, no one need wonder if some thinkers conclude that the lack of hope in our mid-twentieth-century civilization really stems from our lack of faith. One has to believe before one can hope; for the trust we place in another is based on the truth we have found in him. Once we know that Christ is God, then learn the things He has promised, our faith fills our souls with hope.

It is true that many have spoken of "blind faith" — but that adjective, while expressive of fact, is far from expressing all the facts about this fundamental virtue. Some obscurity there will always be in matters pertaining to faith; for we are face to face with Mystery. But faith in itself is light for the blind; it is illumination for our dark intellects; it is insight into things we could never see without it. It is something even more than light; it is life: for "The holy man *lives* by faith" (Rom. 1:17).

But it is essential that we distinguish clearly between faith and fideism; between credence that is based on something as firm as God

85

and that credulity which so often springs from weak man's almost
palpable insecurity. Faith can be fire. It can set mind and heart and
man's whole being burning. But faith can never be mere feeling.
We who live in an age of crisis need to realize that, basically, faith
has nothing to do with feeling. Faith is based on the authority of
God — His knowledge and His veracity. Could anything have firmer
foundation? Could anything be further removed from mere human
feelings, affections, emotions, sensitivity, or susceptibility? There is a
relation between faith and euphoria — that buoyancy and feeling of
well-being that brings joy and peace. But this euphoria is truly of
the soul and substance of man, not merely of his senses and bodily
organs; it is a full pole apart from the euphoria of the psychologists
and the men of medicine. Ultimately it is in and of the intellect; and
while it demands a certain simplicity, let it be stated, and even
stressed, that while the man of faith is a simple soul he need not
have the soul of a simpleton. Thomas of Aquin was a simple soul;
he was anything but a simpleton. So, too, with practically all the
other doctors of the Church, the age-old Fathers, and those early
ecclesiastical writers, from whom, in great part, we have received
what we call Tradition and upon whom, always under the direction
of the Church, of course, we base and build our Theology. Faith
gives certitude; a certitude nothing can shake. That can never be
said about feeling. The unshakableness of our certitude comes from
God, not from ourselves. We believe because *He* has said so — He
who described Himself not as Love, but as Truth: *Ego sum Veri-
tas*. . . . — "I am the Truth" (Jn. 14:6).

I wanted my brother to know a euphoria of soul that would enable
him to sustain all the agonies his body could yet give him. That is
why faith was stressed so strongly. For Paul has put it all in a
sentence: "Faith is the foundation of the blessings for which we
hope, the proof of the realities we do not see" (Hebr. 11:1). Charlie
must hope. Charlie must have proofs for the realities — those realities
we do not see — the only lasting realities. If my letters were urgent in
their appeal for belief, my prayers were more so. Hence, it was
refreshing to read replies that were redolent with faith, and reassuring
to see that it was always based on the fact that "God said so."

When my brother laughingly told how he was thinking about

putting a sign on his door up at Pocasset which would read: "New Wing — Spiritual Advisor," then described the mighty differences between the reactions of those sick people who had faith and those who were without it, I felt I could give him a story that would come in handy when he had to "advise" those whose faith was weak or try to instruct those who had no faith. It was one that he could easily tell and one that would carry force. It is based on a phrase which, in a way, is the basis of our Faith: *"sicut dixit."*

Back in the early twenties, when the Russian Communists were yet young at the task of staging public trials, a huge mass of people had been herded into the Great Square at Moscow where they found a stage already set up and upon it a goodly number of priests and religious. In no time the people learned that they were judge and jury of those upon the stage, but that the verdict had to be "guilty" and the sentence "death." Yet the farce had to be played out. So a so-called public prosecutor arose, presented charges, then delivered an harangue. The prisoners were "dupes" and Religion called "the opiate of the people." On and on he went with the catch phrases that have become so well-known. But this prosecutor made one mistake. He paused in his diatribe, turned to the stage, and cried: "Give me one proof, just one, that Christ was divine." He again paused. This time for dramatic effect. But he paused too long, For, far back on the stage, a gray head rose and an aged priest, with majestic calm and dignity, replied: *Resurrexit sicut dixit* — "He rose as He said He would." That *sicut dixit* rang out clearly above the heads of the people, but its echo had not died when those who had been herded there to be condemned filled that Square with the shout of *Alleluia! Alleluia! Alleluia!*

There can be high feeling where there is deep faith. But it was Charlie himself who told me how low human feelings can sink where there is no faith, and gave me reason to stress the relation between faith and hope.

As "Spiritual Advisor" on the new wing, Charlie had come in contact with another case of incurable cancer in a man who was very close to despair. I recalled how a study of suicide as a phenomenon in human life had shown that in the Middle Ages — a time golden with faith and hope — suicide was practically unknown. But after the

Renaissance, with its rebirth of pagan ideas and consequent loss of faith, the suicide rate rose. From the time of the Protestant Revolt, which so logically leads to Materialism, that rate climbs rapidly. Today the suicide rate is appalling. The real reason being that men have not looked at the empty tomb long enough to take in its full significance. They are without faith. Consequently, they are without hope. Hence, with the shattering of their idols, they themselves are often shattered. The healthy cannot survive a physical or psychological shock. The famous cannot survive a fall. Conquerors cannot survive a defeat. The rich cannot face life after a financial ruin.

With that in mind I told my brother that if he were to be a successful "Spiritual Advisor" he would have to tell his friends how they could be tingling with the *new* life which Christ won for them by going down into the grave, then rising therefrom. He would have to convince them (as I was now trying to persuade him) that the real mystery of life is not life itself, but death — then go on to show them how to solve that mystery by looking at Christ's Resurrection and Ascension and seeing how these two Mysteries were theirs.

He would have no difficulty with the first step in that process; for it is evident to any man who stares life full in the face that he is looking at a death mask. Man is born to die. Then, why give him birth? From Adam on, humanity has been but one long "caravan on the way to death." Since that is true, why join that caravan?

I urged my brother to make his presentation as realistic and logical as possible, to grant the opposition everything they demanded in the way of truth, then demolish their position by the real truth. As an illustration he could use the story of two Japanese youths who before World War II had won their way by scholarship to Tokyo's university. There they sat for a semester under professors who, like so many other university professors, set themselves up as the wrong kind of spiritual advisors. Those in Tokyo taught that life ends at the grave; that man is but an agglomeration of atoms destined to extinction; that earth, this burnt-out cinder which whirls around the sun, is man's only habitat. The two young students were logical enough to push such premises to their logical conclusion. At term holiday they climbed one of Fujiyama's active volcanoes and threw themselves into its boiling depths. Horrible — yet perfectly logical. If there is no afterlife, why live this one?

No one can answer that question satisfactorily unless he has heard Christ saying: "I am the resurrection and the life; he who believes in me will live even if he dies; and no one that lives and believes in me shall be dead forever" (Jn. 11:25). Charlie could make his hearers listen closely enough to realize that the Son of God is speaking those lines to them as personally as He spoke them to the sister of Lazarus. Then when they hear what she heard, namely, "Do you believe this?" they may be able to answer as Martha did: "Yes, Master, I firmly believe. . . ." (Jn. 11:27.) For such a man life holds no unsolved riddles; neither does death. For such there is only the mystery of God's love and mercy.

Hilaire Belloc pointed out that our boastful, and often noisily optimistic century has been really marked by a rising tide of despair. We of the mid-century can appreciate the wisdom of that remark; for we have seen cold fear grip the hearts and chill the lives of millions of our contemporaries; we have watched confidence in governments, trust in nations, and even faith in men die. But how many of us have realized that what is actually killing us is our lack of hope and joy; and that these can be had in abundance if we will but awake to the truth that we can live the Glorious Mysteries of the Rosary — then do so in fullest faith?

That was what I was trying to get my brother to do. I had already told him that "it is Heaven all the way to Heaven," and I meant to prove that by showing that we live the second Glorious Mystery — the Ascension. But before I could proffer proof I had to rethink that Mystery and all it involves.

At first glance one sees little more in this wondrous event than reason to rejoice that Jesus Christ, our Lord, Master, and Model, has at last attained final triumph — His glorification at the right hand of the Father. It really looks as if this Mystery belongs exclusively to Christ. But a little closer study reveals that Jesus was not alone on the Mount of Olives that Thursday noon, nor was He the only one engaged in or affected by this Mystery. One hundred and twenty others, along with Mother Mary, stood on that Mount, witnessed that

Ascension, and were so affected by it that they went back to Jerusalem "in a transport of joy" (Lk. 24:52).

Reflection on these facts throws one off balance. For it is quite
customary to isolate, as it were, this fact and feast, and view both
as personal to Christ and to Him alone. Ascension Thursday looks
like the one feast in the liturgical cycle that was happy for Jesus.
All the others are happy for us. They give us something. But they
do so only because they take something from Christ. Each appears
as but an advance in that "emptying of Himself," of which St.
Paul has made so much. If we begin at the Annunciation, go on to
the Incarnation, Nativity, Circumcision, Presentation, then on and
on, even to Calvary and the empty tomb, we will see that while they
are filled with blessings for us, they meant only humiliation, poverty,
pain, and ultimately that complete "emptying out" — death — for
Jesus. But at the Ascension there was a filling — he was filled with
glory. Up from earth where He had suffered such agonies He went;
up in that very body in which He had made such an outpouring of
Self; up past "every Principality and Power and Virtue and Domination, yes, high above every being, no matter by what title it may be
called, no matter whether it is in this world or in the world to
come" (Eph. 1:21); up He went to the very throne of God.
Justice was done Jesus by this Ascension and consequent Enthrone-
ment. In that justice we have reason to rejoice. But Charlie was to
be shown that in this mighty Mystery he triumphed as well as Christ,
and that this Ascension is a Mystery of the present time as really as
it was of twenty centuries ago. How could I prove that this was all
personal and present?

The solution to this predicament was found in the Liturgy. I
studied the Office and the Mass of the feast and learned, among other
things, how much we miss when we fail to meditate deeply upon the
contents of the feast's Office and Mass, how much treasure, how
much thrilling truth. The Invitatory, which is the beginning of the
Matin song, not only strikes the keynote for the feast, but holds the
solution for my predicament. It is the Christ who sings this Invitatory: "I tell you these things that my joy may be in you, and that
your joy may be full." Surely that says that the dominant emotion of
this feast, and the practical fruit to be garnered, is joy. Equally

obvious is the fact that the joy we are to know is a full sharing of Christ's own joy.

I counted and found that the word "joy" appears no less than eighteen times in the antiphons and hymns of this Office; and, startling as it may appear, it almost always refers not only to the joy of Christ, but to the jubilant joy that should be felt by all Christians. But these discoveries did not completely dispel all my difficulties; for I had to show how Christ's Ascension was a Mystery personal to us in the present time and consequently the joy we were to know was of the present moment. Yet, for quite some time in this prayerful study, all I could see was that the genuine joy of the feast was actually a promise, and our personal triumph lay in the future. For Christ's Ascension in our humanity looked like only a pledge that one day we, too, could ascend. Hope, which really has to do with the future, loomed as a very logical virtue for this feast, but I was out to prove that it should be joy — and joy in the present moment. That meant a restudy of the Mystery of the past to see how it could be depicted as a Mystery of the present.

In both his Acts and Gospel St. Luke tells us the story. The only other Evangelist to treat the fact is St. Mark. St. Paul, of course, makes much of it, especially in his Epistle to the Ephesians. From these three it can be gathered that the Apostles and disciples, along with Mary and the holy women, were in the Cenacle that Thursday morning. It was just forty days since the tomb was found empty — and forty had ever been a symbolic and significant number among the Jews. Suddenly Jesus appears in their midst. He had been doing this off and on ever since the Magdalen first mistook Him for the gardener and was then transformed into an Apostle who was to announce to the other Apostles that "He is risen!" At each new appearance He had told them something further about the Kingdom of God. Yet, even at this late date, there were some among them who did not fully believe! Christ upbraided them for this hardness of heart and head. From the Acts it would appear that He ate with them this fortieth day after Easter, just as He had done on Easter night itself — and for the very same reason: to convince them that it was really He; that they were seeing flesh and blood and not a ghost.

This unbelief as late as Ascension Thursday among those who

had been so favored by the prodigally generous Christ might stir one to impatience with these men unless it be recalled just what it was that they were asked to believe.

These men had seen Christ taken prisoner. They knew He had been crucified. We have no idea of what crucifixion is. The Apostles and disciples had ideas that were, if anything, too clear. They had seen men tied or nailed to trees. They had heard their cries; seen them writhe in agony; watched them as they died. Hence, they well knew what Jesus must have looked like at the ninth hour on that Friday which will ever mark the midmost moment of all time. Suddenly they see Him before them — but He is all glory! How could they trust their senses? The One who had hung, just a little while before, bloody, bedraggled, dead on a cross, now stands before them — and He is more beautiful than any human being had ever been. He speaks. He eats. He touches and is touched. They see the nail prints in the hands and the spear-dug hole in the side. They see the feet. It is He — and yet He is so changed. Then He leaves just as mysteriously as He has come. This kind of thing goes on for six full weeks. He would come and go more swiftly than any breeze, and as suddenly as a flash of light. Yet He was the same Master they had always known. Small wonder they were bewildered. Can that be the explanation of their conduct: they believed, but they were bewildered? It was all true; but it was also too good to be true. They were beside themselves with joy, yet hardly dared credit their senses.

This ambivalence, if you will call it such, in the Apostles and disciples, is not too difficult to understand. Does not the same strike us when we think profoundly enough on any Mystery of our Religion — or even on any one of the Sacraments? Think what Baptism does to man. A supernaturally stillborn person is not only brought to life but to higher than human life; he is "born of God," as St. John says. Hence the early Fathers were justified in their use of such words as "divinized" and "deified." St. Peter, under the inspiration of the Holy Ghost, wrote that we are given a "share in the divine nature." We believe all that; but isn't it bewildering?

St. Mark tells us that Jesus "reproved them for their unbelief and hardness of heart" (Mk. 16:14), but then immediately promised these men He was reproving powers that only God could grant: power to drive out demons, ability to speak new and diverse tongues, and even miraculous healing touch to their hands. But better than all that was contained in the words: "I am going to send down upon you him whom the Father has promised; but you must tarry in the city until you are invested with power from on high" (Lk. 24:29). There is a haunting echo of the words of Gabriel to Mary in that line, so haunting that one is justified in linking the Annunciation of the conception of the physical body of Christ with this "annunciation" of what was to be the "Epiphany" of the Mystical Body of Jesus; for the "Power of the Most High" who overshadowed Mary and this "Power from on High" who is to invest the Apostles is none other than the Holy Spirit, the Blessed Trinity's Third Person.

It would be easy for me now to show my brother why it was that the Apostles and Disciples "retraced their steps to Jerusalem in a *transport of joy*" (Lk. 24:52). Christ had left them, it was true; but He had filled them with powers and promises enough to set anyone staggering back to the Cenacle, drunk with joy. But that would leave me still in the past, and my problem was to prove all this joy something personal and present. I turned again to the Liturgy.

Opening the breviary to the lessons for the feast I began to read, and a line from St. Leo's first sermon on the Ascension leaped out at me: "Christ's Ascension is *our* exaltation." St. Leo uses the present tense. He speaks of our oneness with Christ in such a way that we can only conclude that we should be exulting not only because Christ has gone up to the highest heavens, but because we have ascended with Him.

No one who thinks can fail to be moved to real exultation as he pictures Christ ascending to the Father. For this is greater triumph than was the Resurrection. That was the dawn of Christ's glory, this is its high noon, as St. Augustine noted. Jesus goes to the very throne of God — the bosom of the Father — and does so in that body with which He repaired the Father's outraged glory. Now He can receive the answer to that gravest of all grave prayers — the one He offered just before He went to His Agony: "Father, the hour is come! Glorify your Son, that your Son may glorify you." Eternity sounds and resounds in those words. A moment or two later the Christ of

God repeats that request, and this time that note reminiscent of the unbeginning of endlessness is heard with even greater clarity: "And now for your part, Father, glorify me in your bosom with the glory I possessed in your bosom before the world existed" (Jn. 17:1-5). On Ascension Day Christ went back to the Father's bosom and to that glory of which we sing in every doxology — the glory He had in that beginning which was without beginning. In this return we know a tingling joy, and in some fashion share Christ's happiness; but to make this Mystery truly personal and a Mystery of the present time we have to go deeper into reality: to the truth of our oneness with Jesus Christ.

"One with Christ" — have we any real consciousness of this unity, this actual solidarity? Is there anything real enough to it, vivid and vital enough to make a man who is mortally sick, whose legs swell to elephantine size from thigh to ankle, whose feet will not sustain the slightest weight without excruciating pain, forget that which is so all-absorbing physically, and thrill to this spiritual truth? The latest letters had shown Charlie with pain the most real thing in his world. Could I offer "oneness with Christ" — the risen and ascending Christ — not only as antidote but as stimulant? Could I lift his spirit, his real self, above the pain of his body, and have it soar with the ascending Jesus to the bosom of the Father? Could I have him exult because this triumph was personal — and enable him to show his fellow sufferers that this is a Mystery of the present time? Analogies might help.

I recalled the day in 1919 when I stood on Boston Common and saw the "Yankee Division" — New England's contribution to World War I — come back from France. We did not have so much as a "second cousin twice removed" among those thousands of doughboys, yet I tingled with pride and a certain possessiveness as line after line of "tin hats" marched by. You can be sure that every man, woman, and child in Maine, New Hampshire, Vermont, Connecticut, and Rhode Island, as well as in Massachusetts knew the same pride and tingling possessiveness. These were *our own*. They had been in the San Quentin drive; had battled their way through Belleau Woods; knew Chateau Thierry and all it had cost. They had formed part of that spearhead which had pierced the Hindenburg Line and brought about that sudden silence which marked the eleventh hour of the eleventh day in the eleventh month of the year 1918. And they were *our own*.

That Charlie had experienced the very same thrill many a time during World War II — and for the very same reason, I was sure. All I had to do was recall the day news came that the Marines had landed on Guadalcanal. I stood straighter that day, felt taller, simply because there was a cousin of ours out there with those Marines. I felt I had special share in that victory just because of my "oneness" with him. Would Charlie feel any different?

Then about D-Day. . . . Who in America did not swell with pride when we learned that what had finally stopped Napoleon — one of the greatest military geniuses of all time; what had but recently stopped Germany's war machine — one of the mightiest of any time; namely, the English Channel — had but served as means of passage for our G.I.'s?

The psychology of it all is simple. We look upon these as *our own*. We are "one with them."

When we grasp the reality of it all we see that our "oneness with Christ" is infinitely more intimate. He is the Vine, we the branches. He is the Head, we the members. He is the Word, we the syllables. He is the Breath of Life, and He is still breathing us! The Pauline phrase "in Christ Jesus" is the most comprehensive as well as the most compressed that man can excogitate. It is an atom holding all the energy of time and eternity. Faith plus prayerful thinking will "smash" it for us, and so release its energy that we may well be lifted into ecstasy. We are *one* with Christ Jesus — and Christ Jesus is *God!*

That truth was enough to set anyone tingling. Yet I was still without that satisfaction and rest that comes from a job thoroughly done. I cited the prayer of the Mass for Ascension Day: "Grant, we beseech Thee, Almighty God, that we who believe that Thy Only-Begotten Son, our Redeemer, this day ascended into heaven, may ourselves also dwell there in spirit." That helped show how "it is Heaven all the way to Heaven." But still I was not satisfied.

Finally St Paul was called in to help. His Epistle to the Ephesians tells that "Together with Christ Jesus and in him, he raised us up and enthroned us in the heavenly realm, that in Christ Jesus he might show throughout the ages to come the overflowing riches of his grace springing from his goodness to us" (Eph. 2:6, 7).

That is enough to set one dreaming bright dreams — and dreams that have substance to them; for they are founded on fact. Yet I wanted something more tangible for Charlie. All I could do at this juncture was promise more later — then turn to Mary Immaculate and ask for light.

"Let me show him that 'Christ's Ascension is our exaltation' — *now*," was my prayer.

CHAPTER EIGHT

A Glimpse at God's Throne

IT WAS Father Walter Farrell, O.P., who once wrote that prayer can sometimes be "like talking into a telephone whose wires are cut." As May flowered into June, I felt as if what should be a conversation had become a monologue. The light I desired was denied me for weeks. The proposition that the Glorious Mysteries of the Rosary are mysteries of the present time, for we share in them and are to live them, I knew to be certain. But the proofs for that proposition as applied to the second Mystery eluded me.

The plea of blind Bartimaeus the beggar became my prayer: *Domine, ut videam* — "Lord that I may see." But I did not hear Jesus say: "Go thy way, thy faith hath saved thee" (Mk. 10:51, Confr.). A beggar I remained — but still in blindness. I turned to the Mother of God. I knew the care she was taking of Charlie and his family. I presented my predicament, reminded her of her power, asserted that there must be some palpable proof, then pleaded with her maternal heart, insisting that I needed the help as much as Charlie.

Summer was bringing visitors to the sufferer on the Cape and they so distracted my brother for a time that he did not press me for the fulfillment of my promise about the Ascension. Thus one week after the feast he was writing:

> It has been such an eventful two days that I just cannot go to sleep before telling you about them. First, I have been so elated about the swelling in my legs subsiding that I have been walking on air. I was even able to drive Charlie over to Hyannis for one of his ball games. He played well . . . his team won seven to five. When I got home I learned that Sister Mary Clare had called but did not speak with any-

one since I was not at home. Then Father Joe Doc called to say he would come up from Phillie within the next two weeks. We are all looking forward to his coming.

This morning Kay and I went shopping. When we got back home my heart sank; for I looked down and found that my legs were up like balloons again. They have been most painful all day. I offered that pain up for that man and woman you wrote about who were wavering in their vocations. I asked God to give them the grace of perseverance.

After we put the groceries away I went to bed and was having a grand sleep when Kay woke me to announce none other than Father Tommie Dunn. He has changed over the past twenty-seven years, but I could recognize so many of his mannerisms. As you will recall, Tommie and I were very friendly at Holy Cross. He stayed a couple of hours, meeting all the family except Kathy, who was working. He wants me to call him when Father Joe Doc arrives. It would be fun to get him and Joe together. We'd have many a good laugh over the things we did at the Cross.

After Tommie left I got a call from Sister Mary Clare. She expects to be in Osterville some time next September. She will fly direct from Montreal to Hyannis. We have a large airport there. What a day that will be! . . .

. . . .

I lose patience with myself when I cannot do the things I want to do. But that helplessness has given me a true understanding of my dependence on my Heavenly Father. I do so want to make up what is wanting to the Passion. So many are trying to make it all so easy for me — I know I deserve none of it, but oh! how grateful I am to all who are helping me with prayers and Masses, etc. I could not carry on without their help.

Jack and I had quite a lot of time together during his last visit. He is such a wonderful guy. He suggested that I remember the souls who are away from God but need just a little more grace for salvation. When my pain is at its peak — usually about three in the morning — I make up my list of those I would like helped by my suffering. Then quickly my pain becomes less — or seems so. Sometimes I think I'm cheating by getting such relief, but I guess that's how God wants it.

I continued to plead even more earnestly with Mary for light on the second Mystery of her Glorious Rosary. I was still busy with St. Leo's sermon and his phrase about Christ's Ascension being our exaltation. His sentence saying "on this holy day we have received not only the assurance of entering into possession of eternal glory, but we have already entered the heights of Heaven with Christ Jesus," had me lamenting my lack of consciousness of that wondrous oneness with Christ which would put me in Heaven. How could I make it tangible to my brother when it was so intangible to myself?

At this juncture my prayer was: "Immaculate Mother, it is easy to show Charlie that this second Glorious Mystery is brilliant with promise for the future — and I will do that from time to time; but right now I want to show him how it blazes with spirit-lifting wonder at the present moment. Charlie knows we have been made 'joint heirs with Christ.' He even knows the terms of that inheritance: 'provided we suffer with him that we may also be glorified with him' (Rom. 8:17). But what he may not know is just how we are to live this Mystery of the Ascension while we linger here on earth. Won't you give me some illustration, some proof, some demonstration? I'm sure there must be such, but at the moment I am at a loss. Help this child of yours that I may help others."

Before any answer came I was reading another letter from Cape Cod. As paragraph followed paragraph the wave motion became more intense, for each crest seemed higher and each trough deeper.

> . . . I was on the front lawn today and fell out of my chair. The pains in my legs drive me berserk at times. I'm really sick and tired of being so sick and tired. I know it is all in God's plan, but I must confess there are times when I get tired of it all.
>
> Judge McCarthy sent us a big grocery order last week. It was such a charitable thing for him to do. He is a Cross grad — about the class of '05.
>
> Mrs. Driscoll brought me a beautiful bouquet of gladioli. . . . I have them on the T.V. set in front of the picture of the Christ Child and near the picture of "The Loving Heart of Mary" — my two favorites. Our Crucifix is beneath the picture of the Christ Child telling me: "I suffered for you, won't you suffer a little for me?" That bolsters my determination not to be a crybaby. It sets me whispering: "All for Thee, my Father, in union with the Passion of Thy Son, for the good of my soul."
>
> I go to see Dr. Niles this afternoon. My legs have lost a lot of their swelling. The pain gets worse when the swelling reduces, but the doctor says it is important to get rid of the fluid in them. I walk like "Old Man Mose." . . .

Would anyone in such condition be susceptible to argument about our part in the Ascension? My brother seemed more taken up with the Passion. Yet it was that concept of his oneness with the suffering Christ that spurred me on to find clàrification for his oneness with the ascended and enthroned Christ.

I could truthfully tell him that he was in Heaven *mystically* inasmuch as the Head of the Mystical Body, to whom we are all joined, is enthroned there. But what would such a truth tell a man who was suffering physically the way Charlie was? Yet for a long, long time that is about all I could gather from St. Leo's sermon and reflection on Christ's Ascension.

The temptation to stress the fact that so many confuse the meaning of mystical, and consider it a synonym for unreal, was strong. For I saw that Charlie himself might be led to think along those lines at least subconsciously. For when physical pain grips, any man is liable to think of it as the only reality and to accept all other talk about mystical union as something quite unreal. That must never happen to my brother. Examples to illustrate the truth that mysteriousness in no way negates the reality of the mysterious thing seemed to multiply before me as I thought. Electricity is real; but who can tell just what it is? Gravity is very real; no man understands its essence. The world in which we live and move is filled to the brim with mystery, yet no one questions its reality. I could tell my brother something he very well knew; namely, that pain is real. But who has ever touched it, weighed it, seen its color, shape, or size?

How easy it is to prove the wise old observation of Socrates: "all things end in mystery." But how would that help any sufferer? I could point out that physical reality is the lowest form of reality, then ascend on the scale. I could have my brother reflect on the fact that he and Kay loved one another, but what a gulf lay between the profound spiritual reality of that love and any physical manifestation of it such as a word, a look, an embrace! There is a much deeper consciousness and conviction than that which comes from the physical. Charlie did not have to feel his wife's love or the warm affection of his children. Down deep in his soul he knew he had both. Spiritual consciousness. . . .

The term appealed to me. I could ask Charlie how he knew he was my brother. Surely he needed no birth certificates or other legal testaments. How did he know he was an American? How did he know he was a Catholic? — What a lively letter could be composed along those lines; and all leading to the conclusion: something deep inside us, some "spiritual consciousness," some profound conviction tells us. Then the analogy of our "spiritual consciousness" of being "one with Christ!" Yes, it was appealing; for it would prove that we are *really* in Heaven with Him — that His Ascension is ours.

The appeal intensified when it became clear that the themes that were used in the letters about the Resurrection: "new man," "new life," "new creature" — and all "in Christ Jesus" could be recalled and the constant plea *vivere in Verbo* — "to live in Christ Jesus" — could be given greater force. The reality of that life could be all but felt as he held his beads, recalled the Mysteries, and felt his pain as part of Christ's Passion. Reflection on who he actually was, thanks to the life-giving, transforming power of Baptism, coupled with reflection on what he was actually doing when he offered his every breath to God "in Christ Jesus," would quickly develop and sharpen this "spiritual consciousness" of his oneness with the Man-God who had ascended into Heaven.

That, more than likely, would have been the trend of thought I would have followed had I not one day awakened — or should I say, been illumined? I was pondering the reality, the wonder, the mystery of the Mass and saying to myself, "It is a living memorial of His Passion, Death, Resurrection, and Ascension," when the word "living" suddenly stood out before me. . . . I now had what I wanted!

What are called "lights" in prayer differ in intensity and often appear colored. The "light" contained in this word "living" was very bright, and its color was that of golden flame shot through with quivering red. Indeed I had what I wanted. I wondered now if this was the reason God had kept me from telling Charlie all about prayer when he visited Gethsemani. If François Mauriac is right in saying that "prayer is taking a direction" (and who can question it?) Charlie could be turned full face to the Mass and kept that way until, in all truth, he became a prayer. I believed this could be accomplished by simply pointing him to the Mass and having him see it as a *living* memorial.

That "it is Heaven all the way to Heaven" now appeared as obvious as any of the answers on the first page of the catechism. If

Heaven is knowledge and love of God; if Heaven is that possession of God and possession by God which spells bliss; if Heaven is life with love and a love that is life; what is to prevent anyone from being in Heaven all the days of his earthly exile? The light of faith is not as luminous as the light of glory, but it is strong enough to enable us to see God in everyone and everything; strong enough to give us a knowledge of Him as Father, Son, and Holy Spirit; strong enough to set our hearts pounding with love for Him who loves us with an everlasting love. The vigorous virtue of faith gives us a possession of God that is as actual in time as will be our possession of Him in eternity; and that possession, to a recollected and reflective soul, spells bliss. If we live "in Christ Jesus" and have Him, by grace, living in us, then, assuredly, we live with and in Love — for that is Christ's essence, as the Beloved Disciple once told us. Indeed "it is Heaven all the way to Heaven"; and never is that wonder realized more fully than by those who make the Mass their life, and their lives a Mass. Truly the Mass is a *living* thing!

What slaves we are to formulas! How we allow words and phrases that were meant to reveal reality obscure it for us. How thoughtlessly we subscribe to the formula which says, "The Mass is Calvary, and Calvary is the Mass." After meditating the first Glorious Mystery aright, we should never again remain satisfied with that formula as complete expression of truth. For we know that sacrifice is more than "oblation" and "mactation"; we know that redemption called for more than the death of the God-Man — the dead God-Man had to rise! The Mass is the memorial of the whole Sacrifice of Christ. Hence, it has to be a *living* memorial in which we have the living God-Man, the Jesus Christ who died, rose, and ascended. That is why we can safely say that the Mass is a re-presentation of that Act of Jesus which ended not at three o'clock Good Friday afternoon, nor at dawn Easter Sunday morning, but at noon on Ascension Thursday when He was enthroned on high. That throning is, in all truth, the final sanction of all that He had done on earth. It is the complete, official "accepta-tion" by God the Father of that "oblation" made by God the Son, and that "mactation" He underwent by inspiration, as St. Paul tells us, of God the Holy Ghost.

Thanks to this "light" contained in the word "living" I could take my brother back now to that familiar theme on the Mass being life and life being a Mass. And there was reason to hope that such an exposition of truth might open his eyes to the reality of the Holy Sacrifice as they, perhaps, had never been opened before. For it would show that while the Priest and Victim are the same as they were on Calvary, yet, as Trent teaches, "the manner of offering is different." Very different! In the Mass Jesus Christ, as Priest and Victim, is in a far different state than He was on Calvary. There He was bloodied, bruised, and finally killed. Here He is living! And living in a body that is glorified and ablaze with beauty! Indeed the Mass is a *living* memorial — He who ascended is there in what we see as host and wine.

This second Glorious Mystery would live for Charlie as he learned that vital truth contained in two prayers of the Mass which tell very explicitly just what is going on when Mass is being offered. After the *Lavabo* each celebrating priest must bend over and make offering to the Trinity in "memory of the Passion, Resurrection, and *Ascension* of our Lord, Jesus Christ. . . ." Then immediately after consecrating the bread and wine and elevating the Host and Chalice he must say: "Mindful, therefore, O Lord, not only of the blessed Passion of the same Christ, Thy Son, our Lord, but also of His Resurrection from the dead, and finally of His glorious *Ascension* into Heaven, we, Thy ministers, as also Thy holy people, offer unto Thy supreme Majesty . . . this pure Victim, this holy Victim, this all-perfect Victim . . ." who is, of course, none other than the *living ascended* Christ! Commenting on this prayer a theologian of the Middle Ages, Richard Weddinghusanus, said we have "a *Pure* Victim by the Passion; a *Holy* Victim by the Resurrection; an *Immaculate* Victim by the Ascension."

The Mass, then, is not only a present reality; it is an eternal one; for it catches up the past, present, and future in the here and now. That is so because Jesus Christ did not ascend simply to sit at the right hand of the Father and there reign as King. No! He ascended to *stand* before the throne — to stand there as Priest and Victim; to be a Mass that never ends!

It is the Apocalypse which gives us this truth when it shows us "in front of the throne and in the midst of the four living beings and of the elders, a Lamb as if slain. . . ." The same Apocalypse allows us to hear the song those living beings and those elders are singing about this Lamb: "You are worthy to take the scroll and to open its seals, because you were slain, and with your blood you redeemed for God men of every tribe and tongue and people and nation, and you made them a kingdom and priests for our God" (Apoc. 5:6–10).

"Those ancients are singing about you, Chic," I wrote my brother, "for you were made a priest at Baptism. Not with the same fullness of priesthood that I received at Ordination, it is true; but with a real share in Christ's priesthood nevertheless. You are a priest 'in Christ Jesus.' By your Baptismal character you have been commissioned to *offer* Mass. So let the color and song of the Apocalypse tell you how truly this second Glorious Mystery is yours. It is the ascended Christ you offer in your Mass, and in the ascended Christ you are offered in every Mass.

"St. Paul puts this more soberly: 'We have a great high priest,' he writes, 'who has penetrated the heavens, Jesus, the Son of God' (Hebr. 4:14). Later on in that same Epistle he tells you just why Jesus penetrated those heavens and what He is doing there now: 'Because he continues forever, he has an imperishable priesthood. Consequently he is able at all times to save those that come to God through him, *living* always, as he does, to make intercession on their behalf' (Hebr. 7:26).

"Read that Epistle carefully, Chic, and note how often Paul says 'on our behalf.' The fact that He who ascended is not only our High Priest, but that 'it is not into a holy place made by human hands, a mere type of the genuine, that Christ has entered, but into Heaven itself, where he *now* presents himself in the presence of God *on our behalf,*' proves beyond doubt that the Glorious Mysteries not only celebrate a past event but alert us to a present reality. At this very moment the Christ who ascended is functioning as our High Priest in Heaven. That means He is offering Mass! He is showing the Father the five wounds of His Passion and having them plead with an eloquence that cannot be refused. No wonder Paul says we can 'confidently draw near to God's throne, the source of grace, that we may obtain mercy and find grace when we need it' (Hebr. 4:16). St. John Chrysostom, commenting on this quote, summed it up beautifully by saying: 'Behold in heaven we have a *Priest*. Behold in heaven we have a *Victim!* Behold in heaven we have a *Sacrifice!*'*

"With those truths before us; with that glimpse into Heaven and vision of God's throne; with that realization that the ascended Christ is forever celebrating Mass, and that we, His members, are in His every Mass, who will ever think of the second Glorious Mystery as personal only inasmuch as it gives us promise of the future?"

Through Paul's masterly Epistle to the Hebrews, I was enabled to show my brother that he had part in Christ's Eternal Mass. He needed some such reassurance, for with his swollen legs, daily Mass was out of the question. But with Paul drawing that dramatic picture of the Old Law Ritual for him as he told how in those days the high priest was allowed to enter the Holy of Holies only once a year, and then only on the condition that he observed a fear-filling ritual to the very letter, Charlie's appreciation of our High Priest and His continual offering was heightened. The Old Law Ritual demanded that the high priest enter the Holy of Holies carrying a vessel containing the blood of two victims which he himself had slain, one for his own sins, the other for the sins of the people. If he failed to do this, he was to be put to death. But if he bore that blood before him, he might make intercession for himself and all Israel. Impressive, indeed, was such a ceremony. But what was it compared to the Ascension of Christ when He, our Eternal High Priest, "entered once for all through the greater and more perfect tabernacle . . ." not with "the blood of goats and calves. . . ." It was "his own blood that was the means of his entering the Holy Place and securing eternal salvation" (Hebr. 9:12). That is why Paul could tell us that "we have confident access to the Holy Place, thanks to the blood of Jesus . . ." that we are to "draw near with a sincere heart, in full assurance of faith. . . ." (Hebr. 10:22.) Charlie, Kay, and all their youngsters could assist at Mass every moment of the day — and night — simply by living consciously "in Christ Jesus" who ascended.

To impress both my brother and his wife with the truth about our part in this Mystery of the Ascension, and to show them how easy it is to work for God no matter what our condition, I used a symbol and ceremony familiar to all who have assisted at the Paschal vigils.

* *Hom. 13 on Hebrews.*

Charlie and Kay were told to think of the Paschal candle as it stands in the dimness of the sanctuary just before the long ceremony begins. It is a virginal column of wax standing there unlit — a symbol of the lifeless Christ in the tomb. Soon the celebrant blesses five red grains and inserts them into that candle. No one can fail to see those grains as symbols of the glowing stigmata on the body of Christ. Then the deacon lifts his voice in that joy-filled *Exultet* telling that "this was the night on which Christ snapped the chains of death and rose conqueror from hell." To that swelling eloquence of song, the Liturgy adds the surer eloquence of symbol and sign as she has flame kindled at that candle's tip. Who can fail to see this flame as signifying the soul of Christ returning to the body of Christ not only to revivify it, but to set it ablaze with glory? From that Light — which is Christ — all the other lights in the church are kindled, and each of the faithful should have a smaller Paschal candle which would be quickened from the same flame, signifying that we are alive with, and are to live by, the glorified life of Christ, our one and only Vivifier!

That inspiring lesson is only the beginning of all we are to learn from the Paschal candle. For it will stand in our midst for forty days. In the Roman Rite is will be kindled often to remind the faithful of the many apparitions of the glorified Christ. In our Cistercian Rite, however, it is lit only on the eve of the Ascension, and burns not only all through the night, but all through the feast day itself. Then after Compline on Ascension Thursday the golden flame at that candle's tip is quenched, a tiny spiral of smoke rises up, and the candle itself is taken away. Those who watch that thin spiral of smoke will see that it finally vanishes in the upper air — so very reminiscent of that line in the Acts: "While they looked on he was raised up and a cloud received him out of their sight" (1:10). As the feast ends in this telling ceremony, the real message of the Ascension comes home: Christ, the Light of the World, has gone up to become the Lamp of Heaven. But once He has become the Lamp of Heaven, we Christians *must* become the Light of the World!

Charlie was ever clamoring for reality. This second Glorious Mystery would now give him all he wanted — and perhaps a bit more! For in the very first sermon of His public career, Jesus Christ had looked into the eyes of His disciples and said: "You are the light of the world" (Mt. 5:14). Then, in what was practically his last oral sermon to the world, this same Jesus Christ had looked into the eyes of His enemies and said: "I am the Light of the World" (Jn. 8:12). Those two statements are complementary, for Christ and Christians are one. Hence, what Paul said to his Philippians twenty centuries ago the Paschal candle says to all Christians of this century: "Show yourselves single-minded. . . . You live in an age that is twisted out of its true pattern (in the midst of a crooked and perverse generation); among such people you shine out, *beacons to the world,* upholding the message of life" (Phil. 2:15).*

Obviously, He who ascended, He who went to prepare a place for us in Heaven, left us a work to do for Him on earth. We are to shine out for Him in a darkness that seems to grow denser. That we can do only by being *single-minded,* which means continually and completely Christ-conscious. I confessed to Charlie that the assignment given us on Ascension Day was not easy; but asked: "Could anything be more glorious? The single-mindedness we are to achieve challenges all that is best in us; for, though 'citizens of Heaven,' we live in a complex and an ever increasingly more complex world. But it can be done; because it has been done. Paul did it. In fourteen short Epistles he speaks of being 'in Christ Jesus' one hundred and sixty-four times. That is single-mindedness. That is Christ-consciousness. What is to stop us from a like achievement save inattention and spiritual laziness?"

My brother's sickness was driving me ever deeper and deeper into St. Paul and his Epistles. As I penetrated into the doctrine this Firebrand of God has written I wondered how many human souls — my own among them — are like the Dead Sea. That body of water, often called "The Tomb of the Jordan," has no visible outlet. Yet there are times when the snows of Mt. Hermon melt at such a rate as to swell the Jordan to a flood which daily spills as much as three million gallons of water into the Dead Sea — yet the high water mark of that Sea never rises! Experts think the three million gallons are lost either in the fissures of old craters or are evaporated by the intense heat.

From the Liturgy, through the Sacraments, in the Sacrifice, floods of grace are poured into our souls every day of our earthly lives. In

* Knox translation. Emphasis added.

point of fact, there is not a split second in any day or any night in which there are not waters of grace pouring down from Him who was seen shining as snow on Mt. Thabor, and whom John describes in the Apocalypse as standing with a head of hair "as white as snow-white wool" (1:14). The flood rolls down from that Mass He continually offers in Heaven and from every Mass offered on earth — but in our souls does the high-water mark of grace ever rise?

But that somewhat depressing thought, though faced fully by myself, would not be passed on to the sufferer on Cape Cod. Instead I would have him realize that the second Glorious Mystery does for us what the vision St. John the Beloved had on Patmos did for him: it opens Heaven's door and gives us a glimpse of God and His throne. It allows us to look in and witness the Liturgy of the Lamb. Hence, St. Paul, in speaking of himself and his Ephesians, was really speaking also of us. "God who is rich in mercy, was moved by the intense love with which he has loved us, and when we were dead by reason of our transgressions, he made us live with the life of Christ. . . . Together with Christ Jesus and in him, he has raised us up and enthroned us in the heavenly realm" (Eph. 2:4–6).

While we work our way through this world we live with the life of Christ; for we have been raised from the dead while still on earth. That is actual. It is also actual that we have been enthroned in Heaven — but that enthronment is mystical. To make it physical we must live as Christ would have us live; that is, make our lives *ascensional.* That is what Paul told his Colossians. That is what the Holy Spirit tells us. "Since, then, you have risen with Christ, seek the things that are above, where Christ is seated at the right hand of God. Set your mind on the things that are above, not on the things that are on the earth. For you have died and your life is hidden with Christ in God. When Christ, *your life,* appears, then you shall appear with him in glory" (Col. 3:1–3).

How that passage integrated the truths I was trying to teach my brother and his wife! I had them back now to the original theme: that we are made for glory. I had them seeing that that glory is for tomorrow, but not only for tomorrow; it is for today as well. Paul was pounding on the truth that Christ is our life, and I was just as insistent that it is the Mass that matters. But both Charlie and Kay had a new word now in their religious vocabulary. It was *ascensional*. They were told that if they live "in Christ Jesus," they will rise from grace to grace: more today than yesterday, but not as much as tomorrow. They would ascend from virtue to virtue: more pronounced today than yesterday, but not as pronounced as they would be tomorrow. They would actually mount from glory to glory: more evident today than yesterday, but not as evident as it would be tomorrow.

To make that all practical they were directed to awake each morning with a fresher determination to "put on Christ" that day more firmly and thoroughly than they did yesterday. When they assisted at Mass they were to be so Christ-conscious that the *Agnus Dei* of the priest would throw open the door of Heaven and set them peering at the Lamb of God standing before the throne of God pleading on their behalf. The *Angelus*, toned three times a day, was to tell them that He who became Man ascended with that humanity He had assumed that they might become partakers of His Divinity. That bell would also tell them that they were to pray at least thrice a day, asking God to deepen their souls and into the newer depths pour ever greater Christ-life in such a way that the high-water mark of their Christness would ever be rising and they be ever more completely transformed into Him. They were assured that if they did that not only would their lives be *ascensional* but there was every probability that they would finally *become what they are*.

That Pindaric phrase "become what you are" should never be heard by any Christian without its summoning up remembrances of what he was made by Baptism, what he is made more by every worthy Communion, what his every breath and heartbeat should be helping him become. Baptism makes one Christ. Life on earth is given that we may become what we are! That is why "it is Heaven all the way to Heaven" for those who live conscious of the transformation God worked in them through "water and the Holy Spirit," and conscious of the transformation they are now helping to complete "in Christ Jesus."

The second Glorious Mystery would have been dropped at this point had not Kay written a long letter that was love-filled, but lonely. Charlie was becoming more and more incapacitated. He was still at home and seemed to loathe going back to the hospital — even for a checkup. She said that they had got a hospital bed for Charlie. "He is in it most of the time," she wrote, "but once in a while he sits in a chair that is four feet from the bed. It takes him all of five minutes to get from the bed to the chair. The pain is all in his legs with some ache in his arms. His chest gives him very little bother. His spirits are fair, but not as good as when he could get around and out of doors. Wish I could say the same for my spirits."

I told Kay that the Christ who ascended is King of the universe and Ruler, sole Ruler, of this world of ours which often seems so chaotic. Now that her own little world seemed out of joint, owing to the progress the cancer was making, I urged her to hear Christ saying to her exactly what he Had said so often to His other and earlier followers: "Peace! Have confidence, I have overcome the world" (Jn. 16:33).

"Look through appearances and view reality," I pleaded and then quoted the Council of Trent to the effect that "Our Lord Jesus Christ, when about to ascend to heaven from this earth, commissioned His priests to stay behind as His vicars." "Kay, you are carrying out that commission; for by Baptism you, even though a woman, were given a share in Christ's priesthood. You are 'to stay behind as Christ's vicar.' Hence, no matter how black your horizons seem, look through them and view reality — our world is golden with the glorious light of God; for Mass is ever going on. Therefore, all you need do is remember who you are and what you are doing. What is our world but God's great wine press and mighty flour mill where an ever richer wine must be pressed out and an ever whiter wheat ground so that a more acceptable Chalice can be lifted and a purer Host placed on every paten? You share in that wondrous process as you tend Charlie and do your best to transform the seven youngsters into Christ Jesus."

That bit of encouragement did not satisfy me, so I addressed the next letter to both Kay and Charlie and began with Paul's line to the Colossians: "I rejoice now in the sufferings I bear . . ." (Col. 1:24). Then the almost measureless difference between pleasure and joy was stressed. God made us for happiness, and no human being breathes who does not follow that God-given drive. But the trouble lies in the fact that millions of human beings confuse happiness with pleasure, and while stopping at pleasure are puzzled by the emptiness of their hearts and the vacuity of their lives. Happiness will give pleasure, but pleasure alone will never give lasting happiness. Joy will! Neither Jesus nor His Mother had much pleasure while on earth. Yet the two of them were always filled with joy because they knew they were doing the work God commissioned them to do. Every human being who lives "in Christ Jesus" will know the same joy and for the same reason. But none will know it with greater certainty nor experience it in greater fullness than those who suffer in and for Jesus Christ.

"It calls for high courage and demands special graces," I confessed; "yet both will be given to those who ask for them. Always be mindful of Christ's words at the Last Supper: '. . . should you ask for anything in my name, I will do it' (Jn. 14:14). I sincerely believe that once we become completely Christ-conscious we have both the grace and the courage to do what Paul did: rejoice in our sufferings; and can be as happy as Peter and John were who 'departed from the presence of the Sanhedrin, rejoicing that they had been counted worthy to suffer. . . .' (Acts 5:42.) And if you want me to quote my favorite St. Paul, I'll use his second letter to Timothy where he says: 'Trustworthy is the saying: If we have died with him, we shall also live with him. If we endure, we shall also reign' (2 Tim. 2:12). When the nights seem endless and the pain will not cease tell yourselves the wondrous truth that now you are on the way that leads to glory and thus make 'it Heaven all the way to Heaven!' "

Before that letter reached the Cape I had one from Charlie, written with a very weak and wavery hand, but still showing marvelous spirit. One paragraph ran: "When the going gets real rough I hear the lashes at the pillar, feel the sharp prick of the thorns, and think of the spittle on His face. Then I try to pray with all sincerity: 'Take my body, Jesus, eyes, and ears, and tongue. Never let them, Jesus, help to do Thee wrong. Take my heart and fill it full of love for Thee. All I have I give Thee. . . . Give Thyself to me.' "

I realized that I could make that paragraph apply to the second Glorious Mystery by showing Charlie that Christ's triumph ended where His agony began; for it was from the summit of the mountain at whose base He had sweat blood that Jesus ascended into Heaven. That proves the base of Mt. Olivet — or suffering — is starting point for Heaven. I reminded my brother that between the sufferings of this time and the reward they will win for us "in and through Christ Jesus" there is no proportion. "Since life is a wind, Chic, and eternity is tomorrow — how joyously we should face the wind!"

To close the case for the second Glorious Mystery I claimed that "it is Heaven all the way to Heaven" if we think of ourselves as painting a picture. . . . One day when the Emperor of Japan was still looked upon by Japanese as divine, a little Japanese arrived at the Imperial Palace carrying a huge package. When the guards halted him he said: "I must see the Emperor and show him this." He uncovered the corner of a life-sized painting he was carrying and allowed the guards a glimpse of the face. They gasped and waved him on. The same thing happened when the inner guards halted him. They, too, gasped and waved him on. Through portal after portal and hall after hall the little Japanese went until finally he stood before the Mikado. Then without a word he ripped the wrapping from about the full-length portrait and stepped back. His Imperial Highness gasped; for he was looking at a life-sized portrait of himself. The workmanship was ordinary; but what was far from ordinary was the medium that had been used. The entire picture had been painted in blood.

"Your Worship," the little Japanese said, "I knew no better way of showing my admiration for you than by painting your picture. I knew no better way of expressing my love for you than by painting that picture with my own blood. For twelve years I have been working at it, drawing from my own veins enough blood each day to allow me a few more strokes on the canvas. I finished the portrait yesterday. Will you take it today and know that it is I since it is my blood; but that it is you, since it is your likeness?"

"When we ascend to the truly Imperial realms of Heaven," I wrote Kay, Charlie, and their youngsters, "we will be stopped at the portals. To gain entrance we will have to have on what we may call the canvas of our souls, the life-sized portrait of Him whose Ascension we celebrate every time we say the Glorious Mysteries or assist at Mass. That may mean that, day after day, we will have to give some of our very blood. But be brave — and above all be patient; for it is a life's work; and a life's work can be done only in a life's time!

CHAPTER NINE

The Flame Still Falls

JULY had just burned its way into August of the summer of 1957, when a proposal was made to me which set me searching my soul. A movement was under way to see if John Green Hanning, the Trappist lay-brother who became known to so many as Brother Joachim, "the man who got even with God," should not be beatified. Countless had been the answers received from prayers offered to God through him. Now what was wanted was a real miracle. The monks behind the movement approached me and, with permission of the Abbot, asked if Charlie's case would not be a *bona fide* first-class miracle providing that he was completely cured after prayers offered to God through Brother Joachim. About that, of course, there could be no question. But, to date, no cure had ever been asked for any member of the Cancer Club. It was not that any of us doubted the power of God or the efficacy of prayer; it was only that we all preferred to abandon ourselves completely into His hands. But this proposal, while personal in at least two ways, since it was I who had "christened" Joachim "the man who got even with God," and Charlie was my brother, had other facets to it that were not so personal. America needs an American saint. Gethsemani could do with a *beatus*. Finally it was agreed that a novena of Masses should be offered, asking God for a cure as a manifestation of His will regarding John Green Hanning.

A letter was sent to the Cape informing Kay and Charlie that the Golden Jubilee of Brother Joachim's death was less than a half a year away, and that some monks wanted to celebrate it differently. Hence, they were asking Charlie to apply the "relic" that was enclosed (some

113

grass and soil from Brother Joachim's grave) to his chest, join, by intention, in the novena of Masses, then let us know the results.

That was a difficult letter to write, for it contained a decision that had been almost torn from me. The ordinary in the providence of God is so saturated with His goodness, mercy, and love that an appeal for the extraordinary goes against my grain. To go along with God, trusting Him implicitly, asking for little more than an increase of love, has become so much my life that prayer is almost always adoration, gratitude, and reparation. About the only personal petition, outside of that for more love, is the plea for the grace of final perseverance. Charlie and Kay had been receiving directives along those same lines. This intrusion of a novena of Masses asking a miraculous cure could disturb them to the depths of their souls. That is why the letter informing them of the fact was so carefully worded. They were not told the ultimate aim. They were merely asked to report on any dramatic changes that occurred.

As St. Paul once wrote to the Romans: "How incomprehensible are his judgments and how unsearchable his ways!" (Rom. 11:33.) How often in life I had had to echo the same exclamation. "Who has known the mind of the Lord . . . ?" was Paul's next remark in that same passage. As I looked at what is called the "Cancer Club" that same question framed itself in my mind. For it appeared that if God's ways in general are unsearchable, they are still more unsearchable when it comes to cancer, and when it is a case of cancer of the lung they are most unsearchable of all.

At this late date, summer of 1957, I should not have been shaking my head over the matter. For, from the very beginning, God had shown me that not even the shrewdest of medical experts could discern His ways and His mind with regard to carcinoma. I had flown home from the Pacific Slope in mid-February, 1935, for my father's case of cancer. But the doctors assured me that I could go back, complete my Lenten work in Oregon, do all that was scheduled to be done in the state of Washington that spring, and return east in early summer before my father would be at what is called the "terminal" stage. I went back. But I had just closed a Mission in Corvallis, Oregon, and was packing to go to the next assignment in Bellingham, Washington, when a telegram arrived announcing his death. It was Tuesday in Holy Week — just two months from the day the doctors had assured me he was good until mid-June. With Mother things were different. Her doctors gave her from six to nine months to live. That was January of 1949, just a day or two after my own operation for the same disease. June ninth she was with God. Yet here I am nine years later.

It was the same with the other members of the "Club" — all of whom were either members of my own family, members of Gethsemani's community, or members of the hospital staff where I had to go so often for checkups. One of the earliest members of the "Club" lasted three years; one of the latest members, only three months. Father Richard was given from three months to a year and a half. That was six years ago! He is still alive and very actively working for God. Yet there was Father Rudy who was given the green light by his medical men to go home for Christmas in 1956. His bags were packed, his plane reservations made, and on the morning of Christmas Eve he was ready to take off when he suddenly felt a strange chill, then a burning fever. He was anointed that night. He was dead by the feast of Our Lady of Lourdes.

I should not have been shaking my head this August of 1957, puzzled by God's unpredictable ways with cancer. But I was; for I was thinking very specially of His ways with lung cancers. One of the most promising candidates ever to come to Gethsemani was found with cancer of the lung in June — and buried in September. He had been twenty years younger than my brother and had the build of a champion athlete. Across from me during one of my checkups in the hospital was a powerfully built man of forty-six, who had come in complaining of chest pains. He was found to have cancer of the lung. That was late February. The following November he was dead. One thoracic surgeon, who had all but specialized in cases of cancer of the lung, had stated that it was actually uncanny the way the disease seemed to await the ninth or the eleventh month after the operation before carrying off its victims. We were just nine months away from Charlie's bit of surgery. What would be God's way with him?

One answer came in the very next letter from Cape Cod. It was dated August 24, 1957. It read in part: ". . . Now the good news —

the second night of the Novena to Joachim I slept like a baby. I
have been doing so ever since. As I told you before, I used to dread
the nights. But since Assumption day to the present I have . . . slept
like a log until eight and nine in the morning. I have my pains all
day long, but I've been spared the lonely nights. . . ."

When that news got abroad I was asked what I now thought of
"the man who got even with God." I had no new thoughts about
John Green Hanning. For almost twenty years I had wondered if
Dom Mary Frederic Dunne, the man who had given me Brother
Joachim's entire story, had really selected Gethsemani's best candidate
for beatification and canonization. I had much more reason to think
Dom Frederic himself was the man. But I had no reason whatsoever
to doubt Brother Joachim's power with God. I had heard of it, seen
it, and experienced it myself. Yet, I was neither surprised nor dis-
appointed that God did not see fit to work a first-class miracle in
Charlie's case in order to promote Joachim's cause.

Indian summer was upon the Cape when Sister Mary Clare —
Mazie — came down from Canada for that visit Charlie had been
looking forward to since late spring. Friday, September thirteenth,
my brother was writing: "This has been a heavenly week. I was
unable to meet Mazie at the airport. . . . Doctor Niles had given me
a shot for my legs the night before. . . . But Kay met Mazie and
her companion, Sister John Elizabeth, and got them to '33' all
right. We had a nice steak dinner. I have the most wonderful
neighbors: Tim Driscoll's wife sent the steaks for Saturday night,
then another sent a nice turkey for Sunday dinner. Tonight we are
going to have lobster. . . . Monday I felt better so we went for a
short drive. Tuesday we went out for lunch. Wednesday Father
Jack came down and stayed until eight that night. Thursday I was
bushed. But today we went all over the Cape. Just Mazie, her companion, and myself. . . ."

Sister Mary Clare's version of the same was not quite so buoyant.
She wrote: "We flew directly from Montreal to Hyannis. Kay, with
a neighbor's daughter, met us. They drove us to Osterville. Poor Chic
was miserable that day. It was difficult for me to keep back the
tears, he had changed so much since I had seen him in February.
. . . The next day he was somewhat improved, and then in four days

he made himself move about and even took us for a short drive. I was frightened, but he seemed to know he could do it. Then today . . . he took us for a long drive. . . . I believe it gave him a great deal of pleasure. Surely he is still our 'baby' brother. . . . It was sheer determination that enabled him to move about and drive that car of his. . . ."

Cancer had not yet conquered Charlie. In fact, it had all the family baffled. Father Eddie, O.M.I., had flown home from the Midwest on two occasions already. Father Jack, S.J., managed to drive down to Osterville at least once a month. He wrote: "How long Chic will last is anyone's *guess.* The doctors hazard none."

I had given up guessing long ago. All I dared was echo St. Paul: "How incomprehensible his judgments — how unsearchable his ways!" But when October, with its blazing beauty, came on and we were commemorating, as it were, the anniversary of the first discovery of Charlie's lung cancer, I turned to the Queen of the Rosary with renewed ardor and begged her to let Charlie live her Glorious Mysteries as she prepared him for his Eternity with Love. He had given evidence to satisfy me that he was making those Mysteries of the Resurrection and the Ascension realities of the present time for himself. But with the reports from Sister Mary Clare and Father Jack before me I saw he would need a new influx of grace and a pronounced increase in many virtues. This "Month of the Holy Rosary" was spent in almost uninterrupted communings with the Queen of the Holy Rosary, talking about the graces, gifts, virtues and beatitudes her Spouse could grant my brother.

Charlie was reminded that since there are "no accidents with God" there can be real significance to the time in which things happen. Then he was told to note how it was that Mary's months marked his great crises. It had been in October — her "Month of the Holy Rosary" — that it had been decided to send him to Boston for his exploratory operation. In May — Mary's special month — he had first experienced those leg swellings and the accompanying pain. September — the month in which we celebrate Mary's Birthday, Name Day, Maternity, and Seven Sorrows — marked the time of such physical incapacity that only a strong act of his will enabled him to move about at all. Surely there was some significance in these coincidences of Mary's months and his crises. He was advised to throw himself more fully into her maternal heart and call upon her more frequently as Spouse of the Holy Spirit.

No direct reply came to all that exhorting, for Charlie seemed preoccupied with a new doctor who had come into the case while Doctor Niles was taking a vacation. This new doctor had specialized somewhat in cancer and was much interested in Charlie's case. He managed to reduce the swelling in the legs and even dared promise Charlie that the pain in them would not grow any more intense. But he was anxious that my brother go to Pocasset for a checkup. Charlie's reaction was "I'll do what I'm told, but I'd much prefer to stay at home. I do dread being in a hospital again."

Then came a real confession: "Time surely flies. Here we are nearly at Thanksgiving and I am still far from Home. I know I am losing time, for I do not pray constantly. I have a few hours without pain and my thoughts do not turn to God — I get pain and then I pray. I often ask myself why I must undergo all this and I sometimes rebel against my cross. Then I recall all the wonderful things that have happened to me during the past year and I feel so ashamed and really beg God for forgiveness. I pray that my time on earth will be short, then when I get seizures of pain I cry out: 'Not yet, O God. Not yet!' No consistency there — but that's your brother Charlie."

That candor was most refreshing. All life is undulant. Had Charlie stayed on the crests there would have been reason to grow suspicious. Pious phrases are not difficult to write — and still less difficult to speak. But to live them . . . This confession of inconsistency told me more clearly than pages of professions of abandonment to God's will that my brother was really living as a member of Christ and actualizing the truths that had been presented to him. His reference to Thanksgiving made me ask myself what I should do for him and his family this Christmas.

Last year, 1956, thinking it most likely would be his last Christmas on earth, I had obtained my Abbot's permission to contact a few friends and ask them to make these holydays and holidays unforgettable for the Flanagans on Cape Cod. What a response that plea met with! If anyone thinks Christian charity is dead, let him ask people to contribute to a worthy cause. But now in 1957 I decided to leave it all in the hands of Mary Immaculate. She had given the world its first Christmas and its greatest Christmas Gift. I would trust her to make this Christmas memorable for Charlie and his family.

That she *is* our Mother is demonstrated by Charlie's letter written on December 31, 1957:

I know I wrote you yesterday, but I've been so full of thoughts this morning that I must put some on paper to let you know what this year of 1957 has meant to me. I also want to tell you some of the priceless gifts I received at Christmas.

First, Mary Mahoney had a Novena of Masses said for me starting Christmas day. Father Jack had each and everyone of the family enrolled in the Novena of Masses offered by the Jesuits. Then the thrilling one for me — Father Matt Brennan sent me a card and told me he was offering his three Masses for me. What a thrill that gave me — God is really spoiling me. Here I am, one who deserved nothing from His bountiful love, having Sacrifices offered to Him for the good of my soul from Maine to California, in Canada, and points west, east, north and south. What am I giving in return? I want to give my all, but at times — if I'm feeling good for a short time, I forget to pray — and if I'm feeling real bad, I object to the pain. I have not been able to fully say *Fiat*. I am very ashamed of my shortcoming.

Now the wondrous things that happened to me in the year 1957 — A trip to Kentucky and the meeting of such wonderful people. . . . Then that heavenly ride to the Monastery — the disclosure as to my own condition. . . . I, too, could have gone out and ended it all but for the Grace of God procured for me by Brother Joachim, Sheila Mae, Mom, Dad. . . .

How I loved those days at the Monastery! How many times I have relived those happy hours — our Mass — the Mass with the Community — the prayers — the *Salve Regina* — our tour of the grounds . . . and all the heavenly quiet. The parting was hard, but then on back home and, at last, Kay could breathe easier — for she did not now have to hide anything from me.

Then came the visit with Mazie in February. How good God was to allow me to have such a fine time with her. . . . Why was God so good to me, a sinner? Because so many were beseeching Him by prayer and sacrifices to be kind to me.

In March I heard your voice again. April, May, and June saw my feet swelling. But come July and Fr. Eddie who made me forget for a while. August and our Novena to Joachim. September and another visit from Mazie. November and December and again the thoughtfulness and generosity of your friends made it possible for this family to be happy materially — holy in the sight of Him who made Christmas; for were we not all united with Father Jack in the Holy Sacrifice of the Mass? — You know Jack was here for Christmas. He brought me Holy Communion. Kay and the children went to his private Mass. Such a blessed Christmas day!

An eventful year comes to a close. I am happy, for I feel I am nearer my Creator. I trust my all to Him, through the Immaculate Heart of Mary, and believe that soon He will take me into the Love He has prepared for me from all Eternity. My cup of happiness is filled to the brim.

Ever since the day you said to me: "Remember, Charlie, He is your Father — He can and He will do more for you and your children than you ever could," He has made me conscious of the fact. Perhaps the greatest gift is that He has shown me how to suffer for Him. I often think how bleak and sad it must be for those who suffer for nothing and nobody. . . .

. . . I thought I'd be up in Heaven long before this. But I guess I'll have to wait for a while before I get Home. Pray that I use the time for the Greater Glory of God by doing His Will at all times.

Ever in the Loving Heart of Mary Our Mother,
Chic.

On a separate slip he had noted the names and the gifts he had received. Mother Mary took better care of him and his family in 1957 than she had done in 1956 when I had solicited aid. Small wonder cloistered contemplatives have such confidence in prayer and trust in the Immaculate Heart of Mary!

The New Year got under way quietly enough, but before I entered my annual retreat on January nineteenth I had a letter from Charlie which opened with: "Your Abbot exhorts me to 'Patience! Patience! Patience! For Heaven is Eternal.' You tell me to 'fill up what is wanting' and to 'rejoice in my sufferings.' And I. . . . Well, Joe, I have just gone through a week of sleeplessness with the pain back in my legs twenty-four hours a day. I have actually cried to Jesus to make my offering of pain acceptable to the Father, for the sins of us all, but especially for those who need His help the most. But then the Devil started dictating, and for three days he objected strenuously. But finally your Abbot's advice and the thoughts you have been pounding into me got me back to the prayer I say the most: 'Not my will, but Thine be done.' You would have heard from me sooner if my hand were not so shaky. It's work to push a pen."

When I came out of retreat I was greeted with a letter dated January 22, which began:

Well, I could stand it no longer, and I feared I might kill whatever love the children had for me; for five weeks of sleeplessness had me so short of patience that if anyone so much as looked at me I'd scream. So I finally decided to come up to the "Country Club" and give all at home a rest. Dr. Niles, who has had me on morphine to kill the pain, and a red pill to fight depression, agreed that I should come up here and allow them to experiment to see if they could come up with anything that will make me more comfortable. His morphine and red pill were doing little good. I came up yesterday. But let me tell you how. . . .

I am still an independent sap. I was afraid of putting some people to trouble, so I was going to try to make it with Kay driving me up in our station wagon. Well, the Social Worker heard of it and made a bee line out to the house to forbid me to move. She wanted to call the Cape Cod Hospital ambulance. But I had a better idea. I had Kay call the Osterville Fire Department! You see, I know most of the fellows there quite well. They gladly came and took me up. . . . They actually carried me out of the house and into the hospital.

. . . I am not going to hurry home from here for I want Kay and the kids to enjoy being rid of this crabby old man. I also hope to enjoy the quiet of my private room for thought and prayer. Last night was like the other nights — sleepless — but one good thing is coming out of my sleepless nights: I say the Rosary, the entire fifteen decades, and while I rock with pain I am living with Mary — her life on earth and up to the crowning of her as Queen of Angels.

A year ago this time seems like yesterday to me. . . . At night I often close my eyes and almost feel present at the *Salve Regina*. Then the thrill I got when I was allowed to go up in the Chapel behind you and receive the blessing from the Abbot. I often recall the General Confession. I try to do my penance; that is, live joyously. I feel I have failed often but console myself with the thought that I am trying hard.

Those letters furnished three leads: The Fire Department, the private room, and the living with Mary through the fifteen Mysteries of the Rosary. Blending the three into one enabled me to continue with the fulfillment of that promise made about showing how the Glorious Mysteries are realities both personal and present. Charlie first read a few joshing remarks about being "on fire" then was

pulled up short by the very serious truth that he was actually filled
with "Sacred Flame" thanks not only to what happened in the
Upper Room twenty centuries ago, but to what was going on in his
private room right now in the twentieth century. God the Holy
Spirit was hovering over him just as truly as He did over Mary
and the hundred and twenty in the Cenacle that first Pentecost. The
Flame still falls! Then my brother was reminded that while it was
very wonderful to go over the life of Mary Immaculate during his
sleeplessness by recalling her fifteen Mysteries, there was yet a more
wonderful thing to do — and that was to live those Mysteries in his
own flesh and blood — especially the five Glorious ones. Invisible
tongues of fire — the graces, virtues, gifts, fruits, and beatitudes
commonly associated with God the Holy Spirit — actually hung
over his head, ready to effect in his soul what had been effected in
the souls of Peter, James, John, and the rest. The Holy Spirit would
transform him ever more fully into Christ.

That led into prolonged reflections on the Trinity's Third Person, whom someone has called "The Forgotten God." For while the
experts at the hospital pooled their knowledge and sought means to
ameliorate Charlie's physical condition, my brother was given what
was called "occupational therapy for the spirit." When the reports
of the success the medical men were achieving came in, I could only
pray Our Lady of the Cenacle to parallel their accomplishments in
Charlie's soul. In a very short time these men had my brother's legs
back to normal size; had managed to give him some broken sleep;
had revived his appetite; and restored his happy outlook on life. That
was real accomplishment. When they weighed him, once he was
rid of his edema, the scales showed he was only one hundred and
twenty-six pounds. He had been close to one hundred and eighty
when here at Gethsemani just a year ago. That did not surprise me;
for loss of weight, loss of appetite, loss of energy are three symptoms
of cancer I had come to know quite well. But what did surprise me
was the ability of the doctors to revive that appetite. Charlie said it
was due to cortisone. I had to take his word for it. I waited to see
how long it would last. When Kay wrote telling the way he was
eating, and Charlie himself reported a gain of four pounds in a week,
I began to wonder just what God was doing. The appetite definitely

was back. The weight was coming slowly. And the energy — at least the intellectual energy — was ahead of both weight and appetite. Charlie was writing long letters — and writing almost every day. His handwriting grew firmer daily. His probing into his own soul and the ways and wonders of God deepened.

If cortisone was really the active agent I had a reason to call it a "wonder drug" which those in the medical world would never have thought of. It had me wondering just what God the Holy Spirit had in mind for this brother of mine; for I had evidence not only of grace, but of the Gifts of the Holy Spirit before me in almost every letter. I deemed it advisable to focus my brother's attention on our enormous debt to the Trinity's Third Person because of all He has done and is still doing for us and in us.

Charlie was a father. That fact would be used to sharpen his appreciation of the part played by the Holy Spirit in his own birth to supernatural life. The X-ray department in St. Joseph Infirmary, which he had visited during his stay in Louisville, was recalled to his mind. Then he was told about one X-ray film stored there which held in clearest outline the bodies of quintuplets — who had been stillborn. The skeleton outline of each tiny body, from perfectly shaped head to final articulations of the little toes, was wondrously sharp. When first viewed, that film would call forth the exclamation: "How marvelous is God!" But when one thought of the parents of those stillborn babes, the beauty of the film was seen to hold real heartbreak. It was blighted beauty that would have to be buried. In place of cradles, coffins would have to be prepared.

What would the parents of those five babies give if they could only breathe life into those perfectly formed bodies? Charlie, father of eight, could answer that with finality. Then it was brought home to my brother that he was once as stillborn supernaturally as those quintuplets were naturally; that while his soul was structurally perfect as far as supernatural life was concerned, it could not function supernaturally; for it lacked the breath of life. It was dead! But then God the Father and Holy Mother Church did what no earthly parents can ever do. They bent over his dead soul and breathed into it the breath of supernatural life. He came forth from the waters of Baptism, thanks to God the Holy Spirit, a new creature. He had been reborn, and this time he was "born of God." He was breathing a new life, and that life was a share in the life of Divinity. What gratitude he owed God the Holy Spirit!

"But you well know life is not enough, Chic," I said. "You also need what I call light." Then he was given the analogy of children who are alive physically but handicapped mentally. Charlie knew two such children. He saw that they had bodies that were organically complete and immortal souls that vivified those bodies. But he also saw that those immortal souls were not functioning as they should. Neither the mind, the memory, nor the will acted aright. Looking into those children's eyes Charlie could see the fire of life but never the fire of intellectual light.

I told him to look at his own soul and realize that had God the Holy Spirit not kindled, along with the Fire of Life which is sanctifying grace, the Fire of Light by infusing into that soul the three theological virtues of faith, hope, and charity, he would be supernaturally very like those underprivileged children were naturally. "Are you beginning to see what you owe God the Holy Spirit?" I asked.

"Do you remember Doctor Maguire?" was the way the third analogy was introduced. Doctor "Mickey," as everyone called him, who was a charter member of the Cancer Club, had dropped dead at the operating table just two weeks after Charlie had qualified for membership in that Club. He was gifted with everything an outstanding surgeon must have. In addition to a charming personality and a very sharp intellect, he was blessed with long, agile fingers which enable one to handle scalpel, scissors, needles, and sutures with consummate ease. I once asked him to what he mainly attributed his skill. "I worked like a dog through medical school," he answered, "and I've worked hard ever since. But I have loved it all."

There is the answer to every question about success. Those who are gifted and love, arrive. We all like to do the things we can do well; and we all do well the things we like to do. That is because we are gifted along the line that appeals to us, and it is that gift, or those gifts, which enable us to follow that line with such ease and grace, and achieve success with real finesse.

What is true in the realm of nature is equally true in the supernatural realm. Hence, Charlie was told that he could attain outstanding success in the matter of living supernaturally, thanks to the Gifts the Holy Spirit had given him. He had everything required to make life what it was meant to be — a Divine Romance. He had the wisdom, understanding, and knowledge necessary. He could show real counsel in their use. He had the fortitude that would be in demand as he manifested the piety God had a right to expect. His fear of the Lord would really be filial love.

"But neither grace, the Virtues, or the Gifts work automatically, Charlie. You have to do your part. And you would be very wise if you prayed almost without ceasing for what theologians call 'actual grace.' "

Human eyes can be perfect in every way, yet they will never see a thing unless there is light. Human ears can be flawless, yet they will never hear a single sound unless there be some medium, such as air, to carry sound waves to them. What these media are to physical organs, actual grace is to what can be called our "spiritual organs." A man could be endowed with sanctifying grace, all seven infused Virtues, plus the sevenfold Gifts, yet he would never function supernaturally unless the Holy Spirit gave those impulses which are called actual graces to set those "organs" operating. In other words we depend upon God the Holy Spirit for supernatural life more than we depend upon air for natural living. He is not only the Soul of our souls, He is the soul's very atmosphere.

When these carefully planned lessons in what can be called the "anatomy of the soul" brought back very little response, I wondered if this spiritual occupational therapy was going to help the patient as I had hoped. It had been planned not only to distract, but to instruct, and to develop an awareness of dependence on God the Holy Spirit, and to cause an increase of gratitude to Him. The letter that came as acknowledgment made no mention of the lessons or of the Holy Spirit. It was dated January 27:

> Well, Our Father in Heaven gave me a respite last night for the first time since last June. I slept from 9:30 P.M. to 2:30 A.M. and from 3 A.M. to 6:30 A.M. and I feel full of gratitude this morning; for it's been a long, long time without such sleep.
>
> As you can see from my handwriting, my nerves are quieter and my

hands more mobile. I am not scrawling as I have been. Evidently I have more work to do. God is telling me that there is more to fill up — and I am the one to do it. I still have leg pains, but they are not as bad as they were, but they are being used for Him. Suffice it to say I am feeling better and quite content to go on being used by Him.

That reference to the work God wanted him to do awoke me to an omission that well might explain Charlie's cold reception of this matter on God the Holy Spirit. I had, as yet, said little about Our Lady of the Cenacle, the Spouse of the Holy Spirit, and Mother of the Mystical Body and each of its members. I hastened to make amends.

CHAPTER TEN

Our Lady of the Cenacle — Mother of the "Whole Christ"

"You have asked what many consider an unanswerable question more than once, Charlie," I wrote. "You want to know how long you are going to stay on earth. I know the answer to that unanswerable question. So do you. You have given it in more than one letter but never so clearly as in your last. We both know that Jesus said something about no one knowing 'the day nor the hour' of his death. Yet here I am telling you that we both know just how long you are going to stay on earth. If you push me, I'll say that you are going to stay here 'just as long as Mary Immaculate did.' Don't say no one knows how long that was. For I insist that you know!"

That was provoking enough. To have an answer for the unanswerable, and knowledge of what nobody knows, and to be nonplused about both, was enough to take attention away from his pain, I hoped. So I left Charlie in his puzzlement and went off on what would seem to him like another tack. "Have you ever realized that Mother Mary is in the third Glorious Mystery as prominently as she is in the third Joyful one? And in much the same role. You like parallels. Draw up those of the two middle Mysteries of the Joyful and Glorious Rosary. Look at the cave outside Bethlehem and at the Cenacle within Jerusalem and study Mary's position in those two familiar scenes. If you are as smart as I think you are, you'll find there the answer to what seems unanswerable and come to know just how long you are going to remain on earth."

Those who are fond of parallels have noted that Mary is to be found in the early chapters of the Acts of the Apostles as well as in the early chapters of the Gospel of our Lord Jesus Christ — and in

127

much the same role. It is true that when St. Luke writes as an historian he makes but one mention of Mary Immaculate. But that one, about her being in the Cenacle with the Apostles and disciples, awaiting the coming of the Holy Spirit, is as pregnant with meaning as was the one that tells of her presence in Nazareth the time the Archangel Gabriel was sent from Heaven with a message that was to change the history of God and man. In both places and on both occasions Mary's relations to the Holy Spirit were very similar. At Nazareth He was to overshadow her and she was to conceive the physical Christ. In Jerusalem He was to overshadow her again, as it were, and she was to be instrumental in showing forth the mystical Christ.

The parallels are not perfect; for at the Annunciation she was alone, while at Pentecost she was with others. But Mary's function on each occasion was the same: at Nazareth she was to mother the infant physical Jesus; at Jerusalem she was to mother the infant mystical Christ. That is the fact which explains the descent of the Holy Spirit on one who was already "full of grace." Mary had a new role to fulfill; for it she would need newer graces.

On Calvary the Maid of Nazareth had received a new "annunciation." It fell from the lips of her own Son who was also Son of God, not from those of any mere archangel. When Jesus said: "Woman, behold thy son," He meant St. John the Beloved, it is true; but He meant him not as an individual person only, but as representative of all humankind. Mary was made Mother then just as truly as she was made Mother at Nazareth. And just as nine months had to elapse between Gabriel's Annunciation and the appearance of the "blessed fruit of her womb" at Bethlehem, so more than fifty days had to pass after her second "annunciation" before the world was to see the blessed fruit of her maternal heart: the Christ living again in Simon Peter, James, John, and the rest.

The parallels run on after that. For just as Mary was needed to nourish, teach, and shape the human character of the physical Infant, so she was needed for the same purpose by the mystical Infant Christ who lived in those fishermen and that lone taxgatherer.

It is true that on each occasion God the Holy Spirit was the principal agent. But it is equally true that on each occasion Mary was a contributing cause. The Son of God took flesh "and dwelt amongst us" thanks to the operation of the Holy Spirit and the co-operation of the Maid who said *Fiat*. At Jerusalem, it is true, the Maiden-Mother's co-operation is not made as explicit, but it was nevertheless just as profound. Along with God the Holy Spirit she had her share in shaping those hardhanded, and often hardheaded, fishermen and that lone taxgatherer into the mold of Christ. That, precisely, is why she was left on earth.

If Mary Immaculate had not been needed by the infant mystical Christ just as much, and for the parallel purpose, as she had been needed by the infant physical Jesus, neither God the Father, God the Son, nor God the Holy Spirit would have left her on earth one split second after Christ's Ascension.

That was what I wanted my brother to learn. For what was true of Mary Immaculate is true of every child of God. No one will ever be kept on earth one split second longer than necessary for God to accomplish His will through them. Mother Mary's days were numbered. She, most likely, never knew their exact number until after her Assumption. But Charlie and Kay — and every other human being — learn from Mary that their own days are numbered, and that the number tallies perfectly with the time necessary for them to fulfill their role in the mystical Christ.

There is more than comfort in that truth; there is challenge. For while it is consoling to know that God is watching the sands in the hourglass of our lives, it is challenging to realize that as each one of them falls through we are to be showing forth Christ. That is our mission from God!

To be told that each human has a mission from God just as definitely as did God's only Son and Their Holy Spirit, often brings forth gasps of astonishment. But calm and confidence can be restored by realizing that the Flame which is God still falls! Just as that God of Flame fell on Mary, the Apostles, and disciples to fit them for their specific roles in the Mystical Body of Christ, so does He now descend on each of us — and for the very same purpose.

At His Ascension Christ gave His Apostles their specific mission. They were told to "go into the whole world and preach the Gospel to all creation" (Mk. 16:15). But they could not commence that mission, much less bring it to completion, until after God the Father and God the Son had sent God the Holy Spirit upon them. On Calvary Christ had commissioned Mary Immaculate to mother all men. But, again, though she was "full of grace" and consequently full of the Holy Spirit, she, too, had to wait until after the Flame had fallen before she carried out her commission. Charlie, Kay, myself, all mankind have been created by God and commissioned to manifest His glory, continue the Incarnation of His Word, grow up *in* Christ Jesus and *as* Jesus Christ. But no one of us can so much as begin to carry out that mission until the same Flame of God has fallen on us at Baptism to burn away the "old man" and set us ablaze as little flames in Him who is the "Light of the World."

With those truths as background I returned to the theme that, while God the Holy Spirit was working wonders in Charlie, he had to co-operate and contribute something to the end result desired by God the Father, his Creator, and God the Son, who re-created him. A candle was used as illustration. Charlie was told to look at some such bit of wick and wax and admire the skill that had molded them into the slender beauty and stateliness that we call a candle. But to note that so long as it remained unlit there was something cold, formal, and even forbidding about that beauty. In truth the candle could be called dead. But let someone touch flame to its tiny tip and the dead wax and wick moved, as it were, with life. It had been elevated, so to speak, to a share in the nature of the beautiful flame that had kindled it to life. If Charlie studied that glowing candle closely he would note that the wax and wick had not only been so elevated that they partook of the nature of that flame, but that they were also contributing something to its brightness and beauty. They were yielding their substance, giving up their being, as it were, that that flame might live on.

Charlie was to apply that illustration to his own soul. God the Holy Spirit, the Flame of the Trinity, had touched his soul to life, elevated it above the human, set it glowing with a life that was a share in the very life of God. Now, just as the candle gave its wax and wick, he was to yield his body and soul to this Flame of God that the light, which was he, yet not only he, but Christ also, might enlighten the world with greater brightness.

When he wrote that the pains were back night and day, yet that he managed to get about the hospital a bit in a wheel chair, the illustration of the candle was carried a step farther. Charlie was reminded of the fact that whenever we light another candle from our own burning one, the flame on our own usually leaps up doubled in brilliance and beauty. The same would happen if he would pass on to others the flame wherewith God the Holy Spirit had set him burning. He could do it by word as he wheeled himself from room to room and ward to ward at the hospital. But he would do it much more effectively by example as he suffered not only patiently but even cheerfully.

He was told that "Catholic and Apostolic" are not only marks of the Church, they are supposed to be marks of each individual member of the Church. We have been set aflame by God that we might kindle others. Long centuries before the Holy Spirit fell as Flame He inspired the author of the Book of Proverbs to write the line which depicts the life purpose of every member of Christ: "The spirit of man is the *lamp of the Lord*" (Prov. 20:27). We have been set aflame by God that we may light the way for our fellow men, and bring them to Christ. "Our Lady of the Cenacle is speaking very directly to you, Chic, as you think on this third Glorious Mystery. Listen carefully as you pray this Mystery and you will hear her say that your time on earth is limited to your task on earth; that you are something of a Burning Bush from out of which God will speak to others; that for your God-given work the Holy Spirit will give you all the flame and fire you need. What calm, what confidence, what joy this Mystery brings you." Then with something close kin to awe I added that if he listened aright he would hear his Blessed Mother telling him that he will never have a single spasm of pain that God does not need, nor one tiny touch more than is absolutely necessary for him to complete his specific work for the Trinity.

"Mother Mary is really saying that Pentecost is not only a present reality; it is a very, very personal one as well. You not only live this third Mystery, Chic; you are alive with it."

His next letter told that Kay had been up to see him that very afternoon — the last Sunday in January — and had brought young

Charlie and Kevin with her. "They could not come up to my room," Charlie wrote, "but I was able to look down and see them from my window. They are behaving wonderfully well since I've been up here — especially Charlie. He not only baby-sits for Kay but helps her quite a bit about the house."

If there is a poignancy to that picture of an afflicted father looking down from a hospital window on his two young sons, it is nothing compared to the piercing tenderness in the one Charlie drew in his letter of February third. He opened with the cheerful lines: "Well, this has been a red-letter day for me. I received your letter, two from Mazie, and one from Kay's sister, Grace. I am singing: 'Glory be to the Father, Son, and Holy Ghost.'" That was the first mention of the Holy Spirit he had made since we began this study of the third Glorious Mystery. I smiled at this fact for I suspected that my brother was being shaken by the revelations contained in the study and that he was actually hearing our Lady of the Cenacle speaking to him. I would bide my time, sure that Charlie would speak out when he had assimilated all the truths, or when he was actually unable to grasp them. His letter went on with a detailed report on his physical condition and the various treatments they were giving him. Then came the description: "Well, yesterday afternoon [Sunday, February 2] I had a wonderful visit. Kay arrived with Kathy, Patty, Mary, and Christy. Charlie and Kevin were home with slight fevers. . . . Maureen was to come later with her boy friend, David. Well Kay came up the ramp at the head of which is my room. Christy followed right after her, even though Kathy tried to hold her back. Well, what a delight — her big brown eyes sparkling and that smile of recognition. Then: 'Daddy, Oh, Daddy! And you have a bed just like the one you have at home.' I let her sit in the visitor's chair until the nurse brought me a wheel chair so that I could go down the ramp to the waiting children. Mary was most shy for the longest time, but finally came over and smothered me with affectionate kisses. Patty is not bashful at all. . . . Kathy had her hair cut and looks almost too sweet. . . ."

That description was used to detail for Charlie the opportunity that was his to keep those children of his from ever growing up unmindful of God the Holy Spirit. He could take almost every illus-

tration that had been given him and show them that they were aflame
with this God of Fire. "Though the Spirit is manifest from Genesis to
the Apocalypse," I wrote, "though every day is a Pentecost Day, it
is too true that we can still speak of the Third Person of the Trinity
as 'the Unknown God.'" Then I confessed that it was understandable enough, but insisted it was not any longer pardonable. "As you
know, Chic, to think of God the Father as Father and as God is not
too difficult; for we all know what a father is and what a father
does — and daily, yes, hourly, we come face to face with manifesta-
tions of God's Fatherhood in our regard. I dare say it is even easier
for us to know and love God the Son; for we have seen the Babe
at Bethlehem, the Boy at Nazareth, the Wonder-Worker from Galilee, and every cross and crucifix speaks to us of the God-Man who
loved us to death. Moreover, we have the tabernacle holding the
Bread of Angels, the food for our souls. Hence, it is easy to love
God the Father, easier still to love God the Son — but God the Holy
Spirit. . . . What do we know of Him directly? A Dove was seen
by the Jordan and Tongues of Fire in Jerusalem. So it is all understandable, as I say. But for you and yours, after all the illustrations
you have been given and the consciousness you should have developed, any neglect of the Holy Spirit will be unpardonable."

He was then urged to tell his youngsters how the Holy Spirit
brooded over them, as it were, in Baptism and made them "new
creatures." He brooded over some of them again at Confirmation,
and would so brood over the rest in time, to make them militant
members of Jesus Christ, to "endow them with power from on
high." He was dwelling within them at this very moment. They
were truly aflame with God.

My brother was reminded again of Our Lady of the Cenacle and
told that the Holy Spirit had come down on all in that Upper Room
just that they might "set the world on fire." Then he was reminded
of Fatima and the plea of the Immaculate Heart for prayers and
penance that she might convert Russia; and of the realities of the
present time in which Communism has lit world-wide fires of hate,
which will be conquered only by the fires of love which God the
Holy Spirit kindles. Atheism such as that which comes from Russia
can be killed only by the truth of God and the God of Truth living

in Christ's members. The world needs a Rain of Flame such as it once had at Pentecost. It will have it if enough of us live the third Glorious Mystery. Charlie had a work to do in acquainting his youngsters with the wonders God the Holy Spirit had already worked in them and the wonders He could yet work through them.

Sister Mary Clare had sent some pictures of the children of unmarried mothers she had in her Home of the Angel Guardian, for whom she must try to find adoption homes. While looking at the pictures I was struck with the idea of using them to convey the truth of our divine adoption, thanks to God the Holy Spirit. Charlie and Kay could have their children study these photos, and, surely, it would not be difficult to make them realize what an awful thing it would be for a baby to be without a name, a mother to nurse him, a father to provide for and protect him, or a home to shelter him. Then they could appreciate how wonderful a thing it is for any such child when a couple comes along and gives it not only a name, a home, security, and love — but so plans for that child's future that he or she shall be an heir or an heiress.

The application is easy: when we were without a real name, a lasting home, or any true security, God the Holy Spirit came along, as it were, and very truly "adopted" us. At Baptism He made us "children of God and heirs of Heaven."

Those last two phrases, so familiar to all of us, fail to convey the stupendous reality effected by Baptism and sanctifying grace. We need to dwell on the differences that exist between legal adoption and the Divine Adoption wrought by the Sacrament of Baptism. Kay and Charlie could tell their children that while Sister Mary Clare would see to it that the babies she entrusted to adopting parents would be fully protected by law; that they would be given a name that would be respected by law; she could do nothing about the child's origin or nature that would enable it to be other than simply "adopted by law." The generous couple who took the child would give it a home, an education, social standing, family name, and eventually a share in the family fortune. But that is all they could do. They could never give it a share in the family's blood. There is a limitation in legal adoptions. But in Divine Adoption no such limitation exists.

When God the Holy Spirit takes us into the family of God He actually makes us "children of God." It is not only the name of Christian He gives us, but a real share in the nature of Christ — His Divine Nature. We already possess human nature.

St. John, St. Peter, and St. Paul have all stressed this fact. But Charlie's children were too young as yet for such proofs from Scripture. The pictures Sister Mary Clare sent and the loving instruction by their parents would be enough to have them know their dignity was that of Divinity, and consequently, their devotion should be one of gratitude to the Third Person of the Blessed Trinity.

Both Kay and Charlie were acquainted with Boston's Perkins Institute for the Blind and the wonderful work they do with Braille. I suggested that they take the legend the Braille Press makes use of and impress its truth upon their children: "There is no lovelier way to thank God for your sight than to give a helping hand to someone in the dark." Everyone baptized had been made the "Light of the World!"

The next news from Charlie showed me that he was still in need of the Holy Spirit's Virtues and Gifts. "I am so discouraged," he wrote. "My endurance and patience are wearing thin. . . . Mother Betty Henry has invited Kay and me to stay at her house during your Silver Sacerdotal Jubilee celebration. That, I know, is impossible. But I also know she meant every word of her gracious invitation. . . . Well this is the end of my third week at the 'Country Club' — I wonder if I'll ever leave it."

Such a letter sent me to my knees petitioning Our Lady of the Cenacle to have her Spouse, the Holy Spirit, inflame Charlie with more of the Virtue and the Gift of Fortitude. What I was actually asking was an increase of Christness in my brother and I felt I had the right approach; for our Creed is strikingly exact. It says that we believe "in Jesus Christ . . . who was conceived by the Holy Ghost . . . born of the Virgin Mary . . ." The Spirit and the Bride gave Christ to the world. It is the Bride and the Spirit who still give Christ to the individual soul. The first of Mary's Joyful Mysteries was for Christ and Christians. In it God the Holy Spirit played an essential role. The third of Mary's Glorious Mysteries, dominated again by this same God the Holy Spirit, is also for Christ and Christians. We are wise when we speak to Our Lady of the Cenacle — she is so intimate with God!

That title has overtones that reach back into the "unbeginning of endlessness" when God decreed to create — and re-create; for all was to be in, through, and for Jesus Christ. It also has overtones that stretch out to the last moment of time, and then ring into Eternity; for it is a title that describes, if it does not define, Mary's role as Mediatrix of all grace; which, after all is only a synonym for her title of Mother of all His mystical members. This Handmaid of the Lord will be saying *Fiat* until Time's last tick. By it she will be but becoming again and again Mother of Christ. How this third Glorious Mystery, the Descent of the Holy Spirit, from which Mary gets her title of Our Lady of the Cenacle, speaks to men of the troubled twentieth century, telling them who they are, what they should be doing, and Who they should be becoming! Moreover it tells us where to find calm, confidence, courage, and the chivalry we should show to Jesus Christ.

Charlie was turned toward Our Lady of the Cenacle by my next letter and his brief reply was ample reward. On February tenth, eve of the feast of Our Lady of Lourdes, he wrote: "My pains are more severe than they were. . . . I get great consolation saying my Rosary." That was enough to show that the Holy Spirit was working.

CHAPTER ELEVEN

The Star Above All Storms

THE Centenary Year, marking the apparitions of our Lady-Mother at Lourdes, began for me on February eleventh, the date of the first apparition in 1858 and now the feast day of our Lady-Mother under the title of Our Lady of Lourdes. It was during this first apparition that she summed up all life for me by being silent while Bernadette recited the *Paters* and *Aves* of the Rosary, but joining her fervently when she said, "Glory be to the Father, and to the Son, and to the Holy Spirit." We men were born to give glory to God; were baptized to give greater glory; live, sicken, suffer, die to give glory; then rise, ascend and are to enter Heaven for the selfsame purpose of giving glory to the Three Mary spoke of as she repeated the prayer with the little shepherdess. Man was made to be a living doxology. This feast and the above fact confirmed me in my resolve to keep my sick brother conscious of the truth that God made him for glory — now and forever.

The feast passed prayerfully and quietly for me here in the Monastery, but a few days after it I learned how it had passed for my brother. He awoke at 2:45 a.m. plagued with pain. "My first and only thoughts," he wrote, "were: Jesus and Mary." He prayed ejaculations, Our Fathers, and Hail Marys as he awaited the hypo amid sobs and tears. "I talk to the Angel of Consolation who came to Gethsemani to comfort Jesus. I get no answer. Am I estranged from God?" He went on: "I plead with Mother Mary — asking over and over again for some respite from the pain. I say the *Salve* and the *Memorare*. All to no avail. . . . I plead with Brother Joachim. and Abbot Dunne — my pleas fall on deaf ears . . . my pain conquers

137

my mind . . . I am nearly out of my mind." Then he added: "When I do get somewhat calm I wonder about the validity of my prayers. . . . I know you'll say: 'O ye of little faith.' But you also have said: 'Faith is reasonable.' I'm being reasonable. How reconcile this? Where am I failing? . . ."

At 5:15 the next morning he was writing: "I don't even know how I am writing this for my eyes are filled with tears. I feel so alone. When, oh when, is God going to answer my prayers? Am I demanding too much? How can you reasonably say this is good for me? I believe the hypos they give me are just water! Forgive me for complaining, Joe, but you told me to speak out, to be honest. Formerly I could always say that others were suffering more than I. But now I am conscious only of my own suffering. I know that all things are under God's care. Yes, I know that. But the wheels of my life right now are directionally very wobbly."

He concluded that long lament with the lines: "I woke at 2 — No sleep since. Now I am finally getting a little relief from the pain. It is after eight o'clock. Tell me: am I failing to co-operate with grace? Read me through and through — and tell me how to correct my faults. Know I am trying hard!"

It was a long letter. The writing was wobbly; it was blurred and blotted where tears had fallen. As I stared at it I feared I might blot it some more with my own tears. I thought I knew the power of pain. I also thought I knew my brother.

I reread that letter quite slowly. Before I had finished the final page I gradually awoke to the fact that perhaps never before had Charlie shown such firm faith — or such genuine fortitude. Here were pages that were prayer and penance in one. These lines contained truer offering of self than many he had written when calm and self-composed. Here was severe suffering which was being sublimated into real sacrifice. As I reread Charlie's outpouring, I heard the Christ of Gethsemani and of Golgotha.

Christ's very human, perfectly understandable, yet truly piteous cries gave me all I needed to understand and answer Charlie's long letter. It is St. Mark who has given us what is perhaps the most realistic account of Christ's agony in the Garden, and in his terseness has caught all the tension. What depths are revealed by those words of Christ to His chosen three: "I am plunged in sorrow enough to break my heart! Stay here and keep awake" (Mk. 14:34). What a lesson on the proper way to pray is afforded in that cry: "Abba, Father, you can do all things! Spare me this cup! No, not what I will, but what you will" (Mk. 14:56). In this long letter I saw that my brother was not only doing the will of God, but was doing it willingly. What he failed to understand at the moment was that no follower of Christ has been promised either magic or miracle for saying and meaning: *Fiat Voluntas Tua*. Christ's own valiant cry: "Thy will be done" did not take from the soldiers' scourge its power to sting, bruise, and cut. No Christian's sincere echo of that cry will ever take the piercing pain from the thorns or the nails. But every Christian must distinguish clearly between will-action and the actions of his senses and emotions. He must always remember that faith and feeling are anything but synonymous. There is no pleasure in pain. There never was and never will be — not even for the highest mystic or most generous ascetic. Hence, so long as we are in the flesh, there is no shame in tears, no crime in crying out, no sin in showing evident signs that we are in physical anguish, so long as there is no rebellion in our hearts.

I had an immediate urge to tell Charlie these truths; truths that ought to silence his questionings, even as they explained the very questions themselves. But I recalled that I had told them in substance long ago, and that he himself had once used them to assuage the grief he felt for having grieved. As I sat holding that tear-stained letter, there wakened in my memory psalm after psalm sung first by that "man after God's own Heart," Christ's ancestor — David. How often he had cried out just as Charlie was now crying, wondering if Heaven was brass and God deaf. How often he felt his sufferings were all in vain. Wise Mother Church, knowing human nature as few others know it, has taken these psalms and placed them on the lips of her priests as they go to the altar of God. Is there any Mass whose *Introit* is without a psalm verse, I wondered. Did not Christ Himself, when saying His first Mass — the New Testament's only Mass — say when far beyond His "Introit":

> My God, my God, O why do you abandon me!
> You turn your back upon my prayers, my urgent cries!

My God, I cry the livelong day: you do not hear;
At night: you lend no ear to me!" (Ps. 21:2, 3.)*

Had my brother cried out any differently? Why could I not tell
him that he was saying his "Mass" just as Christ had said His? Why
could I not then go on and show how all these psalms, and especially
the one Christ had used, ended on a strong note of confidence; how
they concluded with an expression of deep resignation and truly
loving acceptance, then point to his own letter and show him the
similarity in its ending? Such a reply was well calculated to lift his
heart and restore his confidence. But, true as such a reply would be,
and inspiring as it would be, it would mark a departure from my
constant theme about glory. Of course I could say that like Christ,
he had to "suffer these things and *thus* enter into his glory"; but
even that did not seem to me to be the proper answer.

As it turned out I did not have to answer that long letter at all;
for the very next mail brought me something that changed the entire
setting. "It is actually late Wednesday night," it began, "but this
good news simply cannot wait. When Dr. Leadbetter arrived at
eleven o'clock yesterday morning I told her the kind of night I had
had and that the shot given me at 7:30 had had no effect. She then
told me that in severe cases of bursitis and arthritis they have injected cortisone into the sore bones with good results lately, and
asked if I would be willing to be a 'guinea pig' and try it. 'I won't
promise a thing,' she said, 'but it may help.' I told her I'd try
anything — and I meant anything! She said she'd consult Dr. Gould,
and if he agreed, they'd try it."

When I got that far in the letter I glanced at my calendar to see
what date Tuesday happened to be. When I found it was February
eleventh, feast of Our Lady of Lourdes, I read on with keener
interest!

"At noon Dr. Gould arrived. He scrubbed up and was pulling on
his rubber gloves when I asked if it was going to hurt; for I wanted
to be prepared. 'Hurt?' he said. 'This will nearly drive you crazy;
for I don't feel good, and besides I have the shakes. Maybe we ought
to wait for someone else to do this job — yet, I owe you plenty, this
is my chance for a pay-off. Where precisely are these pains of yours?'

* Kleist-Lynam translation.

I pointed to the spot on my ankle. He put on a freezing compress, then injected some novocaine. The initial prick of the needle was all I felt. Soon he was taking off his rubber gloves and washing up. 'When is the cortisone injection coming?' I asked. 'I'm waiting a little,' he replied, 'because, boy! is this going to hurt! You need a little rest in preparation. He was cutting some adhesive while talking, he then applied a sterile pad — and it was all over! In less than five minutes there wasn't the tiniest throb of pain in that leg — nor has there been any since! When Dr. Leadbetter dropped around at six that night I gave her the report. 'Well, that was a happy thought on my part, wasn't it?' she said. 'Not taking any credit from you, Doctor,' I replied, 'I say it was God-inspired.'

"They injected the other ankle this morning. And, believe it or not, I'm in no pain whatsoever right now. I've already said two Rosaries in thanksgiving."

I stopped there, smiled, and said: "And I also thank you, Mother!"

Charlie went on to tell how the doctors promised to allow him home soon. However they wanted gradually to taper off the drugs he had been using and see the reaction of his system. They were honest enough to tell him that the relief he was now enjoying might or might not last for a long time.

The last page of this long, excited, and exciting letter told how the entire medical staff at Pocasset was as elated over the success of the injections as my brother was himself. "I may be building myself up for an awful letdown," he wrote, "but if it comes, I think I can honestly say it won't throw me. I have been praying hard these many weeks, and even in my worst pains have managed to say: 'Thy Will be done!' — and mean it. . . . It is now 1 a.m. — and I feel wonderful. It may be that God is but giving me a rest to ready me for what He has in store for me. If so, I think I can say I am prepared."

The doctors had agreed that a day at home would benefit the patient, but the body that had become habituated to drugs rebelled when those drugs were not coming at the usual times and in the usual doses. So the day at home had to be postponed from week to week, until it was actually the eve of St. Patrick's Day. The Irish in Charlie arose. He pleaded — and won permission. He was home for St. Patrick's Day. He spent the next day telling me about it. In the morning he had taken the older children aside to talk to them frankly about what was to be expected in the not too distant future for himself; and what he expected from them. He outlined their duties and their responsibilities; stressed what they owed God, and what, under God, they owed to their mother and to themselves. It must have been a very solemn session. "They listened very attentively," wrote Charlie. "I pray God they do what I asked them. They are a grand family!"

In the afternoon the children treated him to an exhibition — not of Irish, but of modern dancing. In the evening he received what he called a "shock" — for Maureen appeared in an evening gown ready to go out to a ball, and young Charlie was seen shining up for his first dance, for it did seem but a very few years ago that he was concerned about Maureen's baby sicknesses, and only yesterday that Kay and Charlie were gloating over their first boy.

Shortly after this day at home, Charlie was moved from his private room to a four-bed ward. This was a tribute to cortisone and some good psychological therapy on the part of the hospital staff. Charlie's room, in his own words, had been "like Grand Central Station." Visitors, nurses, doctors, orderlies, and aides had kept up a continuous traffic in and out. Yet the constant company of the four-bed ward was both more restful and less lonely.

Beneficial as it was physically and psychologically, it proved even more beneficial religiously; for it opened Charlie's eyes to his riches, and filled him with gratitude to God for the Gift of Faith. His first letter from the ward began: "When I am sick with pain I always talk to Jesus, Mary, and Joseph in this way: 'My Jesus, my Mary, my Joseph.' I feared I might be a bit presumptuous in using the possessive pronoun that way. But further thought, provoked by observing my companions here, convinced me that if They are not mine, then, indeed I am lost."

He then went on with a description of the other three occupants of the ward. One was a man a year younger than himself who had been left with a weak heart after a severe attack of rheumatic fever in childhood. He had a splendid position there on the Cape. "But," said Charlie, "he really has nothing; for he does not pray." Another managed a millionaire's estates on the Cape and boasted he had more hard cash than any of his fellow townsmen. "Yet," said Charlie, "he has nothing; for money is his god." The man whose bed was closest to Charlie's had cancer of the throat. "I am working hard on him," wrote my brother, "for I dread the day he shall be told his fate; for he has absolutely nothing to fall back on — no faith whatsoever. . . . How can we ever be grateful enough . . . for our Faith?"

He then went on to pay a tribute to our parents for inculcating real reverence and a faith that was alive in each of their children. Here he must have had a spasm of pain for he suddenly wrote: "When pain blots out mostly all else, Mary, *my* Mother, is still with me. I know you will ask if I listen to her. Let me assure you I hear her talking to me most intimately. It's all glorious, Joe — even the pains. I should say, 'especially the pains.' For if I feel too well I become less adoring. How frail — how inconsistent we humans can be! We pray for good health, then never pray enough in good health.

"You know there is one conclusion I have come to: No one is in Hell except by his own choice. And, as we used to say in Philosophy, *a pari,* no one is in Heaven except by his own choice. I will not share fully in the Glorious Mysteries you have been talking about; I will never share in the Resurrection and Ascension unless I choose to! I will never see my Mother crowned Queen of Heaven unless I choose to follow His footsteps. God, who made me out of *nothing* (a jolting thought), wants my love so much that He dares to take the chance of giving me the choice of adoring — or ignoring Him. He really wants my love — all of it! What a thought! If a man is what his thoughts are and I keep on thinking this way, I'll be a saint. . . ."

After reading such lines what could a monk do but sit back and prayerfully marvel at the secret, silent work of God the Holy Spirit. How wise is that observation: "being God's son and being led by His Holy Spirit go together." They did for Christ. They do for every thoroughgoing Christian. "Whosoever are led by the Spirit of God, they are the sons of God" (Rom. 8:14). Obviously, my brother was being led by the Spirit. So evident was that to me I hesitated to tell him that he should distinguish clearly between being perfect and being a perfectionist. It is an all-important distinction for all who will be true children of God. But God Himself was doing such an exceptional piece of work on the mind and heart of my brother that I hesitated lest I, instead of being an instrument, become an interference.

If there is to be a full orchestra, some must play second fiddle. But people who are perfectionists never realize that it is possible to play a perfect second fiddle. They go grumbling through life because, no matter how they try, they simply cannot become something God never meant them to be; missing, all the while, the triumph and thrill of becoming the very wonderful persons God intended them to become. It is undeniably true that there is something actually wonderful about every person God has called into being. But the perfectionists are loathe to admit that with all the sparkling assets God has granted them, there are also some very real liabilities. They never seem to grasp the obvious truth that all life is undulant; that tides rise and fall; that each day is born, then dies; that God has an uncanny way of asking of us the unlikely thing — and not too infrequently, the difficult thing — and that He gets His glory from us in ways far different from any we would ever choose. The perfectionists never become perfect — and miss so many God-intended joys in life. They try to be too good, and often fail in being good enough. I would not have Charlie overreaching.

But something — or better, perhaps, Someone — kept me from going off on that tack. Instead I took Pius XII's encyclical defining the Assumption of our Mother into Heaven and quoted the opening paragraph. The Pontiff had spoken of life's ups and downs, attributing both to God's providence. "Say but the first two words of that very important Encyclical, Chic," I wrote, "and you will be saying something tremendous and true. Say but *Munificentissimus Deus*, and you have called God by a name that very properly describes Him — Most Bountiful! That is how His Holiness opened this Letter: 'The most bountiful God, Who is Almighty, the plan of Whose Providence rests upon wisdom and love, tempers, in the secret purpose of His own mind, the sorrows of peoples and of individual men, by means of joys that He interposes in their lives from time to time, in such a way that, under different conditions and in different ways, *all things work together unto good for those who love Him.*"*

"I call your attention to this paragraph and to this Encyclical, for in your many references to the Glorious Mysteries you are now living, you have omitted all mention of Mother Mary's Assumption. Is it because you think it personal only to Mother Mary — or not pertinent to our times? In this century, which has been so filled with astounding events, none will ever surpass in importance the definition of this dogma. We have had two world wars, a world-wide depression; we have split the atom, harnessed hydrogen, and mastered the use of jet-propulsion; we have organized the United Nations, developed intercontinental missiles, sent up satellites, and are readying ships for space travel; we have made gigantic strides in social justice with our various forms of insurance for old age, disability, and unemployment; we have not only paralleled but even surpassed these material accomplishments by triumphs in the world of the spirit. We have made this the Age of Mary and the Age of the Mystical Body. Yet perhaps the most personal and pertinent thing that has occurred in this century of astounding events was that which took place on November 1, 1950, when Pius XII solemnly declared that the Assumption of Mary Immaculate was revealed doctrine."

Naturally that called for an explanation. And it lay in how we live the fourth Glorious Mystery.

* *Munificentissimus Deus,* No. 1. Emphasis added.

CHAPTER TWELVE

Human Flesh Is Sacred

"CHARLIE," I wrote, "I'm going to ask you to focus your gaze on something that is actually dwindling away, but which is destined to be both immortal and glorious — your *flesh*. I choose that word purposely; for in our day it has come to have overtones which should never have been heard, and connotations we should never countenance. Three times a day you and I say the *Angelus,* commemorating the greatest event of all human history. In that prayer we recall the apex of that Mystery by saying: 'The Word was made *flesh.*' We are talking about the all-holy God when we say 'The Word.' We are telling the most magnificent, albeit truly mysterious fact, as far as we are concerned, when we say about Him that He became *flesh.* That is the very word St. John chose for the Prologue of his Gospel. That is the word we priests use every day as we finish Mass: 'The word was made *flesh.*' I stress that word for I want you to realize as never before that human flesh is holy, even sacred.

"I've got a long story to tell you about the flesh — and Mary, our Immaculate Mother, appears many, many times in that story. It really begins in Eden with Eve, the first woman to experience sin in the flesh, and who, through that flesh, brought death to all men. It will end with Mary, the first woman to experience the redemption of the flesh, and who, in and through the flesh, brought eternal life to man."

How modern it seems to speak of the "body beautiful" — and how utterly unreligious! Yet that is a truth as old as creation, and just as religious; for the climaxing act of God the Creator was to fashion the body of man — and He made it beautiful. Our twentieth century has

146

employed every method within its command to call attention to the fact that the human body is beautiful — and can yet be beautified. This glorification of the body has become a cult — a pagan cult, of course; and one that is completely materialistic. But this present day Materialism holds tenets just the opposite to those which marked earlier and even the earliest Materialism. In the olden days many looked upon the flesh as essentially evil and beyond all redemption. Today too many look upon it as so naturally good that it needs no redemption. Both claims are heresies; hence, they are conquered by Mary — for of her it has been truly said: *Cunctas hereses sola interemisti* — "Alone thou hast conquered all heresies."

I recalled a study made by Father Paul Palmer, S.J. — a man who at one time had been a high school student of our brother, Father Jack. Father Palmer's study was a painstaking one of the impact Mary Immaculate had made on what he called a "Theology of the Flesh." The report was a revelation of how wrong men have been to think that Mother Mary's influence on the Theology of the Church begins only at Ephesus and the year 431, when Nestorious — the erring Bishop of Constantinople who would teach that there were two persons in Jesus Christ and that Mary was mother only of the Man and not Mother of God — was so roundly condemned and completely routed by that thundering word *Theotokos* — God-Bearer, which the Council applied to Mary. Long before that, Mary was acting as Queen of Theology. Had she not mothered the Apostles from Christ's Ascension to practically her own Assumption — and wasn't most of that mothering a matter of teaching them true Theology? St. Luke's Gospel, much of which we know must have come from Mary, is evidence enough to win her the title of Queen of Theology. But we have other evidence which proves that even after her Assumption she went on mothering the successors to the Apostles and teaching them true Theology. Ignatius the Martyr, that grand old man who, after ruling the Church in Antioch for more than forty years, wanted, in A.D. 107, nothing more than to become "the wheat of Christ" ground into a host by the teeth of lions in the Roman amphitheater, testified again and again to Mary's place in Theology and her importance when we consider the Theology of the Flesh. In letter after letter he warned many peoples of the heresies springing up about the flesh, but perhaps in none more severely than in those in which he scourges the *Docetists*.

I reminded Charlie that the Greek word *dokein* means "to make believe," and how these earliest of heretics taught that Christ's body was only "make-believe"; that He only "appeared" to take flesh; hence, that He only "seemed" to suffer and die. That surely was a devastating bit of teaching. Ignatius of Antioch gave these heretics their name of "Docetists" — and gave them much else besides. His letter to the people of Tralles in Asia Minor, warning them against these heretics, contains much of the substance of what today we call the "Apostles Creed." For he wrote: "Stop your ears when anyone speaks to you who stands apart from Jesus Christ, David's scion and Mary's Son, who was really born, who really ate and drank, who really suffered under Pontius Pilate, was really crucified, and really died while heaven and earth and the underworld looked on; who also really rose from the dead, since His Father raised Him up — His Father who will likewise raise up all who believe in Him through Jesus Christ, apart from whom we have no real life."*

These earliest of heretics could not believe that God would take flesh from a woman; that God would remain in that same Flesh under the species of bread and wine; that God Himself was the "first-born of the dead"; and, hence, that we humans have flesh that one day will be immortal, impassible, subtile, and agile as is the glorious Flesh of Jesus Christ, if we but cling to the Vine as branches! The Jews could not accept a God who could die. These Docetists could not accept a God who could be born. Actually, these men had what was a real, though perhaps not fully recognized, abhorrence of the flesh.

It was nothing new; though, to me, it is always something puzzling. Five hundred years before God did take flesh from the Virgin Mary, Zoroaster in Persia and Buddha in India were preaching and teaching antagonism to the flesh God had made. Now it is easy to see that there is a great difference between mind and matter, between flesh and spirit, between body and soul. But why have so many in the past, and why do so many today, take this difference to mean inevitable conflict? Why do they look on these opposites as irreconcilable?

* Quoted by Paul Palmer, S.J., in *Mary and Modern Man*, edited by T. J. M. Burke, S.J., (America Press, 1954), p. 112.

One of the earliest lessons in Philosophy teaches that contraries are not necessarily contradictories. Coexistence for these two is not only possible; it is absolutely necessary in this life, and will be gloriously happy in the next for those that love God. But from the most ancient cultures of which we know anything, down to modern times, men who set themselves up as thinkers, even as advanced thinkers, have talked, and still talk about the flesh as something to be despised.

The Gnostics of the first centuries of Christianity can well be considered as the forerunners to today's Rationalists and our modern Intelligentsia. From these ancients it is quite evident that there is nothing new under the sun; especially nothing new in the opposite attitudes toward the flesh that are to be found among out-and-out Materialists. Some will indulge it. Others will not only deny it; they will despise it. That contradiction was evident among the Gnostics of the first three centuries of Christianity; then later among the Manichaeans of the fourth and fifth centuries; still later among the Albigensians of the twelfth and thirteenth centuries, and was not absent from among the Illuminati and Quietists of the sixteenth and seventeenth. Who will dare say it was dead in the nineteenth and twentieth?

As was to be expected, my brother was amused to find a Trappist writing this way about human flesh. That amusement made me ask: "Who isn't tainted with this heresy, call it Gnosticism, Manichaeism, Albigensianism, or whatever you desire? What person, who walks in the flesh, has not wondered, at one time or another, if there was not something in the doctrine which taught that the flesh was evil and, hence, should be despised? Chesterton was right, Chic, when he likened the holding true to correct Theology to walking a tight-rope high above an abyss. There the slightest lack of balance means disaster. Here, in Theology, a missed or a misplaced comma can bring on an ecclesiastical condemnation. We Trappists are ascetics. Therefore, as St. Paul said, we bring our bodies into subjection. But at the same time there is no true Trappist who will not tell you that the human body is beautiful, and that human flesh is to be reverenced — for it is sacred. A Trappist is an adorer, not a blasphemer. He may deny his body, but he will never despise it; for, being a contemplative, he is always peering into Heaven, and there he sees *flesh.* I use the word again, and I use it with a holy emphasis. Looking into Heaven he sees sacred flesh — it is the human flesh of Jesus and Mary. The first, you know, ascended; the second was assumed. So you see how vital the Glorious Mysteries are to a Trappist monk. He wants his own flesh to be one day where Theirs is — and he wants it to be like Theirs; that is, ascended and assumed. Hence, if he is an ascetic, he is such only that he may become a mystic. He renounces the joys of the flesh that he may live a life that really announces the glory of the flesh."

Fearing that I may have been too incisive, I again quoted from Father Paul Palmer who had cited from the Apostolic Constitutions a condemnation that went back to the fourth century. Charlie was told that we Trappists do not want to be put out of the Church, yet we would be if we did not believe that our bodies were beautiful, and deny them only to make them more beautiful for the time that will be timeless and the day that will be without end. "Did you ever know, Chic, that it has been decreed that 'If any bishop, priest, deacon, or any other member of the clergy abstains from marriage, flesh meat, and wine from the motive of contempt and not from the motive of asceticism, he is unmindful of the fact that God made all things exceedingly good, that He made man male and female. In his blasphemy he condemns creation. Therefore, let him be corrected, or deposed, or ejected from the Church; and the same applies to a layman.' " I could not resist adding: "Watch out, Chic."

It was with real joy that I turned to talk about Mary in my next letter and show my suffering but very interested brother that all her stupendous glories are actually connected with the flesh. That statement is a startling one; but we all need to be startled by truth now and then. It is a statement that is easily substantiated; for Mary's Motherhood of God, for which, and, in a way, from which all her other glories stem, was most certainly in the flesh. She herself had been conceived in the flesh immaculately. In the flesh she was virgin before she conceived, and in that same flesh remained virgin both at and after the birth of her Son. In the flesh, and through the flesh, she coredeemed; for the Immaculate Heart which served as scabbard for seven sorrow-sharp swords was a heart of flesh. And in that very same flesh in which she stood beneath His cross, she now

sits beside His throne; for it was that flesh which was assumed into
Heaven.

What did all this mean to my brother whose flesh was being
gnawed away by cancer? With a directness perhaps never used in
any of the other Mysteries, he was shown that this fourth Glorious
Mystery was very particularly his at this very moment in his life.
For it was pointed out that God is pragmatic; He selects the precise
moment to answer the particularly pressing need of His people.
With divinely wise care He had selected this midmost moment of
the sex-preoccupied twentieth century to proclaim the dogma of the
Assumption of Mary Immaculate into Heaven not only to give us
insight into the glorious future of our own human flesh, but to alert
us all to the present-day duty — a glorious duty — we have to discharge in and through our flesh. Charlie, by taking all the agonizing
pains that came from his flesh and sublimating them into sacrifice, in
and through the flesh of Christ, was being a very fruitful branch on
a Vine which restored God's glory and redeemed mankind by allowing
all its Blood to be pressed out on that wine press we name the Cross.

The all-holy Trinity had given my brother flesh — just as It has
given flesh to every living human — that in it and through it glory
might be given to God the Father, God the Son, and God the Holy
Spirit. What is more, Mary Immaculate, moved with pity for her
children, has appeared again and again in this twentieth century
to ask Charlie — and all her other children — to pray and to do
penance in and through the flesh God has given to each. Charlie
was congratulated for the way he was answering his Mother's plea
and His God's purpose. He was urged to go on doing it with even
more generous heart, and assured that if he did so, then eternity in
that flesh of his would be glorious not only for God but for himself.

"You most likely are tempted these days to lay heavy and ever
heavier stress on the last part of the Hail Mary," I wrote. "If we are
honest, we will all admit that 'now and at the hour of our death,'
holds real fascination for each of us — even those who enjoy perfect
health. It is not only understandable, it is all perfectly proper. But,
Chic, did you ever realize what a Heaven-born defiance you hurl at all
who are in any way tainted with Manichaeism, and at all who are
mixed up in and muddled by Materialism, every time you say the

first part of that glorious prayer? To hail Mary as 'full of grace,' to say 'blessed is the fruit of thy womb,' is, in a way, to give a compendium of what theologians call Mariology, and hint strongly at the entire work of God the Redeemer. For, as you know, you touch on that marvelous Mystery which is the heart of our Religion and the center of our worship — the Incarnation — and that, you need not be told, speaks of the Flesh that saved all flesh."

This Angelical Salutation, or Hail Mary, perhaps the most used prayer in all creation, is so replete with revelations that the subtlest minds of the centuries have not exhausted it — while the simplest minds of all centuries will always understand it. To the historian it will speak of Muret, Lepanto, and Vienna, and tell how civilizations were saved; for the Hail Mary was mightier than the sword in the thirteenth, the sixteenth, and the late seventeenth centuries. But this same Hail Mary will take theologians back through all centuries and set them listening to the promise God was making to the first man and woman who stood shamefaced before Him, guilt-laden with the original sin of mankind, and expecting, perhaps, some fate as fearful as that which had been meted out to the first sinner among the angels and to all who followed him. God Himself intoned, as it were, the antiphon for the Angelical Salutation when He said: "I will put enmities between thee and the woman, and thy seed and her seed: she shall crush thy head" (Gen. 3:15). That is why astute theologians can enucleate all Mariology and even all Christology from the simple, brief, beautiful "Hail Mary."

I told my brother that in that prayer he has the scriptural basis for the proof of Mary's Assumption. For when Gabriel saluted Mary as "full of grace" he was telling implicitly and virtually of that crowning grace which was her Assumption. Of course there are other texts which have been accommodated, such as those in the Psalms which tell of the "Queen who stands at your right hand, arrayed in Ophir gold" (44:10) and later when David cries: "Rise, Lord! On to your resting place, you and the Ark that shrines your majesty!" (131:8.) Then there is that one from the Apocalypse which speaks of the "Woman clothed with the sun" (12:1). But none have the weight of the two used by the theologians: the promise of Genesis and the greeting by Gabriel. I would fill my brother's mind with wonder at

God's goodness and admiration for Mary's might as he fingered his Rosary and said his Hail Marys, but there was further purpose in this elucidation of the contents of the Hail Mary. He should have a clear understanding of the dogma contained in the fourth Glorious Mystery and be able to proffer acceptable proofs for the Definition which had set the Protestant world in such a whirl.

"It is closely bound up with the first of her great privileges, Chic, the Immaculate Conception. That is what the Holy Father said almost in his opening lines: 'She, by an entirely unique privilege, completely overcame sin by her Immaculate Conception, and *as a result* she was not subject to the law of remaining in the corruption of the grave, nor did she have to wait until the end of time for the redemption of her body.' "*

That would be easy enough to remember. The theological reasoning on the matter would not prove any more difficult if he tied it in with his Rosary; for it runs: Christ, the Redeemer, scored a triple triumph by His life and death, Resurrection and Ascension: first, over sin; second, over concupiscence; finally, over death — these latter two being the consequences of sin. Mary, the Coredemptress, shares in that triple victory: she was conceived without sin; never knew concupiscence; nor the corruption of the grave.

But the argument that might prove easiest to remember and the most acceptable to give others was the one from "fittingness." Charlie was told first how Dun Scotus had finally won the theological world to the acceptance of his thesis on the Immaculate Conception of Mary by his argument from "fittingness." Then he was shown the magnificent passage from St. John Damascene which Pius XII incorporated into his encyclical. "It was fitting," said St. John, "that she who had kept her virginity intact in childbirth, should keep her own body free from all corruption even after death. It was fitting that she, who had carried the Creator as a child at her breast, should dwell in the divine tabernacles. It was fitting that the spouse, whom the Father had taken to Himself, should live in the divine mansions. It was fitting that she, who had seen her Son upon the Cross and who had thereby received into her heart the sword of sorrow which she had escaped in the act of giving birth to Him, should look upon Him as

* *Munificentissimus Deus*, No. 5. Emphasis added.

He sits with the Father. It was fitting that God's Mother should possess what belongs to her Son, and that she should be honored by every creature as the Mother and the Handmaid of God."*

It was even pointed out that Pius himself argued from "fittingness" later on in the encyclical which he said: "Moreover, it is reasonable and *fitting* that not only the soul and body of a man, but also the soul and body of a woman should have obtained heavenly glory."**

Then, since my brother had shown such a fondness for the "relic" of Brother Joachim that had been sent him, I smiled as I copied out the next few lines from the same encyclical: "Finally, since the Church has never looked for the bodily relics of the Blessed Virgin, nor proposed them for the veneration of the people, we have a proof in the order of sensible experience."***

The reply I received to that lesson made me wonder if my brother was applying the matter too literally to himself. He sounded very close to Heaven:

> Mom and Dad seem very close today. I know they are looking down from Heaven, and I can all but feel their eyes upon me. How our mother must be interceding for me! I can almost hear her telling Mary, our other Mother, all about her youngest son. How often she has been my inspiration to adore. In all truth, Joe, Heaven has begun for me on earth. Of course I long for the last mile Home, but say only *Fiat!* I feel sure that Dad with his unfailing, unfaltering love for the God-Man is now talking to Him about me.
>
> Why am I so sure about all this? — Because of the peace I feel. From the time I entered your holy City of God; from the time I saw that sign at your entrance: *Pax Intrantibus,* I have known peace; for Christ came to me there, and has been with me ever since. That *awful* (at the time I read my sentence) feeling has become a feeling of *awe* — My Jesus has come to abide in, with, and by me!
>
> I'm *longing* for the day when I shall see our Mother Mary face to face for the first time. And you can tell that niece of Brother Joachim, Miss Lucy Hanning, that I'm expecting "the man who got even with God" to do the introducing. What a happy, holy day that will be! Time is short — Eternity is forever.

What is there in our American make-up that leads us to joke when

* *Ibid.,* No. 21.
** *Ibid.,* No. 33.
*** *Ibid.*

most deeply moved, and so frequently to pass on weightiest truth with a laugh? Orientals have accused us of being a profoundly sad people simply because we smile so often. They think they detect a subconscious sorrow beneath our surface appearance of happiness. Few Westerners will agree with them. More likely is the explanation that we mask our emotions because we know them to be so strong, deep, and true. Perhaps it is part of our Anglo-Saxon heritage. At any rate I know I seized on what was the most sacred truth in Charlie's letter, namely, that eternity has already begun for us mortals and, consequently, we should be living with God at all times, and treated it with a very light touch, telling him I was glad that at last he agreed with me; reminding him that I had often insisted that "Heaven begins on earth — or it does not begin at all!" Then I congratulated him on the company he was keeping, thanks to this agreement; for, in the past, whenever quoting from an encyclical to prove a point, I would jokingly say: "See how the Pope agrees with me." Now I welcomed Charlie into the company of the Roman Pontiffs, and went on with the exposition of the dogma of Mary's Assumption as contained in Pius XII's *Munificentissimus Deus.*

This pleasantry about "the Pope agreeing with me" enabled me to knot the entire thesis about the Glorious Mysteries. "If you will but read this encyclical I have been quoting, Chic," I wrote, "you will see how heartily His Holiness agrees with me on this matter of the Glorious Mysteries being yours to live now; and especially is our Holy Father in accord with me in stressing the truth about the Resurrection and Ascension being connected with, and a climax to, Christ's Sacrificial Passion and Death. His Holiness put my argument quite succinctly when he wrote: 'Consequently, just as the glorious resurrection of Christ was an essential part and the final sign of this victory, so that struggle which was common to the Blessed Virgin and her divine Son should be brought to a close by the glorification of her virginal body. . . .' Note how the Pope ties in all the Mysteries you and I have been talking about."

It was enjoyable to write in this vein, for I knew my brother would share the laugh even as he would appreciate and accept the Pope's weighty doctrine. "Look at paragraph forty-two," I commanded, "and learn how thoroughly of one mind are the Pope and your brother.

He tells you there that this Definition is timely and this Mystery personal; for the first reason he gives for exercising his full power as Pastor of the flock of Christ is 'the advantage of human society.' That means present-day human society, Chic; not the society that has gone on, nor the one that is yet to come; though this latter will also profit from it. Secondly, he defines the Dogma 'that all the faithful will be stirred up to a stronger piety towards their heavenly Mother.' Take that word 'piety' in its Latin and theological meaning, my boy; for the Pope was not thinking of, nor talking about, 'pietism'! No, he was telling us to be loving, devoted, obedient children to Mary; children who will take her warnings to heart, and carry out all her requests with generous good will. That puts us back at Paris, La Salette, Lourdes, Pontmain, Fatima, Beauraing and Banneux, doesn't it? We are being told to pray and do penance once again! The next reason given is one that you can devote some of your prayers and pains to — for the Supreme Pastor of Christ's one flock calls to those other sheep who are outside the fold, begging them to come into this fold which has not only one Shepherd but also only one Shepherdess. Pius says he defines the Dogma 'that all those who glory in the Christian name may be moved by the desire of sharing in the unity of Jesus Christ's Mystical Body and of increasing their love for her who shows her motherly heart to all the members of this august Body.' But those three are not the only reasons the Pope had in mind and heart for giving us this Definition. Read on in that same paragraph and learn how thoroughly 'the Pope agrees with me.' "

"There is a Star above the storm," I wrote as I called my brother's attention to the penultimate reason given by His Holiness for the Definition: "It burns brilliantly, Chic. It will lead us — and all who have sense enough to follow it — Home! For it is none other than our Assumed Mother! Pius XII reads the heartbeat of today and gives prognosis for tomorrow. 'Thus,' says he, 'while the illusory teachings of materialism and the corruption of morals that follows from these teachings threaten to extinguish the light of virtue and to ruin the lives of men by exciting discord among them, in this magnificent way *all may see clearly* to what a lofty goal our bodies and souls are destined.'

"He is talking about Red Russia surely. But not only about Red

Russia. He is talking about America, Massachusetts, Cape Cod, Osterville, and Pocasset. For Materialism is in the atmosphere we breathe. It threatens 'to extinguish the light of virtue,' as the Pope put it, and to 'ruin the lives' not only of those on the summit, but even of such lowly mortals as you and me — and the lives of your children. That is why we must live these Mysteries of Mary."

The last reason given by the Pope would apply very directly to my brother. "Finally," he writes in the same paragraph 42, "it is our hope that belief in Mary's bodily Assumption into heaven will make our belief in our own resurrection stronger and render it more effective."

That would have ended the effort to have my brother see how the fourth Glorious Mystery fitted into his life on earth had not a letter come which proved most effectively that life on earth is still very undulant. It had been written on the first day of spring from the hospital and ran in part:

> I was all out of sorts this morning, and my good friend, Tom Molles [an orderly] really laid me out. I deserved it, and I needed it. I was crying with pain and asking for a hypo. I was refused. I guess I got nasty. At any rate Tom spoke up and said that the uppermost concern of all the doctors and nurses in the place was to ease my pain and make me as comfortable as possible, but they did not want to kill me with drugs. That is why they will not administer hypos oftener than every three hours. He then told me I was not bad off. He had seen some cancer patients in the last stages who had real pain. He said he hoped and that he actually prayed that I would not have to go through the anguish he had seen some go through. He really pulled me up short — and I needed to be! Tom and I are really close friends. I needed his bawling out. . . . How I need to remember that my Heavenly Father, who is God, created me out of *nothing*. Then to never forget my complete dependence on Him. . . . But there is a bright side to that thought, too. It tells me that I cannot breathe a moment longer than He wills me to live. I *do* try to remember all this — especially when in great pain. I tell myself then that He does not want me to suffer too much. I know my resignation to His Will is not complete as yet; but I'm working at it — and working hard. Have been since that memorable hour in your "catacomb." Will work harder now after Tom's call-down. But you must keep on praying and helping; for you know I was born baby of the family, and you always insist *"agere sequitur esse"* What can you expect from a baby?

Since my brother could accept such a call-down from a hospital orderly and be as objective as he appeared in this letter, I felt I had just what he needed to distract him from his pain and keep him from "getting nasty" as he called it. It was the philosophical basis for our Doctrine on the Assumption as given by Bishop Fulton J. Sheen. With his usual felicity the Bishop had shown that the darkness and very real despair, which modern philosophies had generated by their preoccupation with sex and death, had been lighted by Holy Mother Church with her Definitions of Mary's Immaculate Conception and her Assumption. Since I wanted Mother Mary to fill Charlie's whole horizon this treatise seemed just the thing.

Darwin, Marx, and John Stuart Mill were not unknown names to Charlie. In his years at Holy Cross and Boston College he had learned how these so-called thinkers had taken man's mind off his divine origin and end by talking about evolution and the unlimited progress possible to man; a progress that would ultimately make man a veritable god. He had seen how Marxian logic did away with all love for God and replaced it not only with a false and exaggerated love for man, but also kindled a very real hatred for the Divinity. And he well knew how Mill's *Essay on Liberty* had brought into being that license which paraded under the name of free love and the like.

Like any other man of his time, my brother knew the modern preoccupation with sex. But I was not sure how much he knew about that preoccupation with pleasure having led them on to what is now a preoccupation with death. So I told him that the Hedonism sponsored by the philosophies of Darwin, Marx, Mill, and Freud, had left man not only unhappy and unsatisfied, but had filled him with such a very real sense of frustration that it led him to despair. I was sure that Heidegger and Sartre were not familiar names to my brother, nor were such titles as Existentialism and Situational Ethics — much less that thing Sartre had named Nausea. But I did not hesitate to call these the children of Darwin, Marx, Mill, and Freud. Once I felt that my brother was sufficiently oriented on the so-called philosophies of the day, I borrowed generously from Bishop Sheen and showed how the agnosticism and pride of the nineteenth and early twentieth centuries, which taught the "immaculate conception" of every man, and his perfectibility by his own efforts, had generated an optimism which, despite its utterly false basis, seemed to grow as wide as the human race and to be hugged to the heart by most men. Two world wars sandwiching a world-wide depression did to that delusion what the A-bomb did to Hiroshima. But long before that pistol shot which ignited World War I had been fired at Sarajevo, Holy Mother Church had swept away all footing beneath such false philosophies by solemnly declaring that there had been but one human person who had been conceived immaculately, and that Conception was due to a special privilege granted by God. The Maid of Nazareth kills philosophical as well as theological heresies!

The two wars and the depression reminded man that he was not naturally good, nor was he due for inevitable progress and ultimate perfection. Man then about faced, and from being the highly optimistic human became the deeply despairing and completely pessimistic one. Holy Mother Church had to step in again and correct man's concepts. She had told him that perfection is not auto-matic by that Definition of Mary's Immaculate Conception. She now had to lift him from his despiar and his preoccupation with death by a Definition that would fill him with hope and tell him of love and life unending. That is what Pius XII presented to the philosophic world when he defined Mary's Assumption; for the twin pillars which support this dogma from a philosophical point of view are, according to Bishop Sheen, *love* and *life*.

"Even the scintillating Sheen agrees with me, Charlie," I wrote. The occasion of that bit of banter was the fact that I had often put forth the claim that every human being has what can be called a "gravitational pull" toward God. Now Fulton Sheen came along with an argument about "Love, like fire, burning upwards, since it is basically desire"; then going on to say: "Our sensate experiences are familiar with the earthly law of gravitation which draws material bodies to earth. But in addition to terrestial gravitation, there is a law of spiritual gravitation, which increases as we get closer to God." The Bishop concluded his argument by asking that if God exerts a gravitational pull on all souls, what must it have been on the all-pure soul of Mother Mary? Then he climaxes his case by stating that, given the ascensional love of Mary for God and the descensional love of God for Mary, the suspicion at least is created that at this intensity, love would be so great that it would "pull the body with it."*

With a wife as devoted and self-sacrificing as Kay, and with seven adoring children, my brother knew something of the power of love to create ecstasy and literally lift one out of this world. He would understand Bishop Sheen's argument that "Love in its nature is an Ascension in Christ and an Assumption in Mary." For, as the Bishop pointed out, since love craves unity with its beloved, what could be more natural then that the Son should return to the Father in the unity of the Divine Nature, and that the Mother should return to Jesus in the unity of human nature?

Here, I reminded Charlie of Father John Banister Tabb's lines:

> Nor heaven itself a home for Him
> Were not His Mother there.

If the first philosophical pillar, *love,* appealed to Charlie, the second, *life,* would hold even greater appeal. Bishop Sheen here based his argument on the fact that while death is divisive, life is unitive. He deftly coupled bodily and spiritual death in this divisiveness. Sin separates from God, the Source of life. Mary was sinless. She knew a union with Eternal Life that no other creature was to know. What could be more natural, then, than that He who named Himself "Life" should take that body, from which He took human life, up to Heaven and give it eternal life?

But after all this reasoning Charlie had to be reminded that it was nothing but prelude to prayer. "It is Mary, Mary, Mary — and always and everywhere Mary," I wrote. "When Death is all around us, and human flesh despised, it is through Mother Mary that Holy Mother Church tells all of life that is unending, and the glory that is to envelope all flesh, if we but follow Mary."

Then he was told that he was now in position to follow Christ's command: "Behold thy Mother." For that accommodation the claim was made that when Jesus looked down upon John the Beloved while speaking those words, He was looking through John down upon every man who would breathe, and very especially did His eyes rest

* *Mary and Modern Man,* edited by T. J. M. Burke, S.J. (America Press, 1954).

on one Charlie Flanagan. " 'Behold thy Mother' is a personal command and commission, Chic, given you by Christ.

"Where are you to look? — Well, if the second Glorious Mystery, the Ascension, opened the door of Heaven for you and let you see the Lamb standing before the Throne, what of this fourth Glorious Mystery, the Assumption? Have I not told you that Mary is present at every Mass? She has to be: for the Mass is Calvary — and 'Mary, the Mother of Jesus was there' much more than she was at Cana. She is present at the Eternal Mass of her only Son, and for the same purpose that she was present on Calvary. Paul says that Christ is in Heaven *semper vivens ad interpellandum pro nobis* — 'ever living to make intercession for us.' I say Mary is there for the same purpose. I dare take Paul's words about Christ and use them about Christ's Mother. I say she is *semper vivens ad interpellandam pro nobis*. She lives — and since she is Mother, what else could she do but intercede for us?

"It is truly thrilling to note the unity of all our dogmas. See how this fits in. We do not supplicate Mary simply because she is a powerful Advocate. Many have taught that, you know. They have said that just as the Jews of old had a powerful advocate in Moses, so we have one in Mary; and that just as God begged Moses to let Him alone, when this leader of the people was pleading with God to spare that people, intimating that Moses' pleading was so powerful that God Himself could not resist it, so we can have unlimited confidence in Mary and her power to plead at the Eternal Throne. All that is true. But it is not nearly basic enough. We supplicate Mary because of her God-given role in Redemption. She, by divine design and eternal decree, is Coredemptress. That changes the picture completely. Back at the Council of Ephesus St. Proclus hailed Mary as 'the only bridge of God to men,' and therein told the whole story. St. Bernard, in his turn and time, summed it up by saying: 'God willed that we have everything through Mary.' We are following God's plan, then, when we go to Him through her. Realize, Chic, that the Assumption is part of that Divine Plan, and that our assumed Mother is still by the side of her Son acting as Coredemptress, and this fourth Glorious Mystery will then breathe with life for you. It is personal and it is present.

"God is talking to us of the twentieth century by this Definition of the Assumption. He is saying first that we have a Mother who truly 'borders on the Infinite'; secondly, that when we now hear the word 'flesh' we need no longer think of sex and sin, but hear those high connotations about real sanctity in the flesh and the ultimate subtility, agility, and glorified immortality of our human bodies; hence, when we read of the 'Body Beautiful' it need not be an exploitation that is called to mind, but holiness and Heaven; finally, that when Death and Despair preoccupy the so-called thinkers of the hour, we Catholics can lift our minds and hearts in brilliant Hope to that throne next to Light Inaccessible and see sitting there as Queen, the Woman we call Mother, and know her to be 'Our Life, Our Sweetness, and our Hope.'"

Too long have we heard that our bodies of flesh are only "sod-born and sod-bent." It is high time to hear the authoritative voice of Christ on earth telling us a truth that makes us realize that these fleshly bodies have been "God-born" and that if we live aright they really are "God-bent."

Indeed there is a Star above all storms! We can look to her at all times, and beg her, as Francis Thompson once begged, that with "the starry treachery of her eyes" she "tempt us back to Paradise."

CHAPTER THIRTEEN

This Is Your Tomorrow ... and Today!

In his letter after St. Patrick's Day my brother had said that he was going to do all in his power to get home for his birthday, March 22. Knowing what Charlie could do once he had set his mind and will to a task, I suspected that the staff at the Pocasset hospital was in for some arguments, pleas, and perhaps a "bit of Blarney." But I also knew how loathe that same staff would be to let my brother home; for they well knew what almost constant care he needed.

It would seem, however, that the cortisone injection given him on Friday had effected such pronounced relief that the doctors decided to allow him home at least for the week end. Kay called for him about 10:30 Saturday morning, March 22. A few minutes later Charlie was off on a unique celebration.

A blizzard had ushered in spring on the Cape, but this second day of the new season was all sunshine. Charlie was happy to be out in the air. Kay drove leisurely up to the Canal, across the bridges, and around many of the places familiar to her husband. It was early afternoon when they reached Blanid Road and the first surprise for his forty-seventh birthday was the presence of his two older sisters, Peg and Beebe, who had driven down that morning from Stoughton. Kay put a huge turkey dinner on the table in an arrestingly short time. It was a happy family gathering. After dinner Charlie called Sister Mary Clare in Halifax.

An hour after Peg and Beebe had left, Kay and Charlie were heading for Armand's, one of the most popular dine and dance places on the Cape. Maureen and Kathleen had claimed they could take care of the children, and since the absent members of the Flanagan

163

family, along with some special friends, had sent checks as birthday presents, Charlie wanted to give Kay an outing. She was a bit fearful, but when her husband insisted that she invite her best friend and her husband along, Kay gave in.

Word reached Armand that Charlie was out of the hospital just for a short while, and that this was his birthday. So, in the middle of the meal, a waitress approached with a huge birthday cake ablaze with candles. The orchestra played, and the grouped waitresses sang: "Happy Birthday to You!" Soon the whole restaurant was ringing with song and applause — and all of it was for the somewhat stunned Charlie. As Charlie rose and led Kay out onto the dance floor, applause increased — for many in that large audience knew Charlie and knew his condition. He and Kay completed the circuit of the floor just once. But that was ever so much more than Kay had ever thought they would dance together again — and very much more than Charlie had dreamed his legs would allow him to accomplish. In the thrill of that unexpected happiness they drove home late that Saturday night.

Sunday night was different. So was the following week. On Sunday the legs that had held him up for the dance swelled again to their old elephantine proportions, and gave him that same fierce pain. By Wednesday a new area of pain appeared. Doctor Bell, who specialized in cancer, was hurriedly summoned to the Blanid Road home. He soon told Charlie that the new pains were caused by a spread of the cancer. He felt sure it had metastasized to the liver. Thursday Charlie went back to Pocasset as an out-patient. A consultation was held. All agreed with Doctor Bell's diagnosis. Doctor Kelley, the superintendent of the hospital, with his usual generosity and kindness, told Charlie that he was free to come and go as he liked but that if he felt he could stay at home with Kay and the children for a while, he was at liberty to do so.

After another injection of cortisone and another prescription, Charlie decided to see if he could stay at home until Easter. He succeeded, but at quite a cost. Passion Week was painful. But Holy Week was made holy by Confession and Communion in his home. Then came Easter day. . . .

This is how Charlie described it:

It is now 6:30 a.m. I've had some sleep and feel like writing. My thoughts this morning are joy-filled; my anticipations, glory-filled. Joy-filled thoughts; for I know this body of mine won't stand much more. Glory-filled anticipations; for I see fulfillment of my work on earth eventually crowned with Glory. But I must also tell you that Satan has been at work of late, trying to crowd my mind with doubts. Thank God Father Jack will be down today. I'll get some things really straightened out. . . .

Right now my spirits are up; for I just had Kay give me a hypo, and she and the two boys are getting ready for Mass. Remember how Ma used to work so hard to have us all looking our best for Easter, then how she'd swell with pride as she saw us off to Mass? Well, I'm just like her at this moment. You should see my wife and my boys! . . . Clean on the outside, pure on the inside; for they went to Confession last night, and these boys so wanted to be with their Mommy at Holy Communion during this seven o'clock Mass.

Kay, you see, gauges her time to suit my ills. I feel pretty good right now, but in an hour may be miserable. My liver sure has been kicking up, and the doctors say that all they can do is kill the pain. I realize now that the end of the road is near.

Don't be alarmed — I only mean that I doubt very much that I'll see next Easter on earth. If God wills it, I'll be singing my "Hosannas" with the Heavenly Host. Isn't that a marvelous thought? . . .

I sat back when I reached that point in the letter; I began to suspect that my brother was genuinely scared. The next page showed how right I was. It ran:

Give Mrs. Henry . . . my love; for next to our Mom she really is the loveliest lady I've had the honor of meeting. How I want her to meet my Kay! I'm so proud of my wife, and have been able to give her so little. Last night my pains so panicked me that I thought I was dying. She clutched me — and what comfort I felt in those arms. She's been so good to me. . . .

The letter broke off there: Then in a different hand and with different ink continued:

Wednesday — Well, here I am back at the Country Club. But before I tell you why, let me complete my story about our wonderful Easter Sunday. . . .

He then went into a detailed description of how lovely the girls looked as they set off for the later Mass. It was a High Mass and, hence, kept them until almost noon. They got home just as Father Jack drove up. They had dinner, took pictures, and had a joyful day.

I was still without information on what had taken him back to the hospital. Kay supplied it in a note written Easter Tuesday. It opened with: "They took Charlie back to the hospital by ambulance last night. He really was in bad shape. The new region of pain has bothered him a lot." Unquestionably, then, the return to Pocasset was sudden and even urgent. I turned the tiny page of Kay's note somewhat anxiously. "I followed the ambulance last night," she wrote. "Dr. Kelley stopped me in the corridor and said: 'You look awfully tired. Come to my office after you finish with Charlie.' When I went down the first thing he asked was: 'Have you contacted Father Raymond?' (What he was getting at I don't know). But, if you get a chance, I hope you'll contact him — even before you do Charlie."

That prompted me to seek the very extraordinary permission to use the phone. It was granted. I called Doctor Kelley, who simply said: "Charlie's chemistry is bad, very bad. Is there any possibility of your coming up?" Of course there wasn't, so after thanking the doctor for all he had done for Charlie, I asked to speak with my brother. It was the most one-sided conversation ever held between the two of us. Charlie had very little to say; and even that little was said in such a listless tone of voice that I could almost see the pain-furrowed face with pain-filled eyes, and almost hear the anguished torment in his chest. His choked "So long, Joe" had a tone of real finality about it. I turned from the phone wondering if I would ever hear that voice again this side of Heaven.

The single sheet of paper I received from Charlie the following week began: "Well, I was anointed this afternoon, and will receive in the morning." Isn't it strange how the thing you have been long expecting always strikes you as sudden when it finally arrives? That opening sentence stated something I had been waiting to read for over a year; yet, when I saw it before me I felt a real shock.

Charlie then explained how he had had a very pain-filled day the Thursday I had phoned, which had been followed by an even more painful night. So he had Kay call Father Leblanc, the priest who acted as chaplain for Pocasset's hospital. The priest came Friday morning and consulted Dr. Sanborne who still thought Charlie was in no immediate danger of death.

When the doctor left, Charlie told the priest how he longed for the Sacraments and how much he would appreciate having Extreme Unction if he were entitled to it. With Doctor Sanborne's words about no immediate danger ringing in his ears, Father Leblanc hesitated. "I'll think it over" was his parting promise.

Friday and Saturday passed rather quietly. But Sunday was another day filled with pain. Father Leblanc came in the late afternoon and quietly said: "I've thought over your case, Charlie, and concluded you are entitled to the last rites."

That announcement was of more therapeutic value than anything the medical world had been able to offer all week. Charlie, with a deep control which spoke to me of majestic calm, had written: "I feel so wonderful! It is such a beautiful rite!"

How utterly true: "It is such a beautiful rite!" Who will ever grasp the complete magnificence of that act which really sees Christ bending over us, caressing each sense, cleansing these fleshy gateways to the soul, and stigmatizing our bodies, as it were, with holiness — the holiness He won through His five wounds! Holy Mother Church seems to take us in her arms during this Sacrament just as any loving mother would take her hurt child, to kiss away the tears, tenderly touch our ears, nostrils and lips, then lovingly pat our hands — assuring us all is well. We can fall asleep after such tender caressing — and wake up refreshed, either here or in the hereafter.

Charlie sensed all that — and more. "I also received the Apostolic Blessing with Plenary Indulgence attached for the hour of death," he wrote. "I feel secure in the arms of Christ. If it be God's Will this anointing will help make me well — if not, then it will surely help me on to sanctification." He added something about not feeling like writing much. I could understand that; for when a man is in such close communion with God, as Charlie seemed to be, any communication with others is not absorbing, nor really welcome.

But what was I to do now? I had taken him through four of the Glorious Mysteries not only as a therapy, but also as a theology. I

meant to distract him, it is true; but only from what should not claim
too much of his attention. My main purpose was to focus his gaze on
God — and thus see himself truly; to rivet his attention on glory —
that which we are to give to God with every breath, and that which
God actually gives to us now in our every bit of breathing — and
which He will increase and make eternal in the hereafter. Theology
is not only truth to be known; it is a life to be lived. And Mary's
Rosary is one of the best compendiums available.

I was now at the last Mystery — the Coronation of Mary as Queen
of Heaven. I had hoped to make it a smashing climax to the course
I had given Charlie. I planned to surprise and even startle him as I
claimed it was a Mystery of the present time and one that was most
personal. My plan was detailed, but, I had reason to question now
whether I had the time to execute it and whether he had the
mental vigor to appreciate it.

In my quandary I turned to Mary, as is my usual custom. After
all, Charlie was dearer to her than he was to me; for he had cost
her more! She had purchased him not only with the last drop of
blood that came from her Son's Sacred Heart, but with the pain the
seven swords of sorrow had brought to her own Immaculate Heart.
In my prayer I claimed I had title to her direction — it was the title
Pilate had written. For under that title, "drawn up in Hebrew, Latin,
and Greek," her only Son had died and all her other children were
born. I begged my Lady of Light to show me the proper thing to
do at this point in Charlie's earthly existence.

She answered my plea almost immediately. Her reply came in the
guise of a long letter from Father Jack in which he described his
Lent, Holy Week, and Easter. The first two had been most laborious.
The last had been flooded with joy. It was a joy that streamed out
to him from the risen Christ through the medium of the family on
the Cape; for after his Mass and colloquy with the risen Saviour,
Jack had headed for Osterville. His description of the day ran:

> It was raining and overcast, but this made little difference to any
> in the group. Kay had the whole family decked out in Easter splendor.
> Both Maureen and Kathleen had made their own dress and coat. The
> entire outfit looked chic and colorful. . . . No question about it, they
> DO make a most beautiful set — Kay with her graying hair, Maureen

and Kathleen in their fresh puberty, Charlie and Kevin real boys, but as different as Jack and Jill, Patricia, Mary-Margaret and Christy in their vivid girlishness — all make an impressive picture, I can assure you. Thank God none of them, as far as I could ascertain, had the faintest realization that this, more than likely, would be their last Easter with their Dad on earth. That undercurrent was with me all day, but it never took over with any pronounced effects. I entered the fun and frolic as far as I could. I took Maureen and Kathleen for a ride in their Easter finery. Like the Queen's beauty, their Easter Parade was all within — the car! The girls directed me about the different roads and got gloriously lost. Eventually, by circuitous roads, we got back to land with which we were familiar. It made for quite a bit of joshing and helped to lighten the whole situation for me. They are two very good-looking girls and will develop into something ravishingly beautiful, or I miss my guess. I then took the four youngest for a ride. Kevin in quite reticent and shy. The three little girls are going to rival their older sisters in good looks. We get along famously.

Chic was his boyish self. Rather insistent on taking pictures of and with the group. There was nothing that would indicate that he was anticipating not being around very long. Nor was there anything morbid in his whole manner. Rather it was the father and husband, very happy and proud to be with his wife and family. During the whole day he never made a single allusion to anything that he foreboded.

What is my unprofessional prognosis? The cancer in the lung seems to me to have made little headway. What has been diagonosed as metastasis to the liver occasions Chic pain. The legs have receded almost to normal, tho' while I was there, evidently due to too much standing and walking about for the pictures, there was a swelling of the feet and of the leg to the knees. Chic is still physically strong. Hence, to my unpracticed eye, I'd say he'd be around for some time yet. How long? I'd say possibly six months.

That last sentence was what I wanted. It set me preparing my presentation of the fifth Glorious Mystery. Before I could write a word, however, I had to adore the love and mercy of God which has destined man for such glory as is revealed in this Coronation of Mary. How breathlessly beautiful is His plan for us! Just as He has placed every single petal in the seed, just as He has secreted the loveliness of the lily in the somewhat ugly bulb, so has He placed our end in our beginning. The waters of Baptism falling on our heads seed our souls with what can bloom as an eternal crown. What simplicity, what unity, what sublimity there is in all God's works! Grace can grow and grow until it bursts into glory. Baptism is the beginning of blessedness, and bliss eternal is but Baptism's full bloom. The God-life given at the baptismal font is the life of Heaven in embryo. Indeed Heaven begins on earth! When in grace, God is nearer to us than breath to our body or marrow to our bone. He is then ours in time just as truly as He will be ours in eternity. We possess Him at the moment we are "born again of water and the Spirit" just as really as we will possess Him from the moment that will mark the beginning of endlessness for all who die in grace. The only difference being the light in which we behold Him — and the awful possibility, during time, of losing sight of Him in the dark!

I came out of that bit of adoration crying: "Mother! Bless Him, thank Him, praise Him for me, and tell Him it is all too beautiful!"

But when I sat down to tell my brother about this Mystery I was suddenly aware of a difficulty. I could readily tell my brother that the Mystery says to him: "This is your tomorrow!" Charlie would accept the fact that glory was only a dawn away; for he had accepted that other statement of mine that "life is a wind; eternity is tomorrow." But would he accept the statement that this fifth Glorious Mystery was his *today*? Would there not be a psychological block brought into being by his whole religious training which is so aptly summed up by Paul's words to his beloved disciple Timothy: "I have fought the good fight, I have finished the course, I have kept the faith. What remains is the crown due to holiness which the Lord, the just Judge, will give me on that day, and not only to me but also to those who love his brilliant coming" (2 Tim. 4:8).

How literally and logically that text could be applied to Charlie! He had fought a very good fight. He had certainly kept the faith. Doubtlessly he was nearing the finish of his course. What was more: I had always described death as a "coming of Christ." I had used His own words: "I shall come like a thief" (Apoc. 3:3), and even more frequently had borrowed from St. Paul and added: "like a thief in the night" (1 Thess. 5:2). For that is the concept of death that makes this dread thing beautiful. This Thief commits Grand Larceny! Let Him come "like a thief"; so long as it is He, who will care? This passage from Paul also dispels that other source of terror

— the Judgment. In Paul's eyes this dread thing was time for awards! It is the moment when the just Judge will give the crown of glory to those who have loved Christ.

It would be easy and pleasant to make both death and Judgment appealing to Charlie. I could even add that his Immaculate Mother Mary would be on hand to give proud maternal touch to his coronation ceremony. He would accept all that without a question and thus have this final Glorious Mystery saying: "This is your tomorrow."

But I wanted him to hear it saying: "This is also your today!"

As I pondered the difficulty and sought the proper approach I heard in my heart what I so often hear when thinking of Mary. It sings itself there almost incessantly, but with variations suited to my every need. At times it is as soft and as soothing as a lullaby. At other times it is as blood-stirring as a military march. Occasionally it is as commanding as a bugle blast. Again it will sound as comforting as the gentle strains that come from strings lightly struck. But, no matter what its form, whenever I hear this song in my soul, I hear what is really a love song. I heard it now, and I could say to Charlie with deepest conviction: "This is your tomorrow — and today!" For I had heard Mary singing in my heart and saying: "I am the Mother of Fair Love . . . and of Holy Hope. . . . In me is all grace of the way. . . . In me is all hope of life. . . . Come over to me, all ye that desire me; and be filled with my fruits" (Ecclus. 24:24–26).

When Mary sings thus in any soul there is something as powerful in her voice as in the one that cried: "Lazarus, come forth!" (Jn. 11:43.) And with Chesterton every real man can say:

> And to hear her calling a man might rise and thunder
> On the doors of the grave.*

These words from Ecclesiasticus, which Mary so often sings in my soul, would be made for Charlie what they had become for me — my Song of Songs. They would serve to make meditation on the fifth Glorious Mystery soul-stirring music. Thanks to them, thunder-

---

* *Regina Angelorum.*

ous truths could be told my brother while he yet lingered in this life, bravely striving to "become what he was" — *Christ!*

Charlie was first asked if he had ever tried to imagine the amazement in Heaven when Christ ascended there — and the far greater amazement as Mary was assumed. I quoted a poem some clever nun had composed describing Christ's descent into Limbo just after His death and before His Resurrection. She has Him lighting that world with the splendor of His presence, astounding patriarchs who had, in their limited way, portrayed Him; amazing prophets who had foretold Him; dumfounding all His ancestors, not only back to David or Jesse, but back to Abraham and even to Adam. But there was one aged man among that waiting throng who was not a bit abashed by the beauty of this Son of God. He greeted the Christ with easy familiarity and asked the tender question: "How is Your Mother, Son?"

That was Limbo and the great St. Joseph with Jesus before He had risen from the dead. But as this same Christ ascended into Heaven who would dare speak save the Eternal Father, or perhaps the Spirit of Love? We are told of one silence in Heaven. It held as Michael battled the Dragon. But what must the silence have been as a Man came into this City of God, a Man who had defeated the Dragon and all his host singlehanded, a Man who had conquered Sin and vanquished Death?

"Can you imagine the amazement of Michael, Raphael, and even of Gabriel, despite the 'annunciation' he had made to Mary at Nazareth about this same Man?" I wrote. "Think how the Angels, Archangels, Thrones, Dominations, Virtues, and Powers must have gazed in astonishment as this Man passed them all and went up beyond the Principalities, beyond even the Cherubim and Seraphim! They would have noted that the Man had holes in His hands and feet, and a gaping hole in His side. Nevertheless, from all about Him — and very especially from these gaping wounds — blinding beauty shone. Perhaps some Seraph dared to whisper what Isaias had one day sung: 'Who is this coming from Edom, coming on the road from Bosra, with garments deep-dyed? Who is this so gaily clad, marching so valiantly?' (Isa. 63:1.)

"If so, you can be positive that the Lord God answered: 'I am the One who is faithful to his promises, a champion bringing deliverance.' Then the dialogue would have gone on. 'And why are thy garments stained with red? Why dost thou go clad like the men who tread out the wine-press?' And Christ would make proud answer: 'None other has trodden the wine-press but I only*. . .' (Isa. 63:2, 3).

"That is the way we monks sing the Mystery of God's pity for man at the Third Nocturne in many an Eastertide Office, Chic. Now parallel that imaginary vision with one of your own making as you think of Mary's entrance into that same Heaven amidst those same nine Choirs of Angels."

I aided him somewhat by referring him to one of Chesterton's poems called *Regina Coeli*, in which Chesterton has Mary passing through the various choirs, and claims that she was not "stayed or questioned." He gives as his reason that she had only to be seen to be recognized for what she is — *Queen*. He even says that the entire angelic host was "broken down under her unbearable beauty," then adds what I anguish and ache to make unchallengeably true: "As we have been." Oh would that that "we" were literally universal! Would that all mankind would look at Mary and see her incomparable beauty. Unquestionably they would be "broken down under it." But there are so many who do not see!

Chesterton has the silence of Heaven broken not by any Seraph, Virtue, or Power, but by the Woman herself. By so doing he shows rare insight into Mary's heart. For her cry bursts forth not when she sees Gabriel who had named her "full of grace"; not when she sees Elizabeth who had named her "blessed among women"; but only when she has glimpsed Him who is the "fruit of her womb"! It was a Mother's cry — different far from the one that had escaped her lips when she found Him in the Temple "seated among the rabbis" (Lk. 2:46) for now He was seated beside that Father, whose call He had answered those three days — and every hour of His earthly life. It was a cry very like that cry which came from those immaculate lips the morning of His Resurrection when He came to her glorious and immortal.

"When you see that Mother and Son embrace," I wrote, "realize that you are looking on the Determination of Almighty God in-

* Knox translation.

carnated in a Man and Woman — the Determination to have as His own us mortals, that He might one day crown us eternally."

That led me on to a quote from my father St. Bernard, who here, as in so many other places, echoes my favorite among the Fathers, St. Augustine of Hippo. "One man and one woman harmed us grievously," wrote Bernard, then added: "Thanks be to God, all things are restored by one Man and one Woman — and that with interest. It is true that Christ would have been adequate, since all our sufficiency is from Him. But it was not good for us that it should be by a Man alone. It was more appropriate that both sexes should take part in our reparation, since both had wrought our ruin. Jesus Christ as Man is, obviously, the trustworthy and powerful Mediator between God and man. But mankind honors in Him His divine majesty. Not only His mercy but also His judgment is sung. There is thus need for a mediator with that Mediator, and none could be more fitting than Mary."*

When I got that far in the quote I suddenly realized Bernard was giving a portrait of Mary which, while true, is not true enough. She is more than "mediator with the Mediator" — and that by the Will of God! So I stopped short and ended my letter with: "This is your tomorrow, Chic. As soon as I get time I'll show you how it is also your today."

* *Serm. de 12 Praerog.,* No. 1; *PL,* clxxxii, 429.

CHAPTER FOURTEEN

This Is the Will of God ...
Today and Tomorrow!

THE promised letter did not demand long reflection, for I have watched our Mariology grow this past quarter of a century and it has been most gratifying to see that our theologians are setting it on a foundation as firm and as immutable as God Himself; for they have found their basic principle to be God's eternally immutable Will. So the first point stressed in the letter was one that had been touched before: that *according to the Will of God* Mary's place in the plan of Redemption is ever so much more intimate and essential than that of the mother of a king who will listen to petitions presented by that mother, but who might not be so amenable were those petitions presented by a lesser person.

Too often that is the only explanation offered by Catholics to those outside the Faith as the reason for our honoring Mary. That explanation is not only inadequate; it may even be misleading. We Catholics do not go to the Queen because the King is a Person we dread to approach. We do not appeal to the Mother because we dare not appeal to the Son. Were this the case, then those who say they approach the Lord directly, insisting that they are so sure of His love that they need no intermediary to intercede for them, would be in a better position than we Catholics are. But that is not the case at all. We do not go to Mary, or through Mary, because we fear the Father, Son, or Holy Spirit. Timidity in dealing with the Holy Trinity is not a Catholic characteristic, far less a Catholic virtue to be cultivated by old and young. We know the love of each Person in the Trinity for each one of us, and we are absolutely sure of our relationship. But we also know something of Almighty God's plan for humankind. We know exactly how Divine Pity was manifest in our regard. It came to us through Mary!

Therefore we see her as God sees her: as part of His principle and plan for the communication of Divine Life to human beings.

There is one word that tells the whole story, the Latin word *Consors*. Mary was Christ's consort — the English transliteration does not do justice to the idea. According to God's eternal, love-filled plan for us sinners, Mary is Coredemptress. Therein lies both marvel and mystery; for she, who coredeemed with Christ, had to be, and was, redeemed by this same Christ. Nevertheless, there can be no doubt about her being Coredemptress. St. Pius X indulgenced a prayer which named her "Coredemptrix of mankind." His successor, Benedict XV, unhesitatingly stated that "it may be truly said that she with Christ redeemed the human race,"* Pius XI on two occasions taught the same truth. And Pius XII insisted on it when he defined the dogma of her Assumption, and when he announced the feast of her Universal Queenship. The principle for all these pronouncements was well expressed by the Citharist of Mary, St. Bernard of Clairvaux, when, at the close of one of his sermons in Mary's honor, he exclaimed: "With our whole heart and with all earnestness let us venerate Mary because *such is the Will of Him* who has *decreed* that we receive everything through Mary."**

So it is not timidity, but truth, that has us approaching Mary. We are following God's plan and doing God's Will; for Mary is so much a part of that plan that unless we see her clearly in the center of it, we do not see His plan at all.

Once that is established, no one can challenge the statement that Mary is not Queen because she was crowned by God the Father, God the Son, and God the Holy Spirit; but that They crowned her because she is Queen. Then all can see how the fifth Glorious Mystery rests on the basic principle of Mariology — the Will of God. Pius XII told us as much when he defined Mary's Assumption. At one point in his encyclical he argued: "Therefore, the august Mother of God, intimately associated with Jesus Christ by 'one and

* *Inter Sodalitia.*
** *In Nativ. B.V.M.* Emphasis added.

the same' decree of predestination, immaculate in her conception, inviolate virgin in her divine maternity, *generous associate* of the Divine Redeemer who fully conquered sin and its consequences, has at last obtained, as the supreme crown of her privileges, that she be preserved immune from the corruption of the sepulcher and, like her Son, conquering death, be borne to heaven in body and soul, there to *shine as Queen* on the right hand of her Son, the immortal King of Ages."*

Even more clearly did this same Marian Pontiff teach this truth in the prayer he composed and recited the day he inaugurated the feast of Mary as Queen, to be celebrated throughout the entire world every year on May 31. In that prayer the Pope tells Mary that we wish to exalt her Queenship and to recognize it as "due to the sovereign excellence of her entire being." Then he pleads with her to reign not only over the angels and saints in Heaven, but over every man on earth. He begs her to reign over "men's minds, that they may seek only what is true; over their wills, that they may follow solely what is good; over their hearts, that they may love nothing but what you yourself love." At the close His Holiness asks Mary to "reign in the streets and in the squares, in the cities and in the villages, in the valleys and in the mountains, in the air, on land and on the sea; and hear the pious prayers of all those who recognize that yours is a reign of mercy, in which every petition is heard, every sorrow comforted, every misfortune relieved, every infirmity healed, and in which, at a gesture from your gentle hands, from death itself there arises smiling life."

After quoting that to Charlie, I told him: "That is the kind of Queen-Mother we have. She can bring smiling life from what men call death. And never forget she is *your* Queen-Mother! You tell me you have often relived your experience here at Gethsemani when you heard the entire Community of almost two hundred and fifty men in virile song, saluting Mary in that moving *Salve Regina.* Many have been impressed as deeply as you seem to have been. It is all understandable; for the setting is quite arresting: the utterly dark church, the sudden burst of a strong solo voice singing the lone word, *Salve,* then the immediate loud chorus on that many-neumed

* No. 40. Emphasis added.

word, *Regina.* The song itself is stirring, but when you have the added effect of the huge window, which fills the entire wall above and in back of the main altar, being slowly lighted — to watch that dim pin point of light grow and grow until the multicolored picture is fully revealed of the Queen of Heaven holding her Child on her lap, while around her throne and enfolded by her blue mantle, which angels hold back, are her Cistercian saints — small wonder that you and others never forget that. But, Chic, have you ever analyzed that song to see what we are actually singing, and what you so often say when you recite that 'Hail Holy Queen'? We not only call our Mother 'Queen,' but we name her 'our life,' 'our sweetness,' and 'our hope.' Doesn't that recall her own words about being the 'Mother of fair love . . . and of holy hope'; about being the one in whom is 'all hope of life' and 'all grace of the way'? Then we go on singing, and credit her with a reign of mercy, when we ask her to turn her 'eyes of mercy' toward us. When we name ourselves her children who are in exile, we implicitly say that Heaven is our Home. That we know what constitutes the essence of eternal happiness is evident from our plea that she 'show us the Fruit of her womb — Jesus.' Has that phrase ever awakened echoes of Christ's own definition of Eternal Life? Jesus once said: 'And this is the sum of eternal life: their knowing you, the only true God, and your ambassador, Jesus Christ' (Jn. 17:3). That's the happiness we are all seeking — and we ask it from her who is the Cause of our Joy. That is the knowledge every soul craves — and we beg it from her who is Seat of Wisdom. That is the love, the life, the bliss we plead for from her who is Mother of Fair Love — of Life — and our Blessedness: Jesus!"

I urged Charlie to pray that prayer and sing that song ever more thoughtfully. He could call Mary by every name in the Litany of Loretto, and she would be pleased. But nothing would gratify her more than for him to know exactly why he named her "Queen."

Most people would be satisfied to say she is Queen because she mothered the King of kings. There is something in the reply. But some heckler might point out that not every woman who gives birth to a child who will one day become king, reigns as queen. The appellation "Queen-Mother" given to such women has no juridical significance; it is mere deference paid to a parent. That, of course, is absolutely true. But Mary is never called "Queen-Mother" in this sense; for she did not give birth to a Child who would one day become king — she brought forth Him who was, and is, and ever will be King of kings. Furthermore, Mary shared her parenthood with no other human being. This Virgin Queen-Mother is sole human parent of God's only Son. Hence, she is related to Him in what lawyers would call the first degree of consanguinity, and in the direct line. That fact makes her literally, and in fullest truth, the highest of all mere human creatures; she "borders on the Infinite"; she belongs to the Hypostatic order! About her no one need say: "Beyond here lies God." No. Right here is God!

But even that is not enough for one who would have "reason for the Faith that is in him." So I cited the address Pius XII made on May 13, 1946, to the throngs gathered in the Cova da Iria for the coronation of the statue of Our Lady of Fatima. "Jesus is King throughout all eternity," His Holiness said, "by nature and by right of conquest. Through Him, with Him, and subordinate to Him, Mary is queen by grace, by divine relationship, by right of conquest, and by singular election." Charlie was urged to study those four reasons; for they will satisfy the most demanding intellect. Then he was told how eight years later, when instituting the feast of Mary Queen of the Universe, the Pope had given the same four reasons for her Queenship. After arguing from Scripture, the Fathers, and the theologians, His Holiness had turned to the Liturgies of the East and the West to show that Mary had always been held and hailed as Queen. At the close of his argument he made use of a beautiful exclamation found in the Ethiopic Missal: "O Mary," it runs, "center of the whole world . . . thou art greater than the many-eyed cherubim and the six-winged seraphim. . . . The heaven and the earth are entirely filled with the sanctity of thy glory."

That reference to the "many-eyed cherubim and six-winged seraphim" would do things to a man steeped in the Old Testament that I could not expect it to do to Charlie, but I knew he would appreciate the color, motion, and sound created by the citation. Then to lighten the exposition a bit I said: "As usual, Chic, His Holiness agrees with me. Just look at this sentence from the pen of Pius XII: 'When they consider the Fifth Glorious Mystery of the Rosary, for many centuries past, Christians have been accustomed to meditate on the ruling power of Mary which embraces heaven and earth.' "*

There is the fact we want to grasp. Mary did not go to Heaven to rest; she went there to reign! Her ruling power is not limited to the courts of Heaven. She rules earth as well. That is the truth which makes the fifth Glorious Mystery a Mystery that is both personal and of the present time! This Queen of Heaven rules us at this very moment; and does so by the Will of God. That is what the Supreme Pontiff made most explicit by saying: ". . . the basic principle upon which Mary's royal dignity rests is without doubt, her divine maternity . . . but not only by reason of this divine maternity is she to be called Queen, but also because, *by the will of God,* she has had an outstanding part in the work of our eternal salvation.** . . . From this association with Christ the King she obtains a splendor and an eminence surpassing the excellence of all created things. From this association with Christ comes the royal function by which she can disperse the treasures of the Divine Redeemer's Kingdom."***

Now we were back to my "Song of Songs." Charlie was told that when Mary says: "I am the Mother of fair love . . . and holy hope"; then adds: "In me is all grace of the way . . . in me is all hope of life"; only to climax it with the invitation: "Come over to me . . . and be filled with my fruits," she was not only telling of her Queenship and the treasures that were hers to dispense, but also of our need for her every moment of our mortal existence as sons of God.

Father Paul Segneri, the celebrated Jesuit, one of Italy's greatest orators of the seventeenth century, said: "The life of man is nothing else than a continual liberality of Mary who with the frequency and number of her graces and benefits, spiritual and temporal, and the greater part hidden, makes herself his guide unto salvation." For us who have been born again, and this time "born of God," grace is life, and life is love, and love is God. That is why we must live this fifth Mystery; for Mary is Mother of Love, Source of Life, and Mediatrix of All Grace. If we would live, we must heed her queenly call: "Come over to me. . . ."

* *Ad Coeli Reginam,* No. 31.
** *Ibid.,* No. 35.
*** *Ibid.,* No. 39.

That I should be talking to him about life just after he had been anointed evoked no protest from Charlie; for by this time he had come to realize what true life is, and to give assent with his whole being to what we healthier members of Christ give assent to too often only with our lips and our speculative minds. "I feel so relaxed after having been anointed," he wrote. "It was truly a thrilling experience. You know I will use every means of gaining grace that I can think of. And be assured that I am offering 'all for Jesus through Mary' — even if it is not 'always with a smile.' I hope you have not been too worried about me. My Brother, Jesus, will help me Home when my work is done. There is a thought that really intoxicates. The Divine Son of God clasping my hand and leading me Home! That is all for now. Keep smiling. Keep praying. Keep helping me. I want to go to God."

From the penmanship I could see that he was feeling stronger, so I pressed on with my presentation of the fifth Mystery. First I told him the picture he drew of the thought that intoxicates him was not quite complete; for if Christ was holding one of his hands, that constant associate of Christ in the work of salvation, whom we call Queen and Mother, was holding his other. I told him this had to be; for such "was the will of God" as St. Bernard had said in the twelfth century. "But don't think that this is not twentieth-century doctrine as well," I wrote. "Leo XII said: 'Of the magnificent treasure of Grace, brought to us by Christ, nothing, *according to the eternal designs* [Note our fundamental Mariological principle] is to be distributed to us except through Mary.' Pius X said: 'She is the neck of our Head, by which all spiritual gifts are communicated to His Mystical Body.' But it was Pius XII, when he was as yet only Cardinal Pacelli, who put the truth I am trying to teach you in briefest, yet clearest and completest form when he said: 'After all, the application of the merits of Christ, together with their acquisition, constitutes a single complete work: that of our Salvation. It was fitting that Mary co-operate equally in the two phases of the same work. The unity of the Divine plan demands it.'"

In that citation my brother could hardly miss the perfect compendium of all that had been stressed for him in this Mystery. The Will of God is there in the words "the Divine plan." The argument from "fittingness" is again in evidence. And the "unity" in the work of Redemption and Salvation planned by Divinity is insisted upon. Has the late Holy Father, Pius XII, been rightly appreciated as an acute theologian? His gifts were so many, and his accomplishments in varied fields so great, that it is possible that his worth as theologian has yet to be evaluated. Surely his many pronouncements on Marian doctrines will win him lasting acclaim for his power of penetration and his skill at adequate expression of some of Theology's profoundest problems.

The month of May — Mary's month — was just opening when I received a letter from Pocasset that was painful to read; and which must have been much more painful to compose. It had taken my brother five days to write it, managing a short paragraph each day. The first ran: "I mean to write more often, but am not up to it most of the time. Because of my Saviour's help, which you say comes to me through Mary, I have been able to bear up. Oh, I do shed tears at times. . . ." It broke off there and was resumed the next day: "I became dopey so just had to stop. It is now 3 a.m. I have been awake half an hour. The Night Nurse has been very nice to me this time. She just gave me a hypo. I feel woozy again, so if I stop suddenly it will be because I am tired out again." The next day he added: "I keep offering my pains as bravely as I can — but sometimes ask God why so much? But He knows what He is doing. . . . If my chest pains are from an ulcer, caused by cortisone — as some of the doctors seem to think — I guess I'll be around for some time. Old Man Cancer is lying dormant. So I presume there is no immediate danger. I was such a healthy cuss I guess I'll take a lot of killing — all that God wants me to suffer with and for His Divine Son. . . ." The next paragraph, written the following day, was in a stronger hand and showed a lighter soul. "I went to Confession this afternoon and will receive my Lord in Holy Communion tomorrow morning. Fr. Leblanc says he will anoint me again when my four weeks are up. Isn't all that just wonderful; for then I will remain in the arms of my Saviour." He finished with a rush Saturday morning. "I feel I'm never going to get this letter finished if I don't do it now. My friend, the alcoholic whom I got to join the AA's, was in to see me last night. He looked wonderful and is still sober. He hasn't missed a week visiting me since he left here last February. The big pains still bother me."

What reply could meet the demand implicit in such a letter? I thought of Leon Bloy and his claim that "the chief stock in trade of man are faith and obedience," of how he insists that "our times call for apostles and not *conferenciers*, for martyrs and not demonstrators. This is no longer the moment to prove that God exists. The hour summons us to give our lives to Christ Jesus." Charlie had faith; submission, or, better still, glad acceptance of his sufferings, would be obedience. He could be a martyr, give his life to Christ, and thus prove that God exists by making his pain all prayer. Then came a cognate idea; one that always rises whenever I think of Bloy. It is contained in that powerful passage in *She Who Weeps*, which runs: "Well, what are we? Lord God! We are the *members* of Jesus Christ! In declaring us members of Jesus Christ, the Holy Spirit has clothed us with the dignity of redeemers. . . . When we shed our blood, it pours down on Calvary's Hill and flows over all the earth. When we shed our tears, which are the 'blood of our souls,' they fall on the heart of the Virgin and thence on to all living hearts. Our standing as members of Jesus Christ and Sons of Mary has made us so great, that we can drown the world with our tears."*

Those would be truths and themes familiar to Charlie, and very much in place at the moment. Bloy has other magnificent passages on suffering, the Mystical Body, and Mary that would fit in too. But finally I fell back on my "Song of Songs" and the closing Glorious Mystery; for they could speak of Paradise in every spasm of pain. As a chivalrous man, Charlie needed a Queen. He had her in Mary. As a child — which every man remains — he needed a Mother. Mary satisfied that need too. And both as Queen and Mother in this fifth Glorious Mystery.

"She is calling, Chic," I wrote. "Hear her in your soul as you say those final Glorious Mysteries of her Rosary. She is saying: 'Come over to me. . . .' That has been her call from your birth. She has sounded it every day of your life. Hear it now and heed it, as you

---

* From: *She Who Weeps*, translated by Emile La Douceur, M.S. (Fresno: California Academy Guild, 1955), p. 40.

never heard it and heeded it before. 'Come over to me all ye that desire me, and be filled with my fruits.'

"That is what the fifth Glorious Mystery sings; for that is precisely what it means. It is the most personal of the fifteen and more timely than the ticking of a clock. It says your Mother is *Queen*. She reigns! That means she enjoys royal power and exercises it with regal authority. You are her loyal subject upon whom she lavishes the wealth of her Kingdom. That is what Pope Pius XII meant when he said 'from her association with Christ comes the royal function by which she can disperse the treasures of the Divine Redeemer's Kingdom.'** That means grace — and grace means life here on earth and glory in our unending future, as you so very well know. So hear her saying 'Come over to me . . .' every time you feel the slightest twinge of pain. As Queen she is asking you to help the King complete Salvation.

"You know I have called this cancer a blessing from God. That has been my theme from the beginning. I do not change it now as I say every pain is a grace from Mary. I am really saying the same thing in different words. But that difference throws clearer light on God's plan for mankind and His Present Will for you. For it tells you just what Leo XIII told the world in one of his encyclicals on the Rosary; namely, that 'every grace which is communicated to the world has a threefold course. For in accord with excellent order, it is dispensed from God to Christ, from Christ to the Virgin, and from the Virgin to us.'* The Queen of Heaven, through your pain, is bestowing an accolade. She is knighting you, Charlie. She is bringing you up higher and ever higher in the ranks of those who follow in the footsteps of her Son who is the King of Kings. Your Mother who is a Queen holds in her hands every grace of the way. Go over to her and 'be filled with her fruits'; one of which is not only confidence in the face of trial, courage in the midst of danger, but joy in the midst of suffering!

"Yes, this Mystery tells you that your Mother is Queen. Does it not necessarily follow then that you are of royal blood; that you are

** *Ad Coeli Reginam,* No. 39.
* *Jucunda Semper,* September 8, 1894.

the son of this Queen? *Noblesse Oblige!* When the Queen Mother calls 'Come over to me . . .' your instantaneous response is not only that of a chivalrous knight, but the joy-filled, love-filled, ecstatic obedience of a stalwart son who is filled with *Pietas*. And that, perhaps, is for you at this moment the more important aspect of this fifth Glorious Mystery: The Woman above all women blessed, who is crowned Queen, is your Mother. And never forget that most important title of hers: *Mater Divinae Gratiae* — Mother of Divine Grace. See now how rightly you call her your 'Life' your 'Sweetness,' and your 'Hope.' "

A brief acknowledgment came to that letter but no direct comment; yet, as I reread the short letter, I saw it contained a perfect response. "Our Patty," it began, "is getting ready to receive her First Holy Communion next Sunday; and though I am disappointed in not being able to be with her physically, I console myself by saying that God must have His reasons." It ended with: "Well, Joe, I guess I'll have to stay in exile a while longer; for it looks as if I am not going to be called Home soon. I believe our Father in Heaven wants me to be purged completely before He gives me that beckoning call. Our Mother Mary is watching over me with her tender care. So . . . I'm just the way God wants me: ever conscious of Him. . . . Our Queen-Mother must want me to sing her praises on earth during her month of May. I want to go Home; but God wills otherwise. But I'm in Heaven on earth, so I bide His call with some show of patience."

That reference to our Queen-Mother and the consciousness of her tender care told me that Charlie had read all I wanted him to in my last effort at orientation. Since Ascension Thursday was nearing, with Pentecost right behind, it was only proper to touch upon all the Mysteries we had reviewed together, even as the final Glorious Mystery was more fully developed. The text "He rose for our sanctification" (Rom. 4:25) served me well. That sanctification is a matter of grace, the virtues, and the gifts was the truth that enabled me to cover the first four Glorious Mysteries with brevity and fresh personal appeal. I climaxed the recapitulation by saying: "From the very beginning, Chic, I have prayed but for two things: not health and happiness; not recovery and re-employment; but only for faith and fortitude. Heaven has answered that prayer in Heaven's own measure, which is always 'a goodly measure — pressed down, shaken together, running over' (Lk. 6:38). Conscious as you have been of your pain, most likely you have been unconscious of the faith demanded of you — and expressed; the fortitude challenged — and unshaken! These Virtues and Gifts have come to you from God the Holy Spirit. But like all gifts, they remained only offerings until they had been accepted. What I mean is that they do not, they did not, work automatically. You had to co-operate with God. You have done so manfully, generously, steadfastly. For that I bless you, praise you, heartily congratulate you — and greatly love you. But now let us both bless, praise, thank, and love the Lovely Giver of these Gifts — not only God the Holy Spirit, but His Spouse, the Queen of the Most Holy Rosary and your Mother."

At that point a doubt arose. We were still on the fifth Glorious Mystery and the Queenship of Mary, which has to do with her mediatrixship of all grace. But I wondered if it was allowable for me to attribute to her the granting of the Gifts of the Holy Spirit. It is so easy to err in Theology when one becomes enthusiastic. Back to the Fathers I went — especially to Bernard, the so-called "Last of the Fathers" — and to St. Bernardine of Siena. The first yielded nothing explicit. But St. Bernardine banished my doubt, and made me blush for ever having had it. He had written: "all gifts, virtues, and graces of the Holy Ghost are administered by her hands to whomsoever she desires, when, and in what manner she desires, and in the degree that she wishes."* Then my memory did me the honor of recalling the closing lines of Pius XII's *Mystici Corporis*: "She it was who through her powerful prayers obtained the grace that the Spirit of the Divine Redeemer, already given to the Church on the Cross, should be bestowed through miraculous gifts on the newly founded Hierarchy on Pentecost."

Reassured by such authorities I joyfully told my brother that our Lady-Mother, who is Queen of the Universe, was leaning out from her throne and stretching toward him hands that were laden with all the graces he needed for the way, all the Gifts required for his further and full Christ-ening, all the Fruits the Holy Spirit had to impart,

---

* *De Nat. B.V.M.*, cap. viii.

so that he might enjoy each and every Beatitude not only tomorrow — but today!

"Now, surely, you can appreciate the wisdom of that eloquent old Jesuit, Paul Segneri, when he said: 'the life of man is nothing else than a continual liberality of Mary.' Who would have it any different? And didn't Pius XII sum up truth neatly when he said: 'let all Christ's faithful glory in the fact that they are subject to the *rule* of the Virgin-Mother who both enjoys royal power and burns with a mother's love'? There's the fifth Glorious Mystery in a sentence, Chic. Live it. Live it, as the Pope says, and as I insisted that you do when I gave you the command to live *gloriously!*"

That letter had not reached Pocasset before I was reading one from Charlie which told how he had suffered what the doctors called "an attack of the nerves." He had been suddenly set twitching from head to foot, and shook thus for three hours. When Doctor Gould had tried to lift him out of it by some friendly joshing, Charlie had broken down completely and cried like a baby. He wrote: "The thought keeps popping up in my mind: 'When the time actually comes for me to leave for my Heavenly Home, will I be a sissy?' Will I break down to such an extent that whatever good I may have done, showing these people how a member of Christ suffers, will all be spoiled?"

After encouraging him, as well as I could, by recalling what Leon Bloy had said about the tears of Christians, I cautioned him about a very common snare of the devil. He will always try to get people to *anticipate*. It is a very clever tactic; for it often ruins the present moment and fills the future with unnecessary and unfounded fears. The best way to avoid the snare and rout the devil is to "receive the Sacrament of the Present Moment"; that is, live to the hilt the moment God gives us with the grace He grants through Mary. We have not the future moment itself, nor the grace that is divinely predestined to accompany it. Hence it is foolish to try to live tomorrow today, tonight this afternoon, or this noontime this morning. Live this present moment — it is all God grants us; it is all God wants of us.

My next point was that all the good he had done there at Pocasset and on the Cape — and it was plentiful! — was really the work of God and the grace that had been granted through Mary. He was but

God's instrument. Nothing would be spoiled, nothing could be spoiled so long as he yielded himself to God and remained pliable in the hands of His Queen-Mother.

He was warmly congratulated on his phrase "leave for my Heavenly Home"; for it showed he was conscious of the fact that we who have been "born of God," we who have "eaten His Flesh and drunk His Blood," do not die. We live now, and we are to live forever. Christ is true to His promises — and this is one of them. When the Church has us sing: *"vita mutatur, non tollitur"* — "life is changed, it is not taken away" — in the Preface of a Requiem Mass, she is not using a sentimental song to soothe aching hearts; she is focusing our gaze on immutable fact: we do not die. Our life is merely changed.

Then I quoted from Leo XIII's letter *Laetitiae Sanctae* — "Sacred Joy" — of September 8, 1893. In it the Pope spoke of those who "by frequent and fervent prayer . . . keep before their minds the glorious mysteries," and assured them that "These mysteries are the means by which, in the soul of a Christian, a most clear light is shed upon good things, hidden to sense but visible to faith, 'which God has prepared for those that love Him.' From them we learn that death is not an annihilation which ends all things, but merely a migration and passage from life to life. By them we are taught that the path to Heaven lies open to all men, and as we behold Christ ascending thither, we recall the sweet words of His promise,' I go to prepare a place for you.' By them we are reminded that a time will come when 'God will wipe away all tears from their eyes'; and that 'nor mourning, nor crying, nor sorrow, shall be any more,' and that 'we shall always be with the Lord,' and 'like to Him: for we shall see Him as He is,' and drink of the torrent of His delight as fellow citizens of the saints, in the blessed companionship of our glorious Queen and Mother. Dwelling upon such a prospect, our hearts are kindled with desire, and we exclaim in the words of a great saint: 'How vile grows the earth when I look up to Heaven!' Then, too, we shall feel the solace of the assurance that 'that which is at present momentary and light of our tribulation, worketh for us above measure exceedingly an eternal weight of glory.' "

"There it is for you, Charlie, and from the pen of a Pope. I have been giving directives and doctrine that are genuinely dogmatic. We live the Glorious Mysteries — or we miss more than half of life! God has set us aglow with glory. That is what actually happened when we were baptized. Our work in life is to fan that fire to a real blaze and become a flaming doxology. That is the meaning of human life — and of all creation. You have been doing your life's work manfully these past painful months. Keep at it now. As Pentecost approaches let 'Glory be to the Father' shine in your eyes; 'Glory be to the Son' sound from your lips; 'Glory be to the Holy Spirit' radiate from your whole body and being. Our Queen-Mother who is calling 'Come over to me . . .' will give you all that is needed. You can be — I dare say you are now — a living doxology. Keep on being so by using this poem as your prayer:

> Maid who wed Infinity,
> Clay that shaped Divinity,
> Lady of the Trinity,
>   Life is filled with fears.
>
> Golden Wheat that made the Host,
> Mortal Woman loved the most
> By Father, Son, and Holy Ghost,
>   Life is wet with tears.
>
> Flame of Wisdom, Holy Shrine,
> Chalice of the Bread and Wine,
> Vineyard that produced the Vine,
>   Death speeds like a dart.
>
> Immaculate Virginity,
> God-filled Femininity,
> Lady of the Trinity,
>   Keep me in your Heart!*

She will, Chic; for that is the secret of the Christly manhood you have shown throughout your sickness: You have been in her Heart."

* From *Martin* by Edward Doherty (New York, 1951). With permission of the author.

CHAPTER FIFTEEN

Grand Larceny at Silver Jubilee

IN THE middle of Mary's month a keener consciousness that I was in my year of Silver Sacerdotal Jubilee came over me. As I knelt one day reviewing that quarter of a century of priestly life, the fact that I had often heard the voice of Christ and felt the very hand of God as I tried to do His work bore in on me. Even more clearly was it evident that I had been under Mary's very special care; for almost incessantly I was aware of her maternal guidance and powerful protection. But then I had to admit that the past twenty months with my brother, Charlie, had been an experience I would have to call unique. The breath of God had not only been over my shoulder and on my neck, His strong hand had not been only under my elbow for support and in my own hand for guidance, but with each new letter from Cape Cod the face of Christ became clearer and the immanence of the Triune God more palpable. I, who thought I was teaching Charlie, was really being taught by him.

Metanoia had become for me a word that summed up all life and living. It had been borrowed from the Greek of the Gospels and it spoke to me of that "putting on of Christ" which is the purpose of all Christian living; that total transformation of the human creature into Christ, which is the end-aim of all our striving while on earth. All the effort put into the proof that we are to live the Rosary — especially the Glorious Mysteries — and not merely recite it, was but a newer way of presenting my old, old proposition. I was but urging Charlie on to a complete *metanoia*. But when I took time to reread the many letters he had sent me since being found with cancer, I saw that I had been actually witnessing what angels worship: the hand of God and the hands of the Mother of God pressing the soul of a Christian man into the mold of Christ. A perfect *metanoia* was taking place before my eyes: for Charlie's mind, his memory, his will were not only focused on Jesus Christ, they were filled to the overflowing with that same Christ Jesus. A moral miracle was manifest before me.

Suddenly I realized that from the moment he had read the doctor's prognosis over my shoulder, up to this present moment a year and a half later, he had written and spoken of little else than of Christ, His Mother, and Our Father, who is God. What a revelation of God's gentle, yet steely strong, guidance and of a full-grown man's childlike submission to God's ways the rereading of those letters afforded me! I sat back abashed — and elated — to find that the tables had been turned: Charlie was the one who had been giving me that God-consciousness, that Christ-consciousness, that God-intoxication, the term of that true *metanoia* which makes a man what God wants him to be, but which other men say makes man a mystic. Cancer in the lung of my youngest brother had shown me the face of Christ with a clarity I had not known since first I was made Christ by Baptism.

With deeper conviction I repeated the truth-laden phrase: "Every happening — be it in the history of a people, a nation or an individual — is nothing but a newer coming of Christ."

But what struck me most forcefully was the way Charlie had kept his sense of humor. How true the statement: "Joy is the secret of the Christian." Even in mid-May, when his pains were really agonizing, he began one of his letters with banter about family and friends. "Kay tells me she sent you the snaps taken last Christmas, those taken as Maureen was going to the Bishop's Ball, and the latest we clicked this past Easter. So I imagine you are still high in the clouds realizing what beautiful nieces and handsome nephews God has given you through Kay and myself. . . . I'll stop at this juncture — for my leg is humming."

It was the next morning before he resumed that letter. After telling how he had managed to get through the night with the help of aspirin for the leg and centrigel for the pain in his chest — since he was trying to get along with as few narcotics as possible — he went on to say: "They have not X-rayed my chest as yet, for they want to keep me off my feet as much as possible. They did X-ray the instep a short while ago — and found it a mess. The calcium has gone from the bones, causing a great softness. The instep is quite swollen and, as yet, they do not know what to do about it. I am finishing up my fourth week here this stretch, and have been out of bed just four times. So you can see why my nerves broke down last week, and why I get so fidgety at times. I find the only way to keep sane is to say my Rosary."

What he had to say about his bones was not news to me; for Doctor Kelley had been kind enough to inform me that Charlie was suffering from what some medical men call "osteoatrophy." It seems that the bones, deprived of their usual nutrition, quickly calcify and deform. Kay had added to that information by telling me that the latest X ray showed that two of the bones in Charlie's foot had completely disappeared. So I had reason to admire my brother's cheerfulness and his mindfulness of others.

The Kentucky Derby had just been run. For it a horse named "Silkey Sullivan" had been brought on from the West Coast where it had shown itself a strong stretch runner. Churchill Downs has a splendid stretch. So more than the Irish, who were taken by the name, had bet heavily on the stranger from the West. Father Matt Brennan, who had been chaplain at St. Joseph Infirmary when Charlie was in Kentucky, had written to the Cape telling the cancer patient how his friend, Sister Margaret, the supervisor of surgery, was insisting that Tim Tam was going to win the race. Father Matt had ended with: "How stubborn — and stupid — can some Irish people be, Chuck?"

Charlie, after telling of his X rays and awful pains, went on to say: "Just dropped a few lines to Father Matt. I cannot understand how he came to overlook Tim Tam; for in my last letter to Sister Margaret I told her to tell him that while my heart was with Silkey Sullivan, my money (if I had any) would be on Tim Tam. Now the Preakness will be another story. For, after all, with mint juleps flowing freely the night before the Derby, what could you expect from an Irishman? But he'll show them something in the Preakness. Yet, I still say put your money on Tim Tam."

His next paragraph wiped away my smile and set me wondering:

"I am going to try to get out for a ride with Kay this afternoon. I need a change of scenery and some fresh air. Moreover, I am anxious to see how the house and grounds look. We have a lot of myrtle, pansies, and jumping-jack violets in bloom already. When Mazie arrives next month our roses, bridal wreath, jonquils, zinnias, etc., will be in full flower. . . . And just think! It is only five weeks away!"

Five weeks. What condition would he be in by that time?

Mazie (Sister Mary Clare) had obtained permission to come from Halifax to Gethsemani in order to celebrate my Silver Jubilee of ordination and first Mass. The actual dates were June 22 and 23; but Mother General was allowing her to anticipate her departure by a few days so that she could visit the invalid on Cape Cod. June 18 had been set as the date of her arrival at Pocasset. Here was Charlie in mid-May counting the weeks.

That I had reason to wonder what condition he would be in when Sister Mary Clare arrived was evident from his next letter, dated May 12. The day before had been Mother's Day and Christine-Marie's third birthday. Charlie had gone riding, as he had determined. "Kay called for me shortly after noon," he wrote. "Out we went in a wheel chair to our beach wagon. . . . We made it into the car finally after much difficulty. Then off to '33.' It was a pleasant ride even if I did have to tell Kay to slow down a few times. She is a splendid driver, but a speed demon. . . .

"Well we got to Blanid Road all right. I had planned to step onto the lawn and crawl to a lawn chair. But Tim Driscoll, our next-door neighbor, came along. So with him on one side and Kay on the other I thought I might make the house. It was a mistake. Halfway to the house my right leg folded under me — and my left leg, which I must keep off of at all costs, began to give me misery in high gear. When I finally got to the studio couch . . . I was in real pain for about a half an hour. But it was all worth it just to see Christy in her new plaid shorts and jersey. It was also a thrill to see the rest of the gang pile into the birthday cake and ice cream. Soon my left leg fired up again and we had one awful struggle getting back into the car. We made it back here by four o'clock.

"I'll not try that again in a hurry. Of course my heart is broken with the realization that in all probability I will not walk again. I'm really down in the dumps at the moment, Joe. But I'll be all right tomorrow. Do pray hard for me. . . ."

My earnest prayer was that he might recapture all his Christ-consciousness and heroic conformity to God's Will.

Three days later a letter came bearing the heading: "All for Thee, my Jesus — Through my loving Mother Mary." That was fitting prelude to: "I know you understand that I would write longer letters and more interesting ones if I were able. Jack came down to see me yesterday afternoon. We had a truly brotherly visit. While he was here Fr. Leblanc dropped in to check on the date of my anointing. As a result I went to Confession, received our Lord and Saviour in Holy Communion, and was anointed again last night. I feel fully reassured that I am in the arms of my Saviour, and that Mother Mary is closer to me than ever before. That's the wonderful news at this moment. Couldn't wait any longer to tell you. Lord love you and keep you ever in His Heart."

Noting that he had not a single reference to his body or his pains, I thanked God for so speedy and so generous an answer to my prayer.

Four days later the patient was writing again. The same heading, "All for Thee, my Jesus — Through my loving Mother Mary," preluded four pages of varied scrawl. "When I'm not in pain," he wrote, "I'm either half asleep or being visited by someone. A man who has been here for two weeks just left my room after saying I had been an inspiration to him by my courage. I told him I was not courageous by myself, but that through, by, and in Jesus Christ I found all the answers to the questions about pain and how to bear suffering. He replied by saying: 'Well, we all believe in God in some fashion, but you have taught me a lot since I've been up here.' I pray to Mother Mary to help him, and all such, to see their way to salvation. In fact, I've been asking her for a little relief from my pain so that I might have more strength to do her work. I want so many to share the heavenly protection of her mantle and cloak!"

Then after a vivid — and almost joyful — description of his help-lessness, which told that now not only his legs, but also his arms had become useless, and that the orderly had to lift him out of his bed, he wrote: "Oh well, it could be a lot worse, and, after all, God is close to me, and that is all that counts. . . ." The letter ended in a scribble with: "May Mother Mary keep us close to her and her Divine Son. . . ."

That was the last complete letter he ever wrote. He began one on May 23, but did not finish the first page. Kay completed it at his dictation. In it he told how further X rays showed that more bones had been completely eaten away. He admitted that he found it very difficult even to move around in bed. "Where we go from here I leave entirely in God's hands. I pray only that I last for Mazie's trip here, if that be God's Will," were the last words Charlie wrote. Kay added her own comment at the end of the letter saying: "I believe he is just hanging on to see Sister Mary Clare. What the incentive will be after that I don't know."

June ninth found me sitting at my desk with my mother's mortuary card before me. This was the ninth anniversary of the day I had first prayed the verses the card held. I prayed them again this day, but with Charlie as much in mind as Mother. The verses will never merit the name of poetry, but assuredly they make a perfect prayer. They bear the title: *Prayer for the Day of My Mother's Demise.* The first verse introduces a "new arrival at the Court of God" to Mother Mary, and begs her to plead with her Son to be merciful to this new arrival. Then Mother Mary is reminded that this new arrival is an old acquaintance, one who lived her entire earthly life with her hands bound to Mary's by her beads. Then I say:

> She had her joys — Dear Lady, Thou wast kind
>   To let her share Thy Joyful Mysteries!
> She had her woes — yes, woes all mothers find.
>   I thank Thee that she shared Thine Agonies.
>
>   And, dear My Lady, she was good to me
>   And taught me how to be God's worshipper.
>   If aught I've done for Jesus or for Thee,
>   Beg God to mark the credit unto her.
>
>   No mighty Panegyric do I say
>   But just the sobbing of my Rosary,
>   To tell Thee, Lady, that I lost today
>   My Mother — who was all the world to me!
>
> I recommend her, Lady, to Thy care.
>   Be good to her — she was a Child of Thine;

She shared Thy pain; let her Thy Glory share!
And be her Mother — just as she was mine!

When I finished praying I realized that those lines of nine years ago held the very story I had been trying to tell Charlie for the past twenty months. But I noted one all-important difference. In the verses I prayed Mother Mary to allow my earthly mother to share her Glorious Mysteries only after she had left this world. For over a year I had been pleading with Charlie to realize that he was sharing them now. As I sat back from my desk I felt that both my prayer and my plea had been heard.

Four days later I learned that at almost the same hour I had been praying for that share in glory, Charlie was dictating a letter to Kay. "Having a secretary isn't all it's cracked up to be," he said, then explained that so many ideas come into his head as he begins to dictate that he gets all mixed up. Comment on his own condition was reduced to the remark that his right arm "for all practical purposes is paralyzed." He immediately added: "I want to offer that to God, too. I tell Brother Joachim I need all his help. You tell him the same!" Then while speaking of the coming visit of Sister Mary Clare, he exclaimed: "Won't it be wonderful! — I pray a little respite from the pain so that she and I can enjoy it."

There the letter broke off. Under different date line Kay finished it on her own, saying that Charlie was not up to completing his dictation — and that it had taken him over an hour to dictate that little bit. It appeared that the awful pain in his right arm had demanded an increase in the dosage of his drugs, and the heavy sedation had him falling into a semislumberous state every few minutes. "It's terrible to see him suffer so. . . ."

A week later a large envelope, inscribed by a strange hand, came to me. I extracted the contents somewhat warily; for by this time I had caught Charlie's spirit and was looking forward to Mary Clare's visit. Could this strange handwriting mean bad news? But, no. The opening lines seemed to sparkle: "All for Thee, my Jesus — through the ever-loving Heart of Mary" they ran. The script was large and flowing. My eyes jumped to the message: "A week from today I'll be saying: 'Hello Mazie!' What a wonderful day that will be! As it looks now, Kay will greet her at the Hyannis Airport, then

drive her and her companion to Pocasset. Looking back now, time
has flown; but when she first told me of her intended visit, that
time stretched like an eternity.

"Vicki Brenize, the occupational therapist here, is now acting as
my secretary. It was she who helped me make that Madonna you
are so crazy about. I have explained to her that you cannot write to
her. She understands. I will thank her for you." Charlie then told
of his pains and his way of meeting them. "I believe Mother Mary
will help me through to the end," was his last sentence before the
cry: "Oh, Joe, please pray for me!"

Vicki added her own P.S. saying: "You have a very fine brother,
and I have enjoyed being able to help him whenever I could. He is
looking forward to seeing his sister; and I am sure it will be a very
happy reunion."

I was reading that postscript just about the hour Mary Clare should
have been landing on the Cape. I again prayed God and His Mother
to make this visit all I had begged Mary Clare to try to make it
when I wrote briefing her on what she would find when she reached
the hospital. I asked Heaven and earth to make this visit what Mary
Immaculate had made of her trip into the hill country just after she
had conceived by the Holy Spirit. I would have Christ radiate from
the person of my sister to set the soul of my sick brother leaping
with joy.

I thought I might get some word as to the effectiveness of that
prayer within the next few days, but my mailbox remained disappoint-
ingly empty. To console myself I set about preparing for the Jubilee
I was to celebrate with Fathers Jack and Eddie along with Sister
Mary Clare and her companion, and telling myself that soon I would
be listening to reports on Charlie's physical and spiritual condition
from eyewitnesses. I suspect I was looking forward to the arrival of
this group with as much eagerness as Charlie had anticipated Mary
Clare's arrival on the Cape.

June twenty-second was a Sunday, which meant that more time
was mine to devote to prayerful recollection than would have been
mine on a weekday. Looking back now, it seems that the day passed
in some sort of stunned awe; yet was entirely aglow with warm
gratitude. It was difficult to believe that a full quarter of a century

had passed since Bishop Emmett, S.J., of Jamaica, B.W.I., had laid his hand on my head to bring down the Holy Spirit in a new descent that He might burn anew and more deeply the character of Christ's Priesthood into my soul. The realization that I had offered the Body and Blood of Christ in the Holy Sacrifice of the Mass almost ten thousand times shook me to my soul's depth. A spasm of fright was exorcised only by recalling that I had often called God a "Gambler" and that He knew just what kind of a gamble He was taking on me before He spoke His first *Fiat* at Creation. If I staggered that day, it was from God-intoxication. If I sang aloud, it was from joyous, grateful exaltation.

But the twenty-third was another day — one I shall never forget. Mass that morning was an almost infinitely more intimate action than had been the First Mass twenty-five years earlier; for in those years Christ and I have become ever so much more consciously one, and the Cenacle, Golgotha, and that Throne in Light Inaccessible have become as familiar as the veins on the back of my hand. I knew now what Mass was, with a knowledge dogmatically the same as then, but dynamically so different that for a moment or two I wondered if I was the same man who had celebrated that First Mass on the feast of the Sacred Heart, June 23, 1933. The actual celebration in the sacred privacy of Gethsemani's dark crypt seemed like the singing of a very short song. Thanksgiving after Mass was something I would want never to end. Bells rang. I obeyed them. But I was still one with the Christ of that Mass; that Mass was still going on; my Priesthood was as new as this morning's dawn, yet I was as old as Christ Himself.

At seven o'clock I found myself with soul still singing and body swaying to the rhythm of that song as I tidied up my workshop in preparation for the Jubilee visit which would begin early that afternoon. There came a knock on the door. Before I could answer, Leo Gannon, the generous gentleman who had not only given two sons and his only daughter to God, but who, on retiring from business, had come to Gethsemani with his wife to conduct our Guest House for Women, entered with outstretched hand and the arresting question: "Well, Father, did you get the word?"

That Leo should come to my "Catacomb" surprised me. That he

should speak surprised me more. For usually he keeps as strict a silence within the Monastery as do the monks themselves. But the cordiality in his handclasp and the sparkle in his eye led me to believe he had some good news about the coming of the visitors. I wondered if they had made a start earlier than originally planned. All these thoughts flashed through my mind in that immeasurable space of time between Leo's entrance and the negative shake of my head. In the same enthusiastic tone, which held overtones of real joy, he went on: "Charlie died at two o'clock this morning. His wife called Brother Alexander, and Brother called me to arrange about the Guest House. I don't suppose your sister will be coming this week. What do you want me to do about the room?"

Can I say that I was stunned by the announcement of something I had been waiting to hear for over a year? Or can I call that death sudden which I had been expecting for full twenty months? Why did I catch my breath at Leo's first statement: "Charlie died at two o 'clock this morning"? Of course there was surprise connected with every element in the announcement. First, that it should be Leo Gannon who made it; second, that he should be making it to me in my "Catacomb" as I stood in the very spot Charlie had occupied when he read Doctor Kelley's letter over my shoulder eighteen months earlier, and learned that he was about to die; third, that it should come so unexpectedly — for I had had no definite word of any pronounced change in Charlie from Kay, from Father Jack, or from Sister Mary Clare, whom I knew to be on the spot. I surmise it was this unexpectedness that finally set me smiling.

Yes, I smiled! For I have always smiled whenever I have found God teasing . . . and to take Charlie Home right in the middle of my Silver Jubilee, precisely between the twenty-fifth anniversary of my ordination and the twenty-fifth anniversary of my First Mass was a bit of divine teasing! I smiled, too, because I could all but see the smile on the face of God as Sister Mary Clare and the two priests had asked permission to go South in order to celebrate my Silver Jubilee. How well He knew that Silver Jubilee would serve to have all present for His Grand Larceny! How He must have smiled as they made their plane reservations for Monday morning, knowing all the while that on that Monday morning they would be gathered near

one who had made a flight much faster and much further than any
earth-bound man can ever make. I smiled again; for I always smile
when I find God keeping His promises. He had said: "I shall come
like a Thief in the night." He had done so. It was in the depth of
the night that He had stolen from the cancer-consumed body of my
youngest brother the soul He had called into being for that body
by an omnipotent *Fiat* of creation forty-seven years earlier. I call
death *grand* larceny because I know the Thief, and I know whither
He carries His quarry!

I thanked Leo Gannon with a Trappist sign and smiled more
broadly when a lay Brother came with the announcement that the
Prior wished to see me. Our Abbot was in New York State, making
a visitation at Our Lady of the Genesee. I entered the young Prior's
office and rather joyfully announced: "Now I have my last chapter."
I meant to spare him embarrassment. I fear now I caused him more
than he ordinarily would have felt; for he knew nothing of the
frame I had used for this book on Mary's Glorious Mysteries, nor
that Leo Gannon had been to see me. He abruptly said: "Your
brother died this morning." I chuckled then and more quietly
replied: "I know it, Father. Let us thank God for His kindness. Leo
Gannon told me. He was concerned about the visitors who were due
today. I'm quite sure no one will come."

"I know nothing more, Father. I think it was your sister-in-law
who called early this morning. Brother Alexander took the message."

"Well, we'll hear more later in the day. In the meanwhile pray
for Charlie — and thank God and His Mother."

Later that day news did come. But it told me nothing of what
I was anxious to learn. It was simply a wire stating that Charlie had
died at 2:15 a.m.; that all reservations had been canceled; and the
visit postponed for a week.

That week would have been interminable had not Father Jack
hurried off a note Tuesday morning telling me that on Monday,
June 16, Charlie had felt that his end was near. He had Kay call
Father Jack that night at 10:30. When Kay reassured Jack that
Charlie had been anointed that day, and had received Viaticum;
that the medical men thought he would easily last the night, in fact,
saw no real immediate danger, Jack said: "There is nothing more

I could do for Charlie's soul right now, Kay. I think it prudent for me to sleep here tonight and hurry down the first thing in the morning." He did that. Charlie's greeting was characteristic: "You'll think I'm nuts, Jack, when you see me now and then know that last night I was sure I was dying — and really wanted to."

Jack did not think him "nuts" — for the man before him was little more than skin and bones. His voice was strong, the light in his eyes was clear, but it demanded no great knowledge of medicine to see that the man's vital being had been eaten away. The wonder was that he was so alive at the moment. Father Jack, of course, allowed none of this to appear in his words or gestures. He sat in and spent the entire day with a younger brother who most of the day sat up in bed clasping his knees and rocking back and forth in intense pain. They talked of Dad and Mother, and all the rest of the family. Charlie spoke lovingly of his wife and children. But according to Father Jack, most of his time was spent in prayer. Jack's last lines were as good as volumes: "Charlie was in great pain, but was most edifying in every way. Ejaculations and Hail Marys were on his lips all the time — especially when the pain grew worse. I told him I was proud of him. You did a splendid job with him. I'll sing Mass Thursday at 10 a.m. Hope to see you Monday."

To win such an encomium from Father Jack, to have this widely experienced missioner say he was edified, told me that God must have been shining through Charlie.

That such was the case I learned when the three religious of my own blood arrived Monday afternoon, June 30. Though physically exhausted and emotionally drained, they made my Silver Jubilee unforgettable by the things they had to tell me of the last days and hours of the man who was now in eternity.

Despite my briefing, Sister Mary Clare had been rendered speechless by the physical appearance of the man who greeted her with the identical words he had used nine months earlier: "Oh, Mazie, I thought you'd never arrive!" That was late Wednesday afternoon, June 18. They spoke little that day, and not much more the next three days and a half. Charlie would pass in and out of what Sister Mary Clare called drugged sleep, but which may well have been semicoma. What wrenched, even as it thrilled, the heart of this nun during those three and a half days was to hear her youngest brother regain consciousness with the cry: "My Jesus! Mercy!" or "Mother Mary! Help me!"

Sunday morning Charlie caught his sister crying. His own exceptionally large brown eyes, deeply sunken now, misted as he said: "Don't cry, May. I'm all right. I'm right in the hands of God." Later that morning he awoke with the cry: "Oh, Jesus! Why was Yours only three hours?" That, I construe as the nearest thing to a complaint that left his lips in over nine months. He then looked at Sister Mary Clare and rather solemnly announced: "You know, Mazie, I'm going to die." They then shot him with a heavy dose of sedative. It was ten o'clock Sunday morning. He soon fell asleep — and never again regained full consciousness.

Sister Mary Clare was tortured with anxiety about the most prudent thing to do. She had her plane reservations. Her permission from higher superiors was limited. The medical people at Pocasset could give her no definite prognosis. They said Charlie could go at any minute, but then added that he could also last for days, and even for weeks. She tried to reach Father Jack by calling Boston, but he was up in Kennebunkport, Maine, assisting the busy pastor over the week end.

When word finally got through to Father Jack in the early afternoon, he hurried to his car, sped to Boston, thence to Stoughton to check with the family there, then down to Pocasset. He arrived at five in the evening. Charlie was still unconscious. Father Jack stayed until 10:30. Once during those hours he thought that death was at hand, so he said the Prayers for the Dying and gave the Apostolic Benediction to which a plenary indulgence is attached. But Charlie's pulse continued strong and his breathing, fairly deep and regular. At 10:30 that night Father Jack asked the nurse on duty if she thought Charlie might pull through until morning. She took his pulse, listened to his chest, then said: "Judging from the condition of his lungs, which are not too congested as yet, I believe he will make the night."

That determined Jack. He sped to Stoughton to tell all concerned that, since it seemed quite certain that Charlie would not last the week, the only thing to do was cancel all plane reservations for the next day. He reached his room in Boston at about 1:30 in the morning.

I got the final details from Kay. She said it was about 11:00 o'clock Sunday morning when Charlie fell into that sleep which evidently turned into a coma. Only once in the afternoon did he cry out — and that was the single name: "Kay!" She was of the opinion that Charlie realized Father Jack had arrived; for a newer calm came over him as soon as Father Jack entered. "As Father Jack was saying the Prayers for the Dying," she added, "I could see Charlie's lips moving. He was either praying his own prayers or answering Jack's. . . . About 1:30 a.m. his breathing grew shallower. He turned his eyes to one side shortly after that. Then he gave a little sigh — and was gone. No struggle. It was just as if he were saying 'Amen.' "

So the Thief Divine committed His Grand Larceny quietly. At first I felt sorry that Fathers Jack and Eddie, along with Sister Mary Clare, had not been at his side at the very end. But then I realized that Christ had given Charlie a greater grace: He had allowed him to die in a manner very reminiscent of the way He Himself had died. Christ was alone at the end, except for that one nearest and dearest to Him — Mary. Charlie had Kay with him physically. Spiritually, I'm sure, he had all Heaven; for he had performed for over eighteen long, pain-filled months the penance I had given him that cold January morning in 1957. He had lived gloriously. Not only with the God of glory, but, thanks to Mother Mary and her Glorious Mysteries, he had lived in the very glory of God.

His had been the joyous optimism of a man redeemed and risen. His mind took a turn that was truly ascensional — and he kept it ever ascending. His was the glad consciousness that, in and through his pain, he had a work to do that was in some way divine; and he glowed with the realization that, thanks to that continual "Descent of the Holy Spirit" which brings grace, virtues and gifts to all who will receive them, he had in his hands the flawless tools with which he could accomplish a perfect task. He gloried in the fact that there was a Woman in Heaven, a being of flesh and blood, who had been crowned Queen of the Universe, but whom he could rightly call

"Mother." Under her maternal guidance he could watch his own fleshly being waste away and rejoice in the fact that, so long as he united himself with all his pains of body and mind, all his psychological and spiritual stresses, with Christ in His ever continuous Mass, and sent his offering through the Immaculate Heart of Mary, he was not only growing hourly in the likeness of Christ, but, every moment, was actually "filling up those things that are wanting to the Passion of Christ." It was this realization that set him reveling in the fact that when he was reduced to utter physical helplessness, and could accomplish absolutely nothing in the material order — then his most glorious hour of life had struck, and with Mary's aid he could achieve his greatest work on earth: he could help Christ save!

My Silver Jubilee turned into an adoring reverie, as I saw with ever greater clarity just what Jesus and Mary had effected in the soul of my youngest brother. Indeed cancer had been his greatest blessing! It taught him, as nothing in forty-seven years of life had taught him, that the very glory of God is meant for man not only in eternity, but in the time we call today!

That close kinship was not coloring my vision became evident from the letters that poured in, congratulating me not so much on my Silver Jubilee as on God's Grand Larceny. A woman in the Pentagon and a parish priest in Louisville will stand as witnesses.

Mary Maginnis, niece of Doctor M. J. Henry, was home from Washington convalescing from a back operation, when Charlie had come South. With Tia Betty, as we all called Mrs. Henry, and Mary White, her unmarried daughter, Charlie and Mary Maginnis would watch television every evening after he had left me at St. Joseph Infirmary. That is why Mary could write from Arlington, Virginia:

Dear Father Raymond:

Tia Betty and my brother Jimmie told me about Charlie's beautiful death. While I know you will miss him, I also know that his long-awaited rendezvous with God and His Blessed Mother could not leave any sadness in your heart. He had a long and painful illness, and how beautifully he bore his crosses! He not only accepted with resignation but with joy.

As I told Tia, I feel very privileged to have known Charlie. I shall never forget his visit to Louisville. He looked so happy and healthy that it was hard to believe the sad news you had to tell him was actually true. My heart wept for him — and for you. He had so much to leave — so much to live for. And yet, what he had to die for he realized, with the grace of God, would more than compensate. How few of us would ever have the faith and courage to die as he did.

That this woman, living in the turmoil of Washington, should have seen faith and fortitude — or "faith and courage" as she put it — indicated that I had not been reading things into my brother's life — and death. But had there been any doubt, the very outspoken and always clear-seeing Father Matt Brennan would have completely dissipated it. He had been chaplain at St. Joseph Infirmary when Charlie was down. He wrote:

I am not writing this as a note of sympathy; for I do not believe that any of you Flanagans need sympathy at this time. By his dying, Charlie has at last accomplished what he and all of us have been praying for — a holy death.

And holy people have holy deaths! Of all the folks I have known, Charlie was far up the road of holiness. Each letter that I received from him was further proof that he had full insight into the meaning of both life and death — the Will of God. I marveled that he understood his suffering so well and the meaning of it. At the same time I blushed that I, a priest of God, am so ignorant by comparison, and so far in the rear in spirituality to a great layman.

I particularly like to recall what he said about the Rosary in his last letter a month ago: "When the pain becomes almost unbearable, then I hold on to my Rosary. It seems to be the only thing that can bring any ease or peace." Charlie knew things that you and I only preach about.

Since he was here a year and a half ago, he has constantly been an inspiration to me. I am a much better person for having known Charlie. . . .

When I offered my Mass on Tuesday for Charlie, I felt that the Blessed Mother (whose Mass I was saying) was standing beside Charlie, adoring her Divine Son and his King. It was not a Requiem Mass — not for saints!

Thanks to such letters it was with greater confidence that I wrote Doctor Julius Kelley. We had become quite intimate over the months. He told me he thought himself an agnostic. But I had assured him he possessed a deeper and livelier faith than he realized. Now as I thanked him and his staff for what they had done for Charlie, and asked permission to publish certain letters of his in this book, I added: "You heard Charlie not only talking about, but actually talking to Jesus and Mary quite often during his illness. Those are not mere names, Julius. They represent historical Personages, People of flesh and blood, who lived on this earth of ours almost two thousand years ago. One of Them, Jesus, died. He rose from the dead. He ascended into Heaven, and sent the Holy Spirit upon His Apostles; as the Acts of those same Apostles testify. The other, Mary, may not have died — though the vast majority of deep-thinking theologians share the opinion that she did. She was assumed into Heaven, enthroned next to her Son, and crowned Queen of the Universe. That Charlie was not calling on mere figments of his imagination is clear from the answers he received to his cries. That They are Persons powerful enough to enable a man to face death not only with courage but with joy — enable a man actually to court what so many cringe from and, if possible, would utterly flee; powerful enough to give laughter to lips that had become purple with pain, happiness to a heart a fatal pathology often set pounding, and absolute surety about his personal immortality to a man whose mortal frame was being eaten away with every tick of time, you have seen with your own eyes. It was this sight that caused you to exclaim in your last letter: 'I am always amazed at your beautiful and marvelous religion. How is it possible for anyone to have such a clear understanding of life and its obligations!'

"Were I to take that last exclamation as a question, Julius, I would reply that you have had your answer incarnated for you before your eyes. Charlie told you. Faith is the secret. A faith that enables one to see Reality as men of mere science can never see it — for their sciences do not give them the necessary light. A faith that gives fortitude (or courage) not only to live — but to gladly and gloriously die!

"God brought Charlie to you, Julius, that you might see and believe! God was speaking to you and all at Pocasset through Charlie. He was saying: 'Man is made for glory — every man! — and made for the very glory of God!' That is the message cancer in the lung of my youngest brother had for you and your world. In effect he was saying: THIS IS YOUR TOMORROW! — and knowing you now as I do, I dare add: If you but will it, Julius, this is your TODAY!"

The Library of Congress has cataloged this publication as follows:

Raymond, *Father,* 1903–
    This is your tomorrow . . . and today. Milwaukee, Bruce
Pub. Co. ₍1959₎
    207 p. 24 cm.

    1. Suffering.   ɪ. Title.
                        Secular name: Joseph David Flanagan.
BV4909.R3   248.8   59–9719 ‡
Library of Congress